"Gerhard is holding a volume of Luther's Works, slightly open. He has his head turned toward some audience and is in the process of speaking. The head, the hand, and the book all stand out from the generally dark background. It's one of my favorite photos of him." —Marianna Forde, letter to Paul Rorem, December 19, 2017. Photo courtesy of Luther Seminary Archives, 1965.

Courtesy of Luther Seminary Archives.

Family portrait. "Timothy and Sarah in back. Marianna, Gerhard, and Geoffrey in front. Circa 1977. Gerhard himself set up this shot with a timer on his own camera."

LUTHERAN QUARTERLY BOOKS

Editor

Paul Rorem, *Princeton Theological Seminary*

Associate Editors

Timothy J. Wengert, *United Lutheran Seminary, Philadelphia*
Mary Jane Haemig, *Luther Seminary, Saint Paul*
Mark C. Mattes, *Grand View University, Des Moines, Iowa*

Lutheran Quarterly Books will advance the same aims as *Lutheran Quarterly* itself, aims repeated by Theodore G. Tappert when he was editor fifty years ago and renewed by Oliver K. Olson when he revived the publication in 1987. The original four aims continue to grace the front matter and to guide the contents of every issue, and can now also indicate the goals of *Lutheran Quarterly Books:* "to provide a forum (1) for the discussion of Christian faith and life on the basis of the Lutheran confession; (2) for the application of the principles of the Lutheran church to the changing problems of religion and society; (3) for the fostering of world Lutheranism; and (4) for the promotion of understanding between Lutherans and other Christians."

For further information, see www.lutheranquarterly.com.

The symbol and motto of *Lutheran Quarterly,* VDMA for *Verbum Domini Manet in Aeternum* (1 Peter 1:25), was adopted as a motto by Luther's sovereign, Frederick the Wise, and his successors. The original "Protestant" princes walking out of the imperial Diet of Speyer in 1529, unruly peasants following Thomas Müntzer, and from 1531 to 1547 the coins, medals, flags, and guns of the Smalcaldic League all bore the most famous Reformation slogan, the first Evangelical confession: The Word of the Lord remains forever.

Lutheran Quarterly Books

Living by Faith: Justification and Sanctification, by Oswald Bayer (2003).

Harvesting Martin Luther's Reflections on Theology, Ethics and the Church, essays from *Lutheran Quarterly*, edited by Timothy J. Wengert, with foreword by David C. Steinmetz (2004).

A More Radical Gospel: Essays on Eschatology, Authority, Atonement, and Ecumenism, by Gerhard O. Forde, edited by Mark Mattes and Steven Paulson (2004).

The Role of Justification in Contemporary Theology, by Mark C. Mattes (2004).

The Captivation of the Will: Luther vs. Erasmus on Freedom and Bondage, by Gerhard O. Forde (2005).

Bound Choice, Election, and Wittenberg Theological Method: From Martin Luther to the Formula of Concord, by Robert Kolb (2005).

A Formula for Parish Practice: Using the Formula of Concord in Congregations, by Timothy J. Wengert (2006).

Luther's Liturgical Music: Principles and Implications, by Robin A. Leaver (2006).

The Preached God: Proclamation in Word and Sacrament, by Gerhard O. Forde, edited by Mark C. Mattes and Steven D. Paulson (2007).

Theology the Lutheran Way, by Oswald Bayer (2007).

A Time for Confessing, by Robert W. Bertram (2008).

The Pastoral Luther: Essays on Martin Luther's Practical Theology, edited by Timothy J. Wengert (2009).

Preaching from Home: The Stories of Seven Lutheran Women Hymn Writers, by Gracia Grindal (2011).

The Early Luther: Stages in a Reformation Reorientation, by Berndt Hamm (2013).

The Life, Works, and Witness of Tsehay Tolessa and Gudina Tumsa, the Ethiopian Bonhoeffer, edited by Samuel Yonas Deressa and Sarah Hinlicky (2017).

The Wittenberg Concord: Creating Space for Dialogue, by Gordon A. Jensen (2018).

Luther's Outlaw God: Volume 1: Hiddenness, Evil, and Predestination, by Steven D. Paulson (2018).

The Essential Forde: Distinguishing Law and Gosepl, by Gerhard O. Forde, edited by Nicholas Hopman, Mark C. Mattes, and Steven D. Paulson (2019).

The Essential Forde

The Essential Forde

Distinguishing Law and Gospel

GERHARD O. FORDE

NICHOLAS HOPMAN, MARK C. MATTES, AND
STEVEN D. PAULSON, EDITORS

FORTRESS PRESS
MINNEAPOLIS

THE ESSENTIAL FORDE
Distinguishing Law and Gospel

Copyright © 2019 Fortress Press. All rights reserved. Except for brief quotations in critical articles or reviews, no part of this book may be reproduced in any manner without prior written permission from the publisher. Email copyright@fortresspress.com or write to Permissions, Fortress Press, PO Box 1209, Minneapolis, MN 55440-1209.

We gratefully acknowledge the following source: Gerhard O. Forde, *On Being a Theologian of the Cross* © 1997. Wm E. Eerdmans Publishing Company, Grand Rapids, MI. Reprinted by permission of the publisher. All rights reserved.

For details of permissions, see sources section

Cover design: Laurie Ingram

Print ISBN: 978-1-5064-4834-3
eBook ISBN: 978-1-5064-4835-0

Contents

Abbreviations	xiii
Foreword James Arne Nestingen	xiv
Introduction	1
Forde's Life Nicholas Hopman	2
Forde's Works: A Guide to *The Essential Forde* Mark C. Mattes	5
"Forde Lives!" Steven D. Paulson	18

Part I. The Law-Gospel Distinction in Modern Lutheranism

The Position of Orthodoxy	37
The Critical Problem: The Place of Law in the Theological System	45
Theodosius Harnack	53
Gospel as the End of the Law	59

Part II. Death and Resurrection

The Lutheran View of Sanctification	83
Two Ways of Being a Theologian	101

Part III. The Bondage of the Will

The Argument about God	111
Luther and Erasmus	124
Heidelberg Disputation: Thesis 15	127

Part IV. Good Works

Heidelberg Disputation: Theses 26–28	133
Luther's "Ethics"	139

Part V. Controversies Concerning the Law

Law and Sexual Behavior	149
The Meaning of *Satis Est*	167
Lex semper accusat? Nineteenth-Century Roots of Our Current Dilemma	178

Part VI. Theological Method

Systematic Theology Is for Proclamation	197
The Preached God	205
Heidelberg Disputation, Theses 19–21	228

Part VII. The Ministry

Speaking the Gospel Today	245
Something to Believe: A Theological Perspective on Infant Baptism	257
The Lord's Supper as the Testament of Jesus	271

Bibliographies	277
Index	285
Sources	289

Abbreviations

LW   *Luther's Works*. 54 vols. St. Louis: Concordia, 1957–1986.

WA   *D. Martin Luthers Werke: kritische Gesammtausgabe*. 120 vols. Weimar: Hermann Böhlau, 1883–2009.

BC   *The Book of Concord: The Confessions of the Evangelical Lutheran Church*. St. Louis: Concordia, 2000.

BC-T   *The Book of Concord*. Edited by Theodore G. Tappert. Minneapolis: Fortress, 1959.

Foreword

JAMES ARNE NESTINGEN

Team teaching with Gerhard Forde, a calling that extended over more than twenty-five years, was always an adventure.

In some ways, it was predictable. The son of a pastor from the old Norwegian Synod, Forde was more orthodox than pious, emphasizing the priority of Word and sacrament over personal experience. He had grown up in Starbuck, a small town of Norwegian immigrants, in northern Minnesota, where he is also buried. In fact, he could still speak the mother tongue and had the sense of humor common among Norwegian Americans. Holding degrees from Luther College in Decorah, Iowa, Luther Seminary in Saint Paul, and Harvard University, his intellectual acumen was legendary.

But for all of this, there was lots of unpredictability in the mixture. He understood teaching as a form of evangelism, so that generations of his students and readers of his books across the globe describe undergoing conversion in his classes or publications. He was an exceptional athlete, and an especially fine tennis player. In fact, he spent his tour in the army living in the Biltmore Hotel in Miami, assigned to play tennis with visiting officers on "temporary leave."

Forde was also a fine singer, with a range from second bass all the way to first tenor and a reliable pitch. Old timers from the Larpenteur-Eustis neighborhood in Saint Paul remember his regular performances at a place long closed, where he played guitar, sang old country-western music, and, when properly prompted, would recite the entirety of the "Ballad of Sam McGee."

Gerhard met his wife, Marianna, when he was out east. She came from New Jersey, won her doctorate in French from Yale, and, after they moved to Saint Paul in the 1960s, taught at several of the local liberal arts schools, including Macalester College. She is a fine painter. Gerhard and

Marianna adopted three children. One of the sons died not so long after he did.

Parkinson's Disease is not generally fatal, it is said. But Gerhard contracted a rare form of it that slowly savages the intellect. It didn't show up in his teaching for some time; when it did, he began to lose himself in his lectures. Challenged with having to quit teaching, he came back with some outstanding lectures. But the disease claimed the final word on his vocation, and he retired. Even then, he would sometimes reappear during a conversation, flashingly insightful.

Throughout his academic career, Forde enjoyed polemics, mixing it up with other theologians. His opponents included former schoolmates like Robert Jenson and Carl Braaten—Jenson wants disciples and Braaten likes to be one, Gerhard joked. He also enjoyed provoking some legally or liturgically minded Missouri Synod critics, especially some few of the Fort Wayne faculty. But his Luther scholarship remains as Gerhard's lasting contribution, recognized as such by the guild of Luther scholars in the United States and Europe.

The documents in this volume, along with others collected and edited by Mark Mattes and Steven Paulson, provide a wonderful sampler of Gerhard's work. Together with the sermons Marianna collected and published, they provide a lasting illumination of the gifts Christ Jesus invested in Gerhard Forde for the church.

James Arne Nestingen
November 2018

Introduction

Martin Luther insisted that the one essential theological distinction was the distinction between God's gospel promises in Christ and his demanding law. No twentieth-century American understood this law-gospel distinction better than Gerhard O. Forde, professor of theology at Luther Theological Seminary in Saint Paul, Minnesota. Because Forde kept this Lutheran distinction razor sharp, his theological writings are an essential inheritance for us today. This volume, *The Essential Forde*, aims to provide the essence of Forde's writing centered upon Luther's and Scripture's essential distinction, that is, the distinction between law and gospel.

Nicholas Hopman first offers a brief biography. Then two of Forde's students, Mark C. Mattes and Steven D. Paulson, introduce the writings collected here and Forde's theological legacy, respectively.

Forde's Life

NICHOLAS HOPMAN

On September 10, 1927, Gerhard Olaf Forde was born in Starbuck, Minnesota.[1] His father, Gerhard Olavus Forde (1884–1964), served as pastor of Indherred Lutheran Church in Starbuck from 1917 to 1961. He succeeded his father, Gerhard Olaf's grandfather, Nils (1849–1917), who served Indherred from 1892 to 1917. The Fordes' roots were in the Norwegian Synod, known as the "Old Synod." This was the American church closest to the Norwegian State Church and followed its Lutheran orthodox theology.

Forde's mother, Hannah (1888–1928), was killed in a car-train accident when he was about six months old. His aunt and uncle moved into the parsonage to help his father until he married Astrid Flack in 1939. Gerhard attended the local public schools and graduated as the valedictorian of the class of 1945 at Starbuck High School. He was musically talented and took part in Indherred's annual performance of Handel's *Messiah*. Later Forde claimed the piece significantly affected his Christology and atonement doctrine.[2]

Gerhard then attended Luther College in Decorah, Iowa, graduating with a BA in mathematics, chemistry, and German in 1950 after a brief stint in the Army Medical Corps. After beginning graduate studies in chemistry at the University of Wisconsin, Forde enrolled at Luther Theological Seminary in St. Paul, Minnesota, graduating in 1955 with a Bachelor of Theology degree. While pursuing a doctoral degree at

---

1. For additional biographical information, see Gerhard Forde, "The One Acted Upon," *Dialog* 36 (1997): 54–61; Marianna Forde, *Gerhard O. Forde: A Life* (Minneapolis: Lutheran University Press, 2014); Mark Lewellyn Nygard, *The Missiological Implications of the Theology of Gerhard Forde* (Minneapolis: Lutheran University Press, 2011), 17–23; James Arne Nestingen, "Examining Sources: Influences on Gerhard Forde's Theology," in *By Faith Alone: Essays on Justification in Honor of Gerhard O. Forde*, ed. Joseph A. Burgess and Marc Kolden (Grand Rapids: Eerdmans, 2004), 10–21.

2. Nygard, *Missiological Implications*, 19.

Harvard, Forde taught at St. Olaf College in Northfield, Minnesota (1955–1956), studied in Germany at Tübingen (1958–1959), and then taught at Luther Theological Seminary (1959–1961) and Luther College (1961–1963) before returning to teach at Luther Theological Seminary in 1964, where he would teach until his retirement in 1998.

In 1964 he married Marianna Carlson of New Jersey, who was a professor of French at Wellesley College in Massachusetts. The couple raised three children, Timothy, Geoffrey, and Sarah. After Gerhard finished his PhD in 1967, they resided in Oxford, England, from 1968 to 1970, where Gerhard was a tutor at Mansfield College. He was ordained in order to serve as a chaplain for the Lutheran students at the university.

In 1971 Forde switched from teaching church history to systematic theology. He saw the difference as negligible, as he believed that all theology should be historically based.[3] Forde taught many different courses involving philosophical and theological issues and thinkers. However, it was a Lutheran Confessions course he taught for thirty years that brought most students into contact with his teaching. The course was team taught, with Forde supplying the theological analysis of the confessional documents and a member of the church history faculty providing their context. For the last twenty-five years of his career, Forde taught the course with his friend James Nestingen.

Forde served as a member of the Lutheran–Roman Catholic dialogues for twenty largely frustrating years beginning in 1979.[4] He was also a member of the Commission for a New Lutheran Church in American between 1982 and 1988, leading up to the creation of the Evangelical Lutheran Church in America.[5] While Forde's theological positions met quite limited success in both contexts, his work bore the fruit of several publications in which he disagreed with the general direction of the ecumenical movement, including the "historic episcopate," as well as the quota system—one of the first symptoms of the ELCA's leftist political course, which would later be fully completed.[6] While others sought political and ecclesial routes beyond confessional Lutheranism, Forde doggedly confessed its faith.

Forde retired from teaching in 1998 as his Parkinson's disease increasingly took its toll. With the assistance of Steven Paulson, Forde completed his final book, *The Captivation of the Will: Luther vs. Erasmus on Freedom and Bondage*. It was published in 2005, joining the list of pre-

---

3. Forde, "The One Acted Upon," 61.
4. Nygard, *Missiological Implications*, 40–42.
5. Nygard, *Missiological Implications*, 22–23.
6. Forde, "The Word on Quotas," *Lutheran Quarterly* 6 (1992): 119–26. Also see the bibliography at the end of this volume.

viously published books, *The Law-Gospel Debate: An Interpretation of Its Historical Development* (1969), *Where God Meets Man: Luther's Down-to-Earth Approach to the Gospel* (1972), *Free to Be: A Handbook to Luther's Small Catechism* (1975, with James Nestingen), *Justification by Faith: A Matter of Death and Life* (1982), *Theology Is for Proclamation* (1990), and *On Being a Theologian of the Cross: Reflections on Luther's Heidelberg Disputation, 1518* (1997). Two published collections of Forde's essays and sermons have been edited by Mark Mattes and Steven Paulson, *A More Radical Gospel: Essays on Eschatology, Authority, Atonement, and Ecumenism* (2004) and *The Preached God: Proclamation in Word and Sacrament* (2007), as well as a collection of sermons edited by Forde's wife, Marianna, *We Preach Christ Crucified: Sermons by Gerhard O. Forde* (2016). Gerhard Forde died on August 9, 2005, and rests in Indherred Lutheran Cemetery.

Forde's Works: A Guide to *The Essential Forde*

MARK C. MATTES

The Essential Forde is offered to pastors, theologians, and laypeople with the anticipation that it will help foster renewal of preaching, pastoral care, theological conversation, and mission throughout the world. Not only does this volume offer selections of Forde's writings essential for understanding his approach to theology, but it also seeks to show that Forde is essential for theology in today's pluralistic context. Gerhard Forde has proved to be one of the most influential and powerful Lutheran theological voices among American Lutheran theologians over the last century. The resilience and value of his thinking is understandable. Forde wrote simply and directly to his audience, free of academic jargon. His thinking, when compared to others, slices through verbiage, particularly arcane scholastic discourse deeply beholden to philosophy, sociology, or psychology. He takes as his guide Luther's conviction that the absolution should be addressed not only as a general statement but also directly to individual sinners: *your* sins are forgiven . . . the body and blood of Christ given and shed *for you*. All too often the third-person voice obscures the direct and personal nature of the gospel. Only by moving theology into the voice of the second person can the gospel accomplish what it is after: securing sinners in Christ's fold. My part in introducing this volume will affirm the value of Forde's thinking for a new generation of pastors and teachers as well as provide an overall glimpse into the content of this book.

Pastors, especially those who have experienced a crisis regarding the value of their vocation over the last several decades, will find Forde's work compelling. After all, why do we need pastors if we have therapists, social workers, and CEOs? What do pastors do that other callings in our society cannot do better? The vitality of the ministry depends on pastors understanding and believing in the essential calling of their vocation. Forde confesses that theology exists for proclamation. Proclamation is the heart of what ministry is all about. Academic theology does not exist to help the church gain access to the proceedings of the academy. Instead, just the opposite: academic work should improve preaching. Theology is done between the events of proclamation, whether in the context of worship or outside it, all for the sake of improving proclamation. Proper theological reflection serves to empower pastors in the chief aspect of their calling, to proclaim God's word—both law, which mortifies sinners, and gospel, which raises new beings in Christ.

Pastors are stewards of a word that both uproots and plants; both the destructive and the constructive aspects are vital to the work that God is doing. All too often theology has been taken captive to other agendas, for example, human self-fulfillment projects, particularly those designed to liberate human potential. Indeed, theology has opted to reconstruct the idea of God in order to make religion more palatable to "cultured despisers." Against the grain, Forde will have nothing of this. Theology's role to serve proclamation is too vital and necessary. It is not theology that needs to be adapted to the world but instead the world that needs accountability to God's word. So, Forde seeks to get to the core of what plagues humans: defensiveness over the fact that they are mortal. Humans employ all manner of means to soften the threat of death, which is part and parcel with their finitude: we are fodder for worms! With religion and other self-justifying enterprises, humans raise up heroes whose ideals transcend death and whom we are to emulate. Or humans postulate an immortal soul, which, at the moment of death, will be liberated from the body as its prison and move on to different, if not greener, pastures. In wider culture, this defensiveness is masked in several ways. First, many contemporary Americans see guilt as a feeling and not as an objective reality, and thereby mitigate their culpability for their insensitivity or even for their violence. Second, Americans have a long-standing conviction that with the right politics, technology, and education, their optimism about improving society is justified. Third, many live according to the "No Harm Principle": you ought to be as free to do whatever you wish provided you do no bodily harm to others. Finally, we are apt to claim victim status whenever we are challenged to limit our entitlement to self-fulfillment.

In contrast, for Forde, as for St. Paul, death is nothing other than the wages of sin. This means that it is unavoidable. God's law, in its theological usage (as opposed to its political usage, in which it curbs violence and helps to order community), exposes sinners to the reality of their death. The classic biblical example of this is when the prophet Nathan counters David, the adulterer and murderer: "You are the man!" God's law not only provides order for the world, but most important, it breaks down all defenses that sinners raise to preserve their egos. The law proves that no one can be just on their own terms but instead that all have fallen short of God's glory (Rom 3:23). The key to preaching the law—as Forde student Timothy Wengert puts it—is simply to tell the truth.[1] It need not entail haranguing others. In most cases, calling out sinners, exactly as Nathan did, is sufficient to get sinners to admit their need.

Such a path is adrenaline-charged. But God works to mortify old beings precisely so that he can create new beings, those who trust in Christ for their forgiveness, life, and salvation. God is precisely in the business of re-creating this world anew. United to Christ, participating in his death and resurrection through the waters of baptism, the new person of faith emerges—honoring God as Creator and trusting in Christ for all things, entrusting one's mortality into the hands of God's mercy, no longer bound to defend oneself on the basis of one's morality before any tribunal. Indeed, "our real death is our dying with Christ, our crucifixion as self-centered, self-justifying, sometimes even pretentiously-pious sinners."[2] Since that is so, Christians are free. Pastors are at the forefront of liberating people.[3] One need no longer appeal to one's own perceived righteousness as achieving merit, and so having a defense that can withstand death. Instead, through faith one entrusts all of life into the hands of one's merciful Savior, Jesus Christ, and lives with humility, wonder, and curiosity in the beauties of creation, eager to share from one's abundance with neighbors.

In sharing the gospel, preachers actually bring sinners to God and protect them from God's own wrath. Far from being the trait of a jealous tribal deity, wrath is a consequence for creatures who refuse to live as creatures and by faith, and instead attempt to secure their own egos in themselves and serve as their own divinities. Wrath is a "real, daily, social experience and not an abstract doctrine of how God presumably will deal with sinners at the end of time or in the afterlife (though, of course, the afterlife and the last judgment are not denied). In a sense, the human quest for self-justification is an attempt to escape this wrath, or at least tame it."[4] To be free of such defensive living is to be free indeed. So, to

---

1. Timothy J. Wengert, "The Lutheran Confessions: A Handbook for Sharing the Faith," *Lutheran Partners* 17 (2001): 24–29.
2. Mark Mattes, "Gerhard Forde on Re-Envisioning Theology in Light of the Gospel," *Lutheran Quarterly* 13, no. 4 (Winter 1999): 382.
3. Hence, Luther wrote, "Christ did not act like a pupil of Moses but as one who now belonged to the New Testament, where Moses' Law was to be abrogated and a new spiritual order was to be established in the entire world by means of the Gospel message." See LW 22:223; WA 46:732.
4. Mattes, "Gerhard Forde on Re-Envisioning," 381.

get at the heart of gospel proclamation: what was Jesus' death all about? "For Forde, Jesus Christ dies in the place we must die and does so in order to claim us." Hence, following Luther, Forde offers us a theology *of* the cross and not merely a theology *about* the cross. "The final difference between the two is that in the former one must suffer the crucifixion of the old being, and thus become a theology of the cross. Theory will not be a defense against this judgment."[5]

Forde proves to be compelling for a variety of Christians burdened by a spirituality that advocates, in one form or another, "my utmost for His highest." Instead of promoting a spirituality that encourages humans to whip up within themselves a love for God and a desire to perfect themselves, Forde stresses God's love, mercy, and forgiveness for sinners. On the basis of that generosity, Forde is confident that lives can change, and that people will spontaneously appreciate the creation in all its wonders, seek to support less-fortunate neighbors, and live into their callings in the world.

Forde's vitality for today is found in that he empowers pastors to do their ministries, and he does so in an accessible way. He also shows us what theology is to be about. Theology exists not to accommodate faith to the wider secular academy but instead to assist the preacher to speak the word from the text of Scriptures to those hungry for a word of grace or those needing to hear about their dependency on God's mercy. Thereby, Christians are empowered to do ministry in the world. This is not because they conform themselves to any program of world transformation engendered by either the political right or left. It is instead because faith issues forth in neighbor-serving love.

THE LAW-GOSPEL DEBATE

The readings in the first section are selected chapters from Forde's Harvard dissertation, published in 1971 as *The Law-Gospel Debate*. This book presents the varied responses of Lutheran theologians, and the Reformed theologian Karl Barth, to J. C. K. von Hofmann's rejection of Lutheran orthodoxy's concepts of "eternal law" (*lex aeterna*), the view that the law is the center of God's being and that atonement is Christ's vicarious satisfaction. In response to von Hofmann's thesis, Forde compares and contrasts how thinkers such as Theodosius Harnack, Albrecht Ritschl, Karl Barth, Lauri Haikola, Werner Elert, and Gerhard Ebeling reinterpret the law-gospel distinction. Countering orthodoxy, Forde's point is to defend the claim that in Luther's view, law is not coterminous with God's eter-

5. Mattes, "Gerhard Forde on Re-Envisioning," 382.

nal essence, and that in place of eternal law, Christ as God's unconditional mercy is made central. Far from being a ladder to God that sinners are capable of climbing provided they are assisted by grace, the law is only and ever accusing. With respect to salvation, its goal is to lead sinners to Christ. It has a necessary role to bring sinners to Christ, but it does not define Christ's atoning work. Christ is then the *telos* (goal) and the *finis* (termination) of the law.

For von Hofmann, the orthodox perspective pictured a static view of God untrue to the biblical witness in which God works within history to save humans (*Heilsgeschichte*). Likewise, the vicarious satisfaction reinforces not that sinners are saved by grace but instead surprisingly by law. The law is seen as a "way of salvation," albeit one that sinners are unable to achieve and that Jesus Christ, the God-man substitute for sinners, achieves on behalf of sinners. In the face of divine wrath, Jesus "buys off" God by fulfilling the law for the sake of humanity's salvation. Again, for von Hofmann, the metaphor of "buying off," that is, Jesus offering his life as a payment to satisfy God's wrath, undermines God's mercy. In response, von Hofmann saw law not as eternal but instead as an epoch within the history of salvation. Likewise, Christ's atonement was no compensatory reckoning—that is, Christ dying in the place of sinners, an execution of a substitute—but instead a *covering* of sinners so that their sin would no longer separate them from a holy God. Christ's righteousness is no longer an achievement reckoned on the basis of an eternal legal scheme but instead his faithfulness to his own even in the face of their opposition to him.

For Forde, Theodosius Harnack, who challenged von Hofmann, is an insightful thinker, but he challenges Harnack's defense of "eternal law" through making a distinction between the law's "essence" and its "office." In its essence, the law is eternal and good, but in relation to sinners, its role is to condemn. For Harnack, in contrast to the orthodox, Jesus's atoning death should not be seen as an "abstract *a priori* necessity" but instead as an "inner-divine necessity" given that God is holy, but humans are offenders. In response, Forde rejects Harnack's distinction between the law's "essence" and "office" because all Harnack achieves is to relativize God's wrath with respect to God's mercy. But to be true to the gospel, Christ does not merely relativize God's wrath but conquers it.

Forde notes that Albrecht Ritschl is so beholden to Kantian moralism that the law-gospel distinction is irreparably compromised in his theology. But Ritschl's anticipation of a "new community" as a result of the gospel, not so very different from von Hofmann's expectation of a "new humanity," has merit. From this approach, Forde proposes that law and gospel refer to two different ages: one (law) is past, and the other (gospel) is promised. Christians live in the intersection between these two ages, one of wrath and the other of mercy, and both bear on Christian existence. That is, "in Adam," Christians ever encounter accusation, but "in Christ," Christians are totally embraced for Jesus's sake.

While Forde finds Karl Barth's formula that the law is the "form of the gospel while the gospel is the content of the law" to be consistent with the former's proposal that God's word is undividedly and unassailably one, its result is to *legalize* the gospel, construing the Christian life as one of obedience rather than freedom. Barth seeks theoretically to loosen the dialectic between judgment and grace, drawing inferences from God's covenant into the being of God. If Christ's atoning work is seen more radically, that is, more eschatologically, than in Barth, then the formula should be revised. Given what has just been said, the law is not the form of the gospel but instead the form of this age. And the gospel is the end of the law, just as Paul claims in Romans 10:4. Despised and rejected by sinners, Christ's crucifixion is the most powerful manifestation of the law for sinners. But Christ's resurrection is God making good on forgiveness, establishing new life through forgiveness, and re-creating a new humanity in fellowship with Christ.

No doubt, changes within society throughout the twentieth century influenced Forde's existentialist understanding of Luther. Advancements in science and technology; the rise of cities as environments where the majority of humans live; greater advances in educational and work opportunities for women and minorities; as well as the crises of two world wars, the Cold War, and the increasing secularization of the academy made the static theological landscape of orthodoxy less plausible. To be sure, the world of orthodoxy was one Forde knew well since his father and grandfather, Norwegian-American pastors, had been affiliated with the version of Norwegian-American Lutheranism, the "Old Synod," that was the closest of Norwegian-American synods to the Lutheran Church Missouri Synod (LCMS). The LCMS endorsed a "repristinating theology," which sought to repeat the masters of Lutheran orthodoxy in the current cultural milieu. But that version of Lutheranism, in contrast to Lutheran Pietism, highly valued C. F. W. Walther's *Law and Gospel*. This text was crucial for how every Old Synod pastor crafted sermons and did ministry. Walther's classic led pastors to look for how the Scriptures function both to accuse sinners by means of the law and then, through Christ, to comfort them. Walther and his disciples held that law and gospel were latent in the text, waiting for a preacher to uncover them and deliver wrath and promise to the congregation in the sermon. Shorn of orthodox assumptions, Walther's classic was an important motivator for Forde to pursue academic perspectives on law and gospel.

While Forde is not explicit in *The Law-Gospel Debate* about how law and gospel bear upon contemporary American culture, his views in time would become more pronounced, even a frontal assault. In a word, the modern American world was increasingly shaped by the "ethics of authenticity," in which the purpose of life is for individuals more and more to become themselves, provided they do no harm to others.[6] Much American preaching has catered to this ethos: if you accept Jesus as your savior, you will be more fulfilled in life. You will become more of yourself through Jesus. Pre-secular perspectives tended to pit eternity against time, and the goal was to climb the law in one way or another in order to secure one's destiny in eternity in the face of death. Contemporary secularism erases the eternal dimension and takes for granted that people live only in the temporal dimension. But it is no less legalistic. The ethics of authenticity's charge to "be all that you can be" is no mere invitation to self-exploration but an imperative to actually develop all one's potential; otherwise one loses out in one's quest to pursue happiness, provided no harm is done to others. In other words, Forde discovers a *death-dealing* side to the alleged life-giving ethos currently governing America and Europe, a matter preachers can decipher for their hearers, bring to the fore, and then release their hearers from it.

GLORY STORY VERSUS CROSS STORY

Having seen Forde's constructive proposal about how law and gospel should be related as two different eras that existentially bear on believers, the second, third, and fourth sections show how this impacts the Christian life and theological anthropology. As a seminary professor, Forde was eager that his students have a passion for this gospel unfettered from law. Forde was appalled that candidates for ministry would be satisfied with merely giving lip service to the confessional tradition. This passionless stance is due somewhat to seeing justification by grace alone through faith alone as solely presented in terms of a legal or forensic framework. According to this framework, for Jesus's sake sinners are acquitted before the court of heaven. Forde notes that this reading of justification by faith misses an equally important theme in Luther (and Paul): death and resurrection. In fact, we cannot properly understand what the tradition means

---

6. See Charles Taylor, *The Ethics of Authenticity* (Cambridge: Harvard University Press, 1991), 25–53.

by "faith alone" when we sideline the language of death and resurrection. Appealing to important passages in Luther but also Paul (Romans 6; 10:4; Galatians 2), Forde sets forth a theory of participation in Christ. To be clear, it is not that we mimetically participate in higher degrees of likeness to God through the infusion of grace. Like Luther, Forde will have nothing to do with Platonic approaches to participation. Instead, those baptized into Christ participate *totally* in Christ's death and *totally* in Christ's resurrection. Indeed, not just in baptism, but in every encounter with the law, the old being is accused to death, just as in baptism and in every proclamation of the gospel, new beings are raised with Christ. For Forde and for Luther, this talk is no mere metaphor. It is the reality that defines believers. In Romans 6:1–11, Paul announces that we have died with Christ; he does not direct us to mortify ourselves in imitation of Jesus's own resignation to death. Instead, a pronouncement is rendered: you have died! Quoting Luther, Forde notes that baptism is no "false sign" but actually dying and rising with Christ.

Forde was aware that the culture is predominantly Pelagian. That is, American and European culture is not running to seek grace, but instead, in a denial of death, as Ernest Becker put it,[7] it is eager to encourage people to develop their full potential. This is simply a restatement of the "ethics of authenticity" mentioned earlier. Given that this is the dominant cultural mode of operating, influencing business, government, politics, therapy, education, and even much of the church, why would Forde advocate such a counter-cultural stance? The answer is simple: because it is the truth. The best recourse for Christian faith is not to conform to the standards and follies of the wider world but instead to help people face the realities of their finite and fragile lives.

Grounding his thinking in Luther's *Heidelberg Disputation*, Forde distinguishes a "glory story" from a "cross story." The glory story is premised on the denial of death indeed, it is a defense against death and the way of the cross. It attempts to surmount death and the cross through some achievement, whether through piety or worldly success, that will make one secure in the face of finitude and one's limitations. Its story feeds the addiction to the self, Forde's way of describing Luther's view of sin as being "turned in on oneself," against the view that sees sin primarily as misdeeds or the failure to do good deeds. Sin as "incurvature" means that sinners are incorrigibly self-centered. They seek to be their own gods for themselves, which can even include the attempt to grow in virtue when it is motivated by the attempt to secure worth both for

---

7. Ernest Becker, *The Denial of Death* (New York: Free Press, 1973). Forde was fond of this book, so much so that it was central to his lectures—albeit read through a law-and-gospel lens.

now and in eternity. In the glory scheme, grace is nothing other than a supplement to whatever is left of the human will and its power.

Instead, the path of the cross is not one of security but of trust or faith. The path of glory is a cul-de-sac that never accomplishes its goal of total security in the frightening face of death and finitude. This is because nothing short of dying in Christ can do it. The flip side of dying with Christ is rising with him into a new life where one lives from the security established in the gospel, in the promise of God's faithfulness to his own. Risen with Christ, oblivious to preserving the continuity or alleged "sacrality" of the self, we as new beings in Christ can enjoy creation as sheer gift; out of the abundance of God's generosity, we can serve others just as Christ has served us.

If Americans are optimistic about human achievement, and if even the church is complicit (as with the late Robert Schuler's acronym about Lent: *L*et's *E*liminate *N*egative *T*hinking!), old beings affirm a free will. In a word, this means that Americans tend to be Erasmians! That is, we align with the thinking of Desiderius Erasmus and his defense of a "free will." After all, why would God give sinners commandments with the full knowledge that they are incapable of obeying them? That would be unfair and unbecoming of God. The law does not exist primarily to show us our absolute need for Christ, but instead it is a metric by which we can secure our status with respect to God and others. Luther finds such an approach to the gospel to be "Christless" and "Spiritless." Forde shows the honesty of Luther's position. All sinners, all the time, are suffering the *pain* of God. Since we wish to be our own gods for ourselves, we resent the God who in fact rules over all things, including our own lives. This is true whether one is a Christian, a practitioner of another faith, or a nonbeliever. Luther refuses to concede God's omnipotence (as Erasmus would), even though that makes us and everything else subordinate to God's will. Why? Because for Luther, Forde notes, God's immutability means that God is immutably kind. In a word, if God does not rule by immutable necessity, then who would believe his promises? On top of that, God does not force anyone to do anything. People do as they will. But because of their incurvature, similar to an addict, they can do nothing other than ever seek to secure themselves in the face of their finitude. For Erasmus, if God is all-powerful, it must be at the expense of human agency. If God has all power, then humans have no power. And to cut to the quick: there is no point for humans to try to be ethical. Luther's perspective on a *bound will* threatens, for Erasmians, to undermine the whole fabric of social ethics.

Luther will have none of this. Erasmus's attempt to whittle down

God's power in order to secure human agency is misguided. For Luther, Christ grants genuine freedom. Humans are free when they believe God's claim that they are God's own. They are free when they then no longer compulsively seek to secure their identity in the face of nothingness, sin, and death but instead trust the story of the cross and the resurrection to mark their lives and define their being. When the law does its work of bringing one addicted to the self to his or her knees and admit powerlessness over the addiction to the self, then the gospel can jump in and secure people in God's goodness and commitment to sinners. Hence Luther's solution to the pain of God is not to re-create God but instead to allow God to re-create oneself. Thereby, the quest to do good is no longer to secure the self but instead to help the neighbor. The self, after all, having died, is no longer an issue. If the Christian faith is about moral reform, as Erasmus seeks it, then the gospel will also appear as immoral. But those who let go of the attempt to secure their identity in the face of death through their virtues will encounter a freedom they will never wish to lose. And they will crave preaching that ever delivers the goods of forgiveness of sins, life, and salvation. For Luther, God is both the problem and the solution. When God is left "unpreached," his omnipotence pains us. This makes us despair of ourselves so that we might seek comfort in God "preached," who is hidden in the suffering of Jesus and gives his life for us so that we might have new life.

THEOLOGICAL POLEMICS

Chapters 5 ("Controversies Concerning the Law") and 6 ("Theological Method") take up some matters in ethics and ecclesiology that are raised when the law loses its status as central to the heart of God. Given Luther's response to Erasmus, it would seem that the project of ethics is over if we are to believe Luther's gospel. That would be a misapprehension, however. Good works are no longer to be seen as "brownie points" or merit—doing others a good turn in order to improve one's status with God—but rather as one's calling or vocation. That is, good works do not secure our status before God because that is already secure in Christ. Nor do such good works establish the kingdom of God on earth, as if the kingdom were a utopian aspiration. Instead, good works are nothing other than collaboration in God's ongoing creative agency in the world. Forde wisely notes that for many, Luther is too pessimistic about human nature since good works do not serve to make a person good. But by the same token, Luther is deemed too optimistic, since he believes that good people spontaneously will do good for their neighbors and creation.

Addressing the question of same-sex relations, which has vexed many contemporary Christians, especially mainline Protestants, Forde notes that sexual behaviors must be understood within a purpose higher than the mere self-fulfillment of genital self-expression. More specifically, the *estate* of marriage, not just the genital expression of the self, is to be honored. But that rules out same-sex sexual behaviors since it is not possible for same-sex partners to "become one flesh" as described in Genesis. Hence, same-sex relations can copy but cannot participate in what the marriage act symbolizes (two becoming one flesh).

MINISTRY

Defying the ecumenical directions of the Evangelical Lutheran Church in America with the Episcopal Church USA, which led to the ELCA adopting the so-called "historic episcopate," Forde questions whether an episcopate is not the attempt of the church to dominate the world through its ruling institutions in contrast to a gospel-centered approach to the church in which the church proclaims a gospel that sets us free from tyranny. Forde agrees with article 7 of the Augsburg Confession that the gospel and sacraments are enough to be true indicators of the church. The episcopate simply transgresses an "eschatological line" since the church is not for the unifying of world history but instead for the preaching of the gospel in this age. The Confession's insistence on the *satis est* concurs with the eschatological limit of the gospel in which the temporal and the eternal are not blurred.

In the last section we see that, unlike most academic approaches to theology, Forde finds theological method and pastoral ministry as intimately joined. Usually, theology makes a distinction between "primary language," language *from* God, and "secondary language," language *about* God. All too often, it is the latter with its theories and systematization that is accorded the highest academic status. Forde will have nothing of this. Instead, he sees secondary discourse as the discussion that occurs among preachers and others between yesterday's and today's proclamation. It is reflection designed to make that proclamation truthful and compelling. All too often, secondary language about God in theology remains lost in what Luther designated as God "not preached," that is, the abstractions of God's traits and attributes indifferent to the proclamation of Jesus Christ as sure gift for sinners. In other words, it abides in God's "masks" even when it designates God as "father," "mother," or even "love." It tends to approach the "God pain" that all humans feel not with preaching God's promises to sinners but instead in order to find loopholes so that God is no longer a threat. But preachers must honestly confront the truth that the word of the cross actually inflicts pain and suffering. The preaching of the law is God's killing and raising, described in Jeremiah as God's word that uproots and plants. No gospel preacher can possibly live by the motto "do no harm." Again, the word of the law effectuates such suffering, such accusation, in order to render humans receptive.

Ministry for Forde is nothing other than doing the word that elects. Surprisingly, the doctrine of election is the *fons et radix* ("font and root") of ministry. Otherwise preachers are inclined to inflate the wills of parishioners and seek to make them in some way or another more moral. All too often "catholic" approaches to ministry seek to ground it in some ontology that sets ministry off from the laity in some higher ontological status. On the other hand, some Protestant views tend to make the preacher a glorified layperson, or even a hired hand of the congregation. In contrast, for Forde, the ministry is neither. The former again tries to surpass the eschatological limit, while the latter disempowers the distinct ministry of doing the word that elects. What Forde advances is that the ministry is a divine institution in which God goes public with his election of sinners; the word of election is given precisely in the absolution; and sinners are claimed as God's own for Jesus's sake. Likewise, "bishops" have no higher status over pastors but are instead administrators for the public good of the church. Baptism is one way whereby God does the electing, and it is appropriate for children. This is because baptism creates faith, not that faith creates baptism. Or, said more abstractly, the external precedes the internal. Forde quotes Luther, who says that God establishes a covenant with all the earth. We should follow Jesus's directive and baptize people, and let God be concerned about the status of their faith. That approach allows for the gospel to be powerful in the church. Likewise, the Lord's Supper is neither a sacrifice nor a memorial but instead a testament. It is not Golgotha repeated but the carrying out of Jesus's will as a real event in the present.

CONCLUSION

Why Forde? Why now? Keep this in mind: it is not that the Pauline understanding of justification by grace alone through faith alone has been tried and found wanting. Instead, it has not been tried. With Forde's work, we are invited to do this specific doctrine as pastoral practice and thereby acknowledge what the doctrine of justification by grace alone was all about in the first place. Free from defenses against death—precisely because in Christ those baptized have died and have risen—one is invited to fullness of life. One can embrace life on its own terms, with all its vicissitudes, high points and low points, with an openness to life in its fullness, in the confidence that "if God is for us, who can be against us?" (Rom 8:31). The gospel empowers people to live their callings in the world, motived through God's boundless and merciful generosity to reach out to those in need and to serve them. One need not measure progress in Christian growth in holiness, since Jesus Christ is our sanctification (1 Cor 1:30), and he is enough. What can be more sanctifying than to stand still and to give God glory for his redemptive generosity? We can be free from spiritual navel-gazing and instead focus on the needs of this good earth and the many creatures God has entrusted to us in it. Last but not least, we can acknowledge the church as the congregation of the faithful whom God nourishes through word and sacrament and through whose fellowship God renews creation.

"Forde Lives!"

STEVEN D. PAULSON

This volume of *The Essential Forde* is collected carefully from the many books, articles, and lectures of this most important Lutheran and American theologian. Those of us who have been fortunate enough to have had him as a teacher or colleague will enjoy reading this collection as a refresher, and likely we will even find some writings not encountered before. But with this volume, we especially want to introduce Forde to a new generation of pastors, theologians, and other church leaders who do not know him directly. Such an introduction is not as hard as it may sound. One of the great gifts of Gerhard Forde was to write as he spoke and to speak as he wrote, and so this influential theologian can be quite well digested and heard from these writings. This also accounts for the many times I see the slogan "Forde Lives!" publicized around the world. It is always a joy for me to hear from students who have fallen upon Forde (or Forde has fallen upon them) in one writing or another. They find they have heard him so clearly and forcefully that they often say, "Everything changed!" without ever meeting the man. We are sure this collection will have the same effect on you and your successors for years to come.

We have selected a wide range of genres of Forde's work and yet have provided a path through these various writings toward becoming a theologian of the cross in Forde's wake. We call this *The Essential Forde* and look forward to your encounter with this most consistent and direct of the teachers of the gospel. When asked by his students over many years to wander to and fro, speculate, or abstract from the word, he always steadfastly refused to answer any questions (as all other teachers instinctively do) in that kind of second-order speech in which one merely speaks *about* things. Instead, Forde steadfastly answered in the first order of speech—that of direct address—since he knew every erstwhile question asked was in fact a public confession either of faith or unbelief. I have never witnessed anyone else pulling this off, because no one else has ever dared. When a student would say, "What about someone in the mountains of New Guinea, who has never heard the gospel?" (ignorant, of course, of the missionaries long since there), Forde always perceived what they actually wanted. And so he would simply ask, "Do you know of any? Then why are you sitting here?" Or when they would ask, "Do you believe in universal salvation?" he would say, "I did, until you asked that question, but the real question is: do you?" In fact, can a free will actually believe in a pure, abstract idea? The difference between a preacher and a speculator quickly becomes clear in such exchanges.

One of my favorite stories about Gerhard Forde happened when I asked him if he ever considered writing a piece for the famous theological genre involving how one's mind has changed. He responded dryly, "But I never did." From anyone else I would have taken this to be an obscure utterance of a Platonic mystic who believed he had found eternal rest outside the world by means of participating in the divine essence. But Forde was not that kind of dreamer or seer at all. He was, as his own common phrase put it, down to earth, because he knew that this is exactly where God meets man. Even his sermons, which have recently been reproduced in growing numbers many years after their delivery, often cannot be dated or placed, and it would not matter much if they could. This may set off danger alarms regarding Barth's old quip that a preacher ought to have the Bible in one hand and the newspaper in another—which is to say that the text is half of preaching, and the context the other half. Of course, we now know the end result of that clever formula for preaching: the context (which is a constructed myth) always drowns the text, whose written word is there not for life but death. Paul was not just "whistling Dixie" when he said, "The letter always kills." That is why the typical writer's notion of "relevance" always amused Forde (along with the fevered attempts by preachers to be germane), as if this yearning would ensure that writers and preachers would not lose their imaginary powers to impact events, change hearts and minds, and thus be "prophetic." Instead, Forde reminded us that Luther's teaching is not in need of being made relevant to America, but America has always been in danger of losing its own relevancy for Luther's teaching, especially when it comes to the cherished dream of "deciding" or committing one's self to something.

PREACHING'S DOCTRINE OF GOD

About what, then, did Forde not change his mind? Well, to start with, it was what theology itself *was*—or better, what it was *for*. Theology is not there to discover God's hidden, inner essence and then encourage the subsequent work of aligning oneself with that essence. Theology is not there to surpass the limits of knowledge (to think beyond the mundane) so that there would be room for faith. Theology is not at the outer limits of human knowing—*meta* physical or *hyper ousia*—helping to discover the highest goals of truth, goodness, or beauty. Specifically, theology is not there in order to assure humans that a law exists somewhere that does not condemn, terrorize, accuse, and kill—metaphysically in God or psychologically in the self. Instead, theology is there to get someone to preach plainly and simply. Theology is for proclamation, which became the name of Forde's handbook on doctrine.

Preaching uses regular human words, of course, but it is not the same thing as normal human discourse, which seeks perpetually to persuade or inform. It is not what the ancients called "Sophism," which shares opinions and tries to convince others of one's position on the issues. Such rhetoric has its place, but it is not preaching. Disputations are, of course, meaningful and necessary as that "second level" of speaking that follows a sermon in preparation for the next proclamation. Luther loved disputation, and Forde could very much enjoy the details of debate, especially when it came to the relevant matter of what exactly the law is and does. However, the first order of preaching is not talking about God but speaking for God. So preaching is not speaking in general or thinking hypothetically, but speaking practically and directly to people.

Furthermore, what this preaching says to people is not one thing but two. The first declaration is an acute accusation: "You are the man!" as Nathan declared to David. It magnifies the sin. The other is a promise. "I forgive you," which Nathan was also equipped to deliver to David the following day: "You will not die." This second word is always declared in the person of Christ, who is the subject of the sentence, "I forgive you," and so is given to the one in need—the accused sinner, who is the direct object of the sentence. The verb of the sentence (forgive) always has the subject (I) doing its work, not the object (you), and this divine work is accomplished quite apart from the "command." This second, or gospel, word is not only a promise in the grammatical sense, but it is the particular theological promise of Christ to sinners while they are yet ungodly. It is a very specific promise, then, which is always and everywhere a promise that forgives the sin that was previously identified.

Delivering these two words—the threatening law and the freeing promise—marks the true job of the theologian. The Holy Spirit uses the theologian as a tool in order to distinguish the law from the gospel for a particular person or persons. The interplay of these two words is not describing a deep structure or underlying law of the world like yin and yang—the two working as paradoxical parts to the greater, integrated whole. The gospel word is always the last, final, eschatological word. That is why Forde recognized true theologians are always eschatologists, who speak in the present about the future, just as the second Isaiah uttered it: "I am the first and the last. . . . Who is like Me? Let him proclaim it, let him declare and set it forth before me. Who has announced from of old the things to come? Let them tell us what is yet to be" (Isa 44:6–7). There is nothing more to preach once this certain future has been delivered, and only the prayer of thanksgiving—what Luther once called the "Amen gloss"—is what one utters once this word has done its work to raise the dead.

Forde made this theological distinction in the same ways and modes that Luther and Scripture do, but he famously did it in terms of what law and gospel actually do to the *theologians* themselves—producing either a theologian of glory or a theologian of the cross. The theologian of glory insists upon working out all theology under the single, simple, unified premise of the eternal law. Consequently, rather than actually distinguishing law and gospel, this glory theologian works out a hypothetical dream world of creatures in relation to the Creator under the dome of the divine law. So instead of law and gospel, glory theologians are only interested in distinguishing two types of law: a temporarily accusing law and a permanent (either static or progressive) blessing law into which one is speculatively launched and will presumably participate in eternity—present, actual experience of law to the contrary. But these glory theologians do not actually get the future right. They have a dream of what is to be, but it never comes to pass. Consequently, when preaching the law and gospel breaks down in churches, it does so by means of working out its own method of proclamation in terms of two laws—the one that coerces and damns, the other that guides, instructs, encourages, and provides joy, peace, justice, and eternal rest or bliss. The theologian of glory is thus born.

This pattern regularly produces the most seductive theology possible. It tells a mythical tale of the prelapsarian joy that Adam and Eve must have experienced in relation to a divine law that did not threaten but rather blessed them. So the source of their garden joy was to say: how wonderful that God has given us a tree from which we may not eat—and if we do, we die. Nevertheless, this little glory myth of a strange fall from the law following the original joy of the law continues. Such a fall is inexplicable except to say that sin seems to be the unfortunate result of the first noble human's original free will. From this unfortunate exit from paradise, theologians of glory then figure that there must be a way to return to this original state and regain the essential blessing of the law. Perhaps this is possible through the example of Christ, who leads the way back to the eternal bliss of God's inner, or relational, law, whose experience must surely produce joy and peace rather than the present fear and terror—if we can only summon it back.

Forde understood how widespread and deep our desires are for this myth. The church's moral teaching and its sacraments are then organized according to this dream of returning to glory as a long-lost bliss. Most especially, Christ and his cross are aligned to remove the accusation from the law altogether—to fulfill, complete, atone, sacrifice, substitute, or pay the debt for a law that is not silenced but acquiesced, appeased, and freed to become the same organizing principle of life that it must have been in the beginning. God must have originally planned for the law to be our friend. And so all of life is subsequently organized according to the myth of an unfortunate exit from paradise and an arduous return (for some hearty souls) to God's original, integral, universal law.

PREACHING'S ATONEMENT DOCTRINE

Of course, Christ's cross can and must be said to do all that such verbs as *atone* and *sacrifice* and their like want to do, but it must say them without the assumption that God is the law and that Christ is the means to reestablish that law. For this reason, Forde points out in *On Being a Theologian of the Cross* the shattering truth that first and foremost the cross is not recovery of original glory but God's attack on sinners. The cross is not the strange, twisted call to disciples to love the crucifixion against all expectations or natural human desires. Instead this attack by the cross is God's own doing, and not simply a "function" of law or an existential feeling of sinners. God is actually out to get me! He does not simply try to move, persuade, motivate, or change my will, mind, or disposition in order to get his recalcitrant sheep to return to the fold. God hunts bigger game. Indeed, unlike our theories of returning to heaven, which never succeed, this cross/attack actually works! It kills us. Subsequently, we do not ever learn to love that attacking cross or accept it as part of a bigger plan in which God eventually comes around to rewarding our faithfulness. Once the cross hits, we are not returning, following, trusting, or doing much of anything anymore—as is the usual case with dead people.

This is why, from early on, the atonement controversies of the nineteenth century (especially joined by J. C. K von Hofmann), along with the revisionist Protestant attempts to rescue the law's positive function for salvation in the twentieth century (especially Barth), interested Forde. It became his doctoral thesis and first book on *The Law-Gospel Debate*. But he also recognized that any way of describing the cross in some atonement "theory" was first and foremost a way of avoiding the most troubling (especially for Protestants)—and yet valuable—teaching that Luther ever produced: the law ended with Christ. Christian freedom was exactly what Paul said—freedom from sin, the devil, death, and shockingly even the law. The cross was not a fulfillment of the law that restored the true non-accusatory voice of the law, but it silenced the law's voice once and for all. The cross did not produce the old saw that one is freed *from* law (like cheap grace) only in order to be freed *for* it in a new way—a joyful obedience. There were two rejoinders to God's cross attack, both of which refuted the law's end (and both happened so quickly among Luther's best friends and colleagues that you could hardly say "jack rabbit" before Luther was beset by both): the antinomian and the nomian. On the one hand were those who wanted to get rid of law by a verbal fiat—do not preach the law! What better way to get to the gospel! On the other hand were those who wanted to make the eternal, blessed, hypothetical law into the heart of the gospel itself, lest the gospel actually mute the law forever—the single, eternal monolith of God's unshakeable will as law. Otherwise, how would anyone become good—who would even try?—if sinners are not somehow in the eschaton reconciled to God's law?

Thus, on one hand Luther found himself dealing with his good friend Agricola, and on the other with the cleverer and dearer Melanchthon (or at least Melanchthon's experimentally minded students). Luther recognized that what all sides wanted was the same dream: to find a law that does not accuse. Since it was not possible to find such a blessed law on earth, the search had to take the form of pure speculation—looking into the mystical divine essence and/or uniting the primordial and eschatological relation of the Creator to his creatures (Eden and heaven) in order to find a hypothetical, necessary law that aided and abetted Christians to become sanctified. With Agricola, this speculative theology determined to keep the law in the old world under the office of earthly judgment—in the town hall, where laws are made and enforced. Agricola attempted to ban this accusatory, town-hall law from ever entering the church by keeping it out of the pulpit—at least in name. What better way to keep the attack of the law from biting than to check it at the door? Instead of the law, the preacher would paint the picture of Christ and his suffering cross along with Christ's victory over the terror of God's wrath and law in glory. Thus, he was attempting to make God's attack of the cross something appealing. So Agricola's principal text became Luke 24:46–47: "Thus it was necessary for the Christ to die, and to enter into his glory in this way, so that repentance and forgiveness of sins might be preached in his name."

Accordingly, the cross was to be preached without the law in such a way as to elicit the pity that would bring repentance, along with Christ's glory. Christ's glory was taken to be his forgiveness of sins in the sense of fulfilling the law on one's behalf in the act of the cross, so that Christians no longer need to fear this law. Christ tames the wildcat-like law so that it will no longer bite you. He took the law's teeth out so that you can pet and befriend it. In this dream you can have every bit of a *solus Christus*, but Christ is then simply navigating the waters of the law and showing us how to survive. Of course, the gospel then becomes an appeal—a motivator of the will, which Luther caught Agricola sneaking back into the church through the backdoor—as if the cross motivated what the law suppressed. Forde used to say that in the end it was no better to be gnashed by the teeth of a tiger than to be gummed to death by thousands of guppies. The agony is only protracted.

As Luther recognized quickly, this attempt at exiling the *name* "accusation" or "law" did not actually get rid of the thing itself. Nominalists can only help to a certain extent before they fail to free anyone. The law is not just operating in the mode of a "function" when it accuses, but in accusing it is revealing both its essence and existence for us and for itself. Meanwhile the ire of the normally steady Melanchthon was enflamed by this antinomian nonsense, and so the great educator attempted to make his way to the true evangelical teaching from the other side of the equation: the nomian rather than antinomian way. To use Forde's language, Melanchthon tried to heal his leprous students with a second-order remedy to a first-order problem. Melanchthon began seeking a non-accusatory law that could be preached in the church in such a way as to guide, befriend, and encourage the baptized into their sanctification. And behold, the nomian ends up oddly with the same conclusion Agricola had reached: though we cannot find it, the law must be used by God to justify us in the end.

This remedy is why Luther recognized quickly that the problem between Agricola and Melanchthon was really a war of words dealing with, and sharing, the exact same problem. They both wanted the same thing in the end: a law that blessed rather than cursed. But in response to the antinomian syllogism (grace justifies, the law does not, therefore law is not to be taught), Luther concluded in his *Antinomian Disputations*, "This consequence is invalid, because the law is to be taught precisely because it does not justify."[1] Who but Luther (and a few who have followed in his wake) has ever stated such blunt truths? So Luther concludes with a pox on both houses: "Who denies that the condemning law is to be taught, by that simply denies the law itself . . . a law that does not condemn is a fake and counterfeit law, like a chimera or a goat stag."[2]

FORDE'S FAITHFULNESS TO LUTHER'S TEACHING

Forde is one of the few who determined to stay with Luther on this matter of the law and how it is preached. Lutherans have historically run from Luther for shelter elsewhere, say in a Wittenberg cohort, a new orthodoxy, or in a way that thinks of the law in Christ's mouth—especially in the Sermon on the Mount—as not really law at all but the pure, non-condemning law. The law always accuses; it does not justify and never will, because God made it that way from the beginning. Furthermore, God does not resurrect the law at the end to organize or form the new kingdom. This freedom from the law is what makes the current effort at teaching the evangelical proclamation into what Forde called "radical Lutheranism." Radical means *root* here, though it can also take on its secondary meaning of overthrowing the status quo, because it refuses to blame the gospel for the disaster of parishes and morally corrupt people. It refuses the dream of conservative law or of liberal law as the real secret of building a missional church.

In fact, Forde refuses to blame the gospel for God's electing, necessarily, whom he wants and hardening the hearts of people like Pharaoh—who, after all, are just doing their jobs. When Melanchthon took on the terrible job of cleaning up parishes by using the law to correct what was ailing them in his Saxon Visitation Articles, he introduced the whole antinomian problem. Agricola at least recognized that terror would not make churches better. His half-cocked solution was to quarantine the law to lawyers and let preachers run free to give Christ as an example who would entice the congregation to do better. Melanchthon used the stick, and Agricola the carrot.

---

1. *Solus Decalogus Est Aeternus: Martin Luther's Complete Antinomian Theses and Disputations*, ed. Holger Sonntag (Minneapolis: Cygnus, 2008), 295 (disputation 5, argument 8).
2. Sonntag, *Solus Decalogus Est Aeternus*, 375 (disputation 6, theses 12, 14).

But just as it was earlier with Erasmus, Luther recognized that preachers naturally worried about the state of their congregations and yet ended up backing themselves into a corner by searching for a non-accusatory law (goat-stag). When attempting to quell the mass of perdition found in the world—and God knows it is a mess out there—they always arrive at a point in which the gospel itself, the forgiveness of sins, is blamed for the trouble of their awful churches. It either makes grace so cheap that the Epicureans can buy stock, or it makes grace so expensive that only those who can overcome the law's threat are able to buy. No wonder that Agricola ended up re-joining the sophist papalists in foisting the foul Interim plan upon his own evangelical congregations. His big plan of removing the law from the pulpit ended up in the imposition of the law in what was considered its churchly, non-threatening form.

From the beginning, Forde saw clearly that the place of the law in the theological system determined everything the theologian said thereafter. The antinomian hypothesis is always a play performed before an empty house. It may feel good to certain players, but the audience is off seeking freedom and truth elsewhere. It is a game in which theologians dress up the gospel as a non-threatening law in the person of Christ and then tell people that Christ will help them follow the law without any threat—*if only* they can manage to embrace the cross. If Jesus gives a law, such as "You shall not even look upon a woman with lust," it is not an accusation if you love him enough and follow his example sufficiently to live and remain in his orbit. Only the sanctified are able to do this, thus the cross itself will not terrorize when one looks piously upon it. In the end, the play's script says that we have found the way to the non-accusatory law; just follow its lead.

Luther recognized that when Agricola's play is performed, the theater is always empty. No one has followed this experimental path, at least wittingly, because in fact all preachers want to preach the law in their churches. How else can they possibly get the rabble to improve? The form and content of law shifts, sometimes wildly, between Sadducee and Pharisee, between conservative and liberal, but Forde recognized that it was all the same impotent game. Indeed, the law is to be preached; it cannot be any other way. But that law does not justify, and it rarely even improves anything in a church, even for a little while—although admittedly the only way to speak with Epicureans pursuing their own pleasures is to give them law, the whole law, and nothing but the law.

And it should not surprise us, as it did not surprise Luther, that churches are full of Epicurean hedonists who behave like pigs at a trough. To these one does not simply say, "I forgive you," as if there were no law or sin, or as if the law were to be kept for later once their Christian journey had begun. That is a fraudulent future or eschaton drawn out by those who do not want to hear any word from God. But neither can preachers give such animals the law as if it were to attract them into righteousness—as if they would agree with it if they looked at the thing in the right fashion and saw the sense. For Epicureans there is no truth in the dream that they will finally discover something beneficial in this law if they see it through to the end.

FORDE'S PREACHING OF THE CROSS: AGAINST THE *LEX AETERNA* AND ITS THIRD USE OF THE LAW

The biggest problem for preachers, however, is what happens once Christ is dragged into this chimera of giving a congregation laws that will bless it. One devolves into encouraging the flock, improving them, perfecting them, and so sanctifying them by telling stories about how well Adam liked the non-threatening law before the fall. Then the preacher doubles the problem by telling the ready audience about how much Christ likes the law in the by and by—so they will also love it when one day they get to heaven. After all, the law is the very love found in the inner heart of God himself, is it not? And in fact, obedience to the law does indeed make for a better life in this world. What have you to fear if the law has not been transgressed (Romans 13)? But the law preached to a congregation specifically includes the threat of God's wrath, since the law is not and never was given for righteousness in God's eternal kingdom.

Forde's work is so powerful because he knew enough to focus on the place of the law for creatures, especially sinners, as God sees them. The law is not to be speculated about abstractly as something that God needs for his own being. Rather the merciful Father heard the cries of his people, who were being oppressed by the law. He determined to liberate them from that very law and his own wrath by taking the sins from them and putting them on Christ. Nowhere is this understanding of the oppression of the law more important than when it comes to preaching Christ crucified, since the cross cannot be loved, as both Agricola and Melanchthon mistakenly hoped. We could address this basic theological situation in a simple yet counterintuitive way in the form of a theological question: What did the law do to Christ, and what did Christ do to the law? The answer to these adjoined questions, however, is that the law ends up playing a secondary and alien role in the crucifixion—it does not set the rules by which the cross must be understood. In fact, Father and

Son use mercy—outside the law—to steal the precious possession of sin by sinners, and the law only reacts as it must after the heist is pulled—to condemn and kill Christ according to our bidding. As Isaiah declares, "You gave me nothing . . . except you burdened me with your sins . . . and I will not remember your sins" (Isa 43:24–25). And again, "Beside me there is no Christ" (Isa 43:11).

So, what did the law do to Christ? It did an alien work—it judged and testified that the sins of the world no longer belong to the sinners (the normal work of the law) but to the innocent Christ. It damns him unjustly but very effectively. How did this happen? In the first place, the eternal word of God did not count equality with God a thing to be grasped (Philippians 2) and so humbled himself precisely by being born of a woman under the law (Galatians 4). The one who was over the law was born under the law. What, then, did the law do to Christ once the incarnation placed him under its power? It preserved his life under its divine rule, as when he was protected from Herod's attack on infants or from the attempt to throw him from a cliff after preaching his first sermon. It set him out as example since Christ perfectly fulfilled the law. He was the one wholly innocent man on earth. But then the one who knew no sin took the sins of the world and became sin (Isaiah 53; 2 Corinthians 5), and he was crucified by ungodly men.

Forde, more than anyone in recent times, recalled for us that the cross of Jesus Christ was, after all, a murder. And the murderer was us. The cross caught humans, one by one and collectively, in the act of hating Christ more than anything else in the world—the very one whom the law calls us to love above all. This is what Forde meant when he repeatedly said that he wanted something down to earth, concrete, real, and honest about what happened when Christ was hoisted on the tree—not just a hypothetical treatment of pure abstractions of supposed eternal truths about what the law seems to need in order to make the cross something salvific. He did not want to hypothesize about the law in its essence apart from what, in fact, happened to get Jesus killed. He refused to treat Jesus's humiliation as an idea within the logical, necessary requirements of the law. That is, sinners routinely make up atonement theories and then conclude that all the pictures they paint have some aspect of the larger, mysterious truth. It is therefore best not to choose one metaphor for the effectiveness of Christ's death but rather employ and celebrate the diversity of ideas about what makes the cross so effective and so glorious. Such is the real, rotten root of what we today call the principle of diversity and its demand that we think of the cross in multiple metaphors with plenteous analogies, since the mystery is greater than minds can adequately grasp. Speculation on the cross is our best option, and the only possible way to make the cross something lovable.

Instead, for Forde, these kinds of theories of atonement overtake the actual events. What we actually discover when we set aside the vaunted "theories" and "tell it like it is" is in fact a smoking gun with our blackened fingers on the trigger. The story of Christ's incarnation under the law and his path to the cross is the opposite of what we wanted to find (that Christ is our shining example and highest desire, going the extra mile to fulfill the law where we fell short). Instead, what was revealed when the Son of man came into our darkness is that Christ is truly the hated God, despised and rejected by men. For what? Why was it "inevitable" or "necessary"? Christ refused to use his own innocence as merit, but in fulfilling the law he gave his betrayers not just love but the gospel that forgives sin—apart from the law altogether. He gave his righteousness to the unrighteous, apart from the law—he abrogated and silenced the law. Christ ended the law after it had ended him.

As Forde points out, if we ask the simple question, "Why could not God just up and forgive?" we will see that it is not that God could not do this for reasons of the law or would not do it in order to make room for humans to contribute something to the cause. In fact, forgiving is just what God has done from Adam and Eve to the present—and with extraordinary power when Christ himself began to preach. He forgave sin, and we hated him for it. The stupefied atonement question—Why could God not just up and forgive?—is answered simply: He did! We don't want mercy, especially not the free kind. We want justice, just as the law has told us we should desire, and which would be our glory. We want the law, and we would rather kill the holy one of Israel, the only redeemer, rather than lose it. As Forde points out, when we are thus brought to trial for the killing of Christ, the plea is always the same: it was self-defense! Self-defense is the only time murder is justified, since it is better that one man die than that we lose the only path and point of connection between ourselves and our Creator—the only possible path to God's righteousness. Thus, as Forde likes to say, Christ came not merely talking about or referring to the new kingdom but actually *doing* it—with a simple word of mercy that is not law.

So the essence of the law, its heart or will, came strangely to be exercised upon the innocent man—by lawless men who insisted on saving the law—murdered by all. And Christ passively suffered the law's judgment and damnation. In this way, at great cost, Christ pays for the sins of the world—including our own—and makes satisfaction for the sins, that is, takes them and blots them out of the book. Yet the law was not calling the shots here. The "book" of law does not remain. It was the mercy of the almighty Father, who insisted that his Son do this. He insisted on this neither in order to right the ship of God's inner attributes of justice and mercy and bring God back to equilibrium, nor to make the law the reigning power of God's new kingdom. Rather, the Father wanted to take away the sins of sinners and would not be stopped by anyone or anything, including his own, most holy law. God's mercy to take sins burns like a fiery love that will not be quenched by anything other than having Christ take these sins so that in him, not on us, the Father would forget them once and for all. Thus, Forde reasoned backward from God's love born of Christ's cross to the law rather than forward from the needs of eternal law to the cross. Christ will alone teach you what the law is and was.

It is this hot mercy that drives God, not a love of the law's norm and rightness. So the law became a tool in God's horrible insistence that Christ suffer to get to his chosen sinners. Law, exercised through its practitioners on earth, threatened, accused, and attacked Jesus. After all, this attack of self-preservation is both the sinner's and the law's true reason for existing, and it neither could nor wanted to do anything else. Both sinners and law looked around at the hour of the cross and found no more sin remaining in the world—the entirety was laid upon Christ, and they mocked him. The one raised on the tree is concretely, historically, absolutely, unquestionably cursed by God, and from this curse everyone must flee. You not only will not ever love the cross, but you cannot. Your will is bound precisely at this point.

This teaching of the cross of Christ is not a theory of what God or humans have long needed in order to fulfill the law; it is rather the judgment of every judge on earth, starting with the Sanhedrin and Pilate right down to the individuals like Judas, Peter, and Paul. And, of course, this extends to us, who murder Christ daily by murdering his word of forgiveness when it is applied to us by a preacher. The law thus attacked Jesus Christ with its full force of accusation, cursing him with his Father's wrath. It was not a mistake or a blunder that the law attacked the innocent one; it was not avoidable. Nor was this attack of the cross halfhearted on behalf of law itself or its officers, either because it was undeserved or since Christ was, after all, committing a noble act of selflessness—a selfless martyr exercising agape love. This horror was what the law did to Christ—it cursed him with its entire, divine curse, and the Father insisted on this—not for the sake of the law itself but so he could free his chosen sinners by mercy. The central matter of all Scripture was hereby exercised—Christ has borne our griefs and our iniquities

(Isa 53:4, 11). For this reason, Forde often said he learned his whole theology from singing Handel's *Messiah* (and especially this chapter of Isaiah) at his country church.

THE CROSS AND BAPTISM: THE END OF THE LAW

But the story is not finished by what happened between Christ and the law and therefore what it meant for Christ to suffer. Not only did the law do something to Christ, but Christ did something to the law. Christ, the curse, was raised on the third day by his Father and the Holy Spirit. But at this new thing, or in this new kingdom, the law had played itself out. The law had nothing more to say or do. It was now, eternally, in a state of quiescence—quiet, dumb. The law was abrogated by the propitiator. It was emptied of content and void of form, never to rise and speak again—eternally, because Christ suffered it in full. The law remains eternally silent when and where Christ is present.[3]

Even this would mean much for Christ's person but nothing for us sinners, who very much remain under the law with its full accusation—even while the law protects and preserves our lives in this old world. The law still has much to say to the old Adam or Eve, including the baptized Christian who is not yet perfectly fulfilling the law as Christ promised we would—that is, to the extent that he or she is not a Christian. The resurrected Christ is not simply the hope of an empty tomb, nor is Christ the victor over sin, death, devil—and the law itself—only in and for himself. The resurrection itself is not the good news, as the disciples roundly learned upon seeing the thing of the empty tomb—they ran away! But the final matter of Christ and the law is this: while the law lies dumb, Christ now speaks. Christ did all of this not just to show that God has power over everything, even the law. It was to comfort sinners whose conscience is accused by the law and especially by what the law shows us—that we murdered the Son. The cross's purpose was to make faith in us. What he says, therefore, is not the old law—you must pay for this betrayal! Nor is it a new law like the old: whereas before you hated me, you now have a second chance to love me. It is rather a new word altogether: "I forgive you, apart from the law, with a promise that Christ himself and alone shall keep, since he has determined that no principle, power or authority on earth or in heaven can keep me from this absolution."

Christ's kingdom is not organized or ruled by the law but by the

---

3. Nicholas Hopman, "Luther's *Antinomian Disputations* and *Lex aeterna*," *Lutheran Quarterly* 30, no. 2 (Summer 2016): 158–60.

gospel. That is, the Christian life is now free from sin and the sting of death (and so Satan's sermons that try to improve us and promise us glory) because it is free from the law, thus fulfilling the law without the law as the work and gift of the Holy Spirit. There is only freedom on account of Christ's promise, not duty, virtue, or obedience. Thus, wherever Christ is preaching, there and then the law is not only fulfilled, but it comes to an end. Christ fulfills the law; we do not. However, Christ's own fulfillment is not what unleashes God's burning mercy. It occasions an unheard-of and truly terrible duel between all the forces of sin and death and law, including God's own wrath and God's righteousness outside the law in eternal, free life. God against God! Christ raised from the dead is the arrival of the promised new kingdom where God's righteousness defeats sin, law, the devil, and even the last enemy, death. God's faithfulness to this promise is certain, not only for Christ's sake, but for the very sinners who belong to Christ. Faith is then in Christ's blood as a mercy seat (Rom 3:25). Christ is not only present as resurrected but speaking to his sinners in such a way that they are crucified in his death and raised in a resurrection like his—that is, baptized (Romans 6).

This end to the law is what alone satisfies God, who not only wants to be merciful in himself but actually to have mercy on sinners in the middle of their acts of sin, including deicide. God necessarily is satisfied only when the Holy Spirit sends a preacher who forgives as Christ forgives—and it actually works! That is, it actually creates faith where there was none. But this necessity and satisfaction is apart from the law because (to our great shock, surprise, and dismay) God is not the law. Forde first became a theologian by taking up the great and nearly unceasing debates over atonement, and he finished the same way, by recognizing that these debates are merely a tool to get to what the Holy Spirit really wants. And what does this Holy Spirit want but to deliver the word of the cross from the mouth of the resurrected Jesus Christ? He himself knows well what we did to him, and he has the one power that overcomes this betrayal by forgiving the sinner, thus raising the dead. God used the law as a tool and then disposed of it when the mercy (apart from the law) was delivered in the absolution to the sinners God necessarily wanted. He will not stop wanting it until this burning love of mercy is satisfied and he actually gets a preacher to deliver his goods to you.

What happens to the law, then, once God discards it so shabbily? The law continues to be preached in its fullness in this old world until the gospel is applied to the bruised reed. Then the law finds its one and only end—quiet, silent, and empty. As Luther liked to say, the law is thus behind you rather than ahead of you. Either the law will compose the theological system, or the gospel will break out of the legal system into something new. That is why Forde—first a church historian, then a systematic theologian—was nevertheless unsystematic. Of course, the same is routinely said of Luther—not that Luther had a different pastoral style or was constantly replying to disparate contextual situations that arose helter-skelter. Luther was unsystematic not because he failed to produce a system of thought to compare with Aquinas's or Calvin's. Rather, both Luther and Forde broke free of the legal system and are both doing something the old world hates: operating outside the system. Of course, this is always hated until it dawns on one that Christ's promise really is not a law at all. But this change does not happen by faith seeking understanding. It requires a much greater change than the will or mind can muster itself. This change is that which moves from death to life. The law is satisfied only when the sinner dies; God is satisfied only when the sinner is joined to him in a true reconciliation without the law intervening. We have learned to tolerate just about any act or thought known to humankind, but we will not tolerate absolute forgiveness by God until we die of our hatred and are raised outside this law entirely.

This is where both antinomians and orthodox nomians find their own limits, and Forde recognized what it meant for evangelical teaching to be free of both. He was also aware of the problems that arise for theology when either the law or the gospel is ignored. Thus, as he often said, what he wanted from his teaching was merely to improve preaching—here or there—by getting people to *do* the gospel rather than talk about it. That means to give the promise rather than merely describe it. Just so, the fruit of Forde's labor continues. Many more preachers have actually begun to elect the ungodly, even while they are ungodly, through the declaration of God's mercy as a pure promise. Although he would have rejected this conclusion and probably is rejecting it right now, he appears to have been used to produce an actual good work—even sanctification—by getting us used to being justified by faith alone and free to just do it. He never changed his mind about this, and in eternity will never have reason to.

PART I

The Law–Gospel Distinction in Modern Lutheranism

The Position of Orthodoxy

The beginning of the modern debate about law and gospel took the form of a controversy over the doctrine of the atonement. The controversy erupted when J. C. K. von Hofmann attacked the orthodox doctrine of vicarious satisfaction in the name of a *heilsgeschichtliche* theology. Although the law-gospel issue is seldom mentioned as such, when we look back on the controversy from our present vantage point it is apparent that this was really the central issue. In this more or less forgotten chapter of 19th century theology *Heilsgeschichte* confronts Orthodoxy,[1] and this confrontation begins a crisis of major proportions—so much so that it is still a key to understanding many later developments, most especially the debate over law and gospel.

Before turning to the controversy over the atonement precipitated by Hofmann, it will be necessary briefly to outline the orthodox position against which he directed his attack. This will lead us into the orthodox conception of the relationship between law and gospel.

The key to the traditional orthodox position is the understanding of the place of the law in the theological system. Protestant orthodoxy operated with what we shall refer to in this study as a static-ontological concept of divine law. This idea of law provides the basic structure for the whole orthodox system and so determines the understanding of all other related doctrines—the nature of the gospel, revelation, and of course, the doctrine of the atonement.

The orthodox understanding of law stemmed, no doubt, from its theology of justification. Orthodoxy made the doctrine of justification of central importance; this led quite naturally to a system based on

---

1. We shall use the term "Orthodoxy" in this study primarily with reference to the orthodox doctrine of law and gospel. Even though many of the theologians we refer to could not be classified as "orthodox" in the 17th century sense, nevertheless they were orthodox in their view of law, gospel, and atonement, and it is to this complex of ideas that I refer.

divine law and justice,² for the theology of justification by faith posits a God who alone justifies and decides man's fate. In his absolute freedom (*agens liberrimum*), God acts according to his own good pleasure;³ to the orthodox this freedom could make him seem almost arbitrary in his motives and actions. There was, consequently, a pronounced attempt in Lutheran dogmatics, to avoid assigning God this whimsical freedom. God, they said, acts freely indeed, but only in accordance with the inner law of his own essence.⁴

If in his essence God is righteous and acts only according to the law of his own being, then this must also be true in God's relationship with man. God's righteousness, God's claim upon man, expresses itself in the form of law, and justification must take place in accordance with this law. Law is, therefore, an eternal, objective order, a *lex aeterna* which sets forth the ideal to which human life must attain in order to find favor with God.⁵ In the law man encounters the personal will of God, so that relationship to this will becomes the decisive problem of his existence. Only a righteousness which is *absoluta conformitas* with the divine law can count in justification. Here the basic structure of the orthodox system is already given; the entire orthodox theology of sin and grace is formulated against this background.⁶

Furthermore, this divine law finds its "echo" in the "natural law," the law which speaks in the conscience of man. The righteousness of God makes its claim upon man, demanding absolute conformity, threatening the conscience. The remnant of the divine law in the conscience of man, the natural law which has persisted even after the fall, provides the point of contact. This basic understanding of the law enabled the orthodox to build a rationally coherent system.⁷

The law provided, therefore, the structure which governed the understanding of other doctrines. This is most apparent in the doctrine of the atonement. The law is, in effect, the "way" of salvation, but because of his sin man cannot traverse this "way." Since he cannot meet God's demands, he is guilty and subject to just punishment under the law. Atonement takes place only when another as man's "substitute" bears the

---

2. Hans Emil Weber, *Reformation, Orthodoxie und Rationalismus*, 3 vols. (Gütersloh: C. Bertelsmann Verlag, 1937–1951), 2:1–11.

3. Weber, *Reformation*, 3.

4. Weber, *Reformation*, 3.

5. Lauri Haikola, *Studien zu Luther und zum Luthertum*, Uppsala Universitets Aarsskrift, no. 2 (Uppsala: Lundequistika Bokhandeln, 1953), 9.

6. Weber, *Reformation*, 5–7.

7. See Ernst Troeltsch, *Vernunft und Offenbarung bei Johann Gerhard und Melanchthon* (Göttingen: Vandenhöck & Ruprecht, 1891), 135–40.

punishment and succeeds in going the "way" instead of man. Since the law was understood as an objective scheme of demands and prohibitions, as a legal order which must be fulfilled, it was quite easy to conceive of a substitutionary fulfillment by Christ.[8]

Vicarious satisfaction of the demands of the divine law is therefore the heart of the orthodox doctrine of the atonement.[9] Here orthodoxy follows mainly in the tradition of Anselm, although with some alterations.[10] Their main point is Anselmian: that Christ made the satisfaction which was necessary to allow God to meet man in mercy.

The alterations come in two places. First, the Anselmian alternative, either punishment or satisfaction (*poena aut satisfactio*), was rejected. The law demands punishment for sin, so that satisfaction can be made only if the necessary punishment has been suffered. For orthodoxy the punishment *is* the satisfaction. Second, orthodoxy differs from Anselm in its emphasis upon active obedience in the fulfillment of the law as well as passive obedience. If man cannot fulfill the law, Christ must do it actively as man's substitute; the demands of the law must be fulfilled under all circumstances. It is important to note here that both alterations serve the same end: they strengthen and magnify the place of law in the system.[11]

Thus the elevation and insistence upon the law as *lex aeterna* were the distinctive features of the orthodox system. The demand for satisfaction was even more insistent than it was in Anselm; the Anselmian view is magnified and made more legalistic. This is shown by the position of some of the orthodox teachers on the necessity of the atonement. Quenstedt, for instance, rejected the "scholastic" idea that God could forgive by virtue of his absolute power without satisfaction[12]; because his essence is righteousness God can do nothing other than be wrathful against sin until satisfaction has been made. Others, like Hollaz, admitted that God could, as absolute Lord, forgive without satisfaction, but they went on to say that in justification God acts not as absolute but as a righteous judge (*iudex iustissimus*) who has the law in himself and whose righteousness is part of his nature. For Hollaz, then, the absolute power to forgive without satisfaction is only an abstract possibility which can have no actuality. The idea that God's righteousness necessarily demands satisfaction is still basic.[13]

I shall refer to this orthodox doctrine of the atonement as a speculative

---

8. Haikola, *Studien*, 10–11.
9. Gustav Aulén, *Das Christliche Gottesbild* (Gütersloh: C. Bertelsmann Verlag, 1930), 256.
10. Aulén, *Das Christliche Gottesbild*, 257.
11. Aulén, *Das Christliche Gottesbild*, 257.
12. Aulén, *Das Christliche Gottesbild*, 258.
13. Aulén, *Das Christliche Gottesbild*, 258.

construction based on the static-ontological concept of divine law. I do this because, in contrast with the more historically orientated view of Hofmann, orthodoxy understood the atonement against the background of a concept of the law which is rooted in the divine being as an eternal and unchangeable standard. The law provides the rational framework for understanding what takes place in the atonement. This can be called a speculative construction because it seeks to posit what is necessary "from God's point of view" before atonement can take place. By using this framework orthodoxy is forced to think in terms of a rational equivalence between the punishment inflicted on Christ, the divine-human substitute, and the demands of the divine righteousness.

This orthodox doctrine of law has several consequences for the rest of the theological system. These consequences are evident in the orthodox conception of the relationship between the law and the gospel, for orthodoxy was driven to make what can be called an abstract and material distinction between the law and the gospel. Law was distinguished from gospel in the same way that one group of propositions is distinguished from another according to the given content or matter of each proposition. Those propositions which contain the *demands* of the divine righteousness are law whether they be "natural" or "revealed." On the other hand, those propositions which contain the divine promises and gifts are "gospel," and come, of course, only through "revelation." This distinction can be called abstract and material because, as we shall see later, it is to be contrasted with a more concrete and formal type of distinction which emerges from the modern debate.

The fact that law and gospel were understood as composed of propositions had the further consequence that revelation itself was understood quite strictly in a propositional sense. Orthodoxy said that revelation is the impartation of divine truth in the form of propositions which "must be believed" if one is to "be saved." Faith, therefore, is understood as an act of cognition—the acceptance of the propositions of revelation—and one is led quite necessarily into the knowledge, assent, trust (*notitia, assensus, fiducia*) scheme characteristic of the orthodox system.

Since revelation is propositional, the law-gospel distinction as such has little or nothing to do with the problem of how revelation is to be received and validated; as a result the distinction never affected the dogmatic prolegomena of orthodoxy and was relegated to the practical sections having to do with the preaching of the word.

This meant that orthodox theology had to depend upon some other means for validating the propositions of revelation. Here it was the doctrine of scriptural infallibility which filled the breach. Since revelation was propositional truth, the orthodox theologians had to establish first the reliability of the propositions before they could go on to other matters. They were virtually driven therefore to a doctrine of verbal infallibility. Starting from assumptions about the eternal standard of the law, the system produced a chain of consequences which are difficult, if not impossible, to avoid—up to and including a view of scripture which could hardly survive the crisis presented by the development of the historical-critical method. In addition to these more or less formal consequences of the orthodox conception of law and gospel, there are consequences more intrinsic to the system itself which became the object of considerable attention in the controversy over the atonement. Because the law was seen as a static, eternal order, orthodoxy committed itself to a system which became extremely difficult to operate.

This difficulty is evident in the orthodox doctrine of justification itself. In order to guarantee a justification *sola gratia*, faith had to be described as the appropriation of the entirely "objective" work of Christ. Justification had to be purely "forensic." One therefore became entangled in the difficult question of "objective" versus "subjective." Justification is supposed to be entirely the work of God, something "outside of" man and therefore entirely "objective." But this makes it seem as though man subjectively has nothing whatever to say about it and that God's justifying action is entirely arbitrary. On the other hand, if one reacts to this by asserting the place of man's subjectivity, seeking a place for man's "decision" or "response," and making justification somehow dependent on such subjective response, one is hard pressed to avoid the charge of synergism. Thus traditional piety was torn between the poles of orthodoxist "objectivism" and pietistic "subjectivism."

The nature of the ethical life is also obscured by the orthodox view of law. Works must be excluded from justification; consequently, careful distinctions must be made between justification and sanctification, even if they tend artificially to fragment the Christian life.

Starting from certain assumptions about the law, then, the orthodox system spun a web from which it was difficult to escape. When the law is thought of as a static-ontological scheme, atonement must be understood as an "entirely objective" act, a satisfaction of the demands of the law. The gospel then becomes a proposition to the effect that the demands of the law have been met, that a "once-for-all" act has occurred within an eternally fixed scheme. God's action in Christ then loses any dimension of present actuality; one is confronted instead with a doctrine about a past event which "must be believed." In order that the doctrine possess credibility the reliability of the historical sources must be assured;

thus the doctrine of scriptural infallibility must be added. All this follows quite naturally and inevitably from the original starting point. The orthodox system was a system wedded to a particular conception of law; this meant that the entire edifice was permeated by a stringent legalism which it could not avoid.

Admittedly, this sketch of the orthodox system is exceedingly brief, as is the case with most brief sketches it runs the risk of caricature. There are no doubt many devices and distinctions which the orthodox theologian could and did use to ameliorate the difficulties of the system, but those are not our concern here What I have sought to do is simply to expose the main structural components which bear upon the problem of law and gospel and which lead into a controversy about the atonement. It is necessary to do this in order to understand that when the battle was joined over the doctrine of the atonement it was really the fundamental structure of orthodoxy that was being attacked, and that that structure is based upon a particular conception of law and gospel.

Of course, the orthodoxy of the early 19th century was not exactly that of the 17th century. The orthodoxy of the early 19th century, variously called Biblicism, Supernaturalism, or Repristination Theology, arose out of the religious awakenings of the time and was a reaction to the erosion of the traditional theology by the Enlightenment. It was inspired by different conditions and used a somewhat different methodology, but the end result was in most cases the same as the orthodoxy of the 17th century. This is especially true in the areas of our concern here, the doctrine of law and gospel and the doctrine of the atonement.

A good example of 19th century orthodox theology can be seen in the work of E.W. Hengstenberg (Professor in Berlin, 1828–1869), a theologian whom Hofmann attacks in much of his early work. In opposition to the Enlightenment and the encroachment of historical criticism, Hengstenberg sought to base his theology entirely and objectively on the Bible. From the religious awakening he drew the belief that rebirth is necessary for true theological work and that obedience to the word of scripture is the only possible procedure.[14] In opposition to the rationalists he held that there was no philosophical road to the knowledge of God. Revelation, in his view, was contrary to human reason and so could not be buttressed by appeal to universal truths.[15] Unlike the orthodox of the 17th century, he made no attempt at a synthesis of natural and revealed truth.

---

14. Werner Elert, *Der Kampf um das Christentum* (München: C. H. Beck, 1921), 87.

15. Emanuel Hirsch, *Geschichte der neueren Evangelischen Theologie* (Gütersloh: C. Bertelsmann Verlag, 1954), 5:119–23.

To avoid the charge that he based his theology purely on subjective experience, Hengstenberg appealed to the Bible as the sole objective basis for faith. His aim, which involved excluding all subjectivity and human reason, was to listen simply and completely to the words of the Bible as the objectively given source of revelation. His only goal was to learn to think and to teach biblically.

Hengstenberg made a kind of substitution of biblical objectivity for rational objectivity. Rationalism sought its "scientific" objectivity in the universally valid truths of reason. Hengstenberg's repristination theology sought its objectivity solely in its object, the Bible. This kind of Biblicism, Hengstenberg thought, could be the only real defense against historical criticism. Historical criticism, he felt, was contaminated by alien subjective concerns stemming from human reason. Like other Biblicists, he carried on a kind of negative apologetic in that he sought to defend the authenticity of scripture by demonstrating that the arguments of the critics were not necessarily conclusive.

The complete subjection of man's mind to the objective authority of scripture brought with it for Hengstenberg a return to orthodoxy in doctrine. The Bible became the sourcebook for church doctrine. In Hengstenberg's view, the doctrine of the Bible and that of the Church Confessions (The Augsburg Confession) were one.[16] The Bible was treated, even more than in orthodoxy, as a compendium of doctrines.

As a theologian and as an influential church politician, Hengstenberg worked unceasingly for the renewal of orthodoxy. It is significant that he devoted a good share of his theological energy to a renewal of the orthodox doctrine of vicarious satisfaction.[17] The net result of Hengstenberg's work was simply a restoration of orthodoxy under the aegis of Biblicism. This meant, of course, the reinstatement of the orthodox position on law and gospel.

Through men like Hengstenberg, orthodoxy was revitalized and offered to the "awakened Christian" of the 19th century as an alternative to the rationalism of the Enlightenment and as a defense against historical criticism. But for those who really took historical criticism seriously and who could not simply dismiss the developing historical world view as something antithetical to Christianity, Hengstenberg's Biblicism could hardly be a viable alternative.

---

16. Hirsch, *Geschichte*, 122.
17. Hirsch, *Geschichte*, 127.

To attack this Biblicism, though, meant to attack the entire system of which it was a part. The man who saw this most clearly was J. C. K. von Hofmann. His attempt to reconstruct the entire system on the basis of a *heilsgeschichtliche* scheme was an attack on the basic presuppositions of the orthodox-biblicistic system.

The Critical Problem: The Place of Law in the Theological System

The 19th century controversy over the atonement was inconclusive. We have suggested that this was so because both parties failed to locate the critical problem in the debate. Here we must seek briefly to spell out this contention before turning to an account of the manner in which the debate continued.

The critical problem is the manner in which one conceives the place of law in the theological system. Is law, as the orthodox system implied, the structure through which man is related to God, the expression of the eternal will of God for man, or is it, as Hofmann has said, only a part of a historical dispensation, so that man's relationship to God must be understood more in terms of the historical realization of the divine will to love? This is the question which we must examine more closely.

Hofmann was quite astute in exposing the difficulties in the orthodox view. For when one assumes that the law is the eternal standard governing man's relationship to God one can hardly avoid a number of problems. These problems are all reflected in the perennial problem of the relationship between wrath and love in God. When law is the standard, one can hardly avoid the implication that "before" the atonement God is wrathful and only "after" being satisfied does his attitude change to love. By this, of course, the orthodox intended to give real significance to the historical event of atonement itself. It brought about a real and "objective" change in God's attitude towards man and, supposedly, established justification as an *actus forensis* (declarative act) on a solid basis.

The difficulties in this scheme are manifest, though, as Hofmann was quick to point out. They can be summed up by saying that it becomes difficult, in such a view, to give systematic expression to the divine love. There is, of course, the old question: If God was simply wrathful "before" the atonement why was Christ sent? Further, there is the equally perennial question: If God's wrath has been "bought off," how can one call it an act of mercy? And when, in seeking to explain how such "payment" could take place, one is drawn into a computation of the equivalence between the payment due and the "infinite worth" of the God-man's sufferings, the problems are only compounded and the legalistic web is spun even tighter at the expense of the divine love.

Hofmann's opponents, as we have seen, generally attempted to disassociate themselves from such computation; they took refuge instead in the idea that it was not abstract reckoning that demanded payment but the sinner's experience of guilt. But this simply substantiated Hofmann's charge that the whole doctrine was a *theory* constructed according to *man's* ideas about what God *must* do to atone for sin, and does nothing to alleviate the difficulties of the system. In general, it can be said that since the question of God's eternal attitude has been preempted by law, it becomes exceedingly difficult to give systematic expression to the divine love. Wrath tends to become the primary category and love always comes off second best. And this leads in turn to the legalistic attitude toward scripture and revelation which we noted at the outset.[1]

Hofmann, on the other hand, wanted to give the primary place in the system to the divine love-will. He asserted that God was eternal love even "before" the event of the atonement. The event itself is the *realization* of the eternal love-will. This makes Hofmann the object of orthodox criticism because he seems to make the historical event a mere *demonstration* of an eternal truth and he is hard pressed to explain why the sufferings and death of the Godman are really necessary. But Hofmann's view, of course, is not that simple. That God is love is not a *general* truth; rather it is a conclusion reached only by "thinking in" the new situation "after" one has experienced the benefits of the cross. His system was supposed to be strictly the result of *ex post facto* reasoning.

This is where the difficulty of comparing Hofmann's system with the orthodox system arises. It raises the difficult question of whether in fact one can really reason in this manner and still give the historical event of atonement crucial significance—a question with which subsequent debate will become increasingly involved. The orthodox theologian argues on the basis of a more-or-less natural logic of law and retribution common to everyday experience available to everyone. Hofmann, however, wants to argue on the basis of a special *heilsgeschichtliche* logic available, supposedly, only to the man of faith. Thinking in the situation of faith leads, in Hofmann's view, to the demand for a continuous

1. Above, pp. 42–43.

historical scheme describing the progressive self-realization of the divine love. It was the orthodox inability really to cope with the problem posed by Hofmann's type of reasoning that lay at the root of the difficulties introduced by the atonement controversy. Hofmann actually proposed that by "thinking in" the situation of being a Christian one can penetrate behind the events of history into the divine intent in such a way as to deduce therefrom the whole sweep of the process. When this is judged to be possible, one can simply put law in its proper place in the historical scheme. The law is something which comes "between the times" and pertains only to a particular stage in the process. This means that a theory of history—a historical continuum—has displaced the law as the "system" for understanding the atonement.

The orthodox objection at this point was that such a view does not take law and wrath in its ultimate seriousness. There was a certain legitimacy to this objection, but the real difficulty is in the system which Hofmann proposed. For Hofmann, just as much as the orthodox, could insist that it is only in the historical event that the law was "fulfilled." But when in theologizing about that event he reasoned *behind* the event so as to make it seem that the fulfillment of the law was from the outset a foregone conclusion, that Jesus by his very nature could not do otherwise, then he had assimilated law into a scheme in which it is easily disposed of. And this means that the real threat of the law has been removed by a theological construction. The "theory" to which the Christian is privy has depotentiated the law.

This means, in effect, that the wrath of God has been "seen through." Even though he asserted the place of wrath in no uncertain terms, Hofmann fit it into a scheme in which it is no longer very terrifying. He had "figured God out." When Hofmann reasoned behind the cross to set up his historical scheme he ran the risk of making the divine wrath seem fictive. It is because he did this that his system in turn threatened to rob the historical event of atonement of its decisiveness. Hofmann's Jesus suffered as he has said, in consciousness of and faithfulness to his calling. This means that Jesus himself is all the while privy to the divine plan, that he knows its outcome, and that since at all times he preserves his relationship to God he cannot suffer "what man should have suffered"—the desolation of ultimate defeat and despair. The atonement then appears as the working out of the divine plan which was from the outset a foregone conclusion. The historical event threatens to become mere demonstration, in spite of all the insistence upon "history." An element of docetism comes to the surface for, when all is said and done, Hofmann's Jesus is "protected" from the full reality of historical death, despair, and defeat.

The "system" which Hofmann proposed demanded a Jesus who at all times preserved his *Berufstreue* and whose suffering had to be a *Berufsleiden*.

In effect, Hofmann's Jesus died the death of a good *heilsgeschichtliche* theologian. He knew what the eventual outcome would be and thus he was protected from its ultimate seriousness. This, really, is the point at which Gottfried Thomasius' objection that in Hofmann Jesus never experienced wrath *personally* receives its due. And it is hardly to the point for Hofmann to defend himself by saying that a Jesus who suffers in consciousness of his calling does not suffer *less* but *more* than man, for then he is indulging in the same kind of *quantitative* speculation for which he has castigated his opponents. It does nothing to rescue the fact that by means of the system the wrath of God had been "seen through."

Orthodox criticism of Hofmann was therefore in a certain sense justified. Nevertheless, the difficulty in the controversy lay in the fact that the orthodox attack on Hofmann was based upon a set of assumptions which were equally as vulnerable. They too assumed that it was possible to reason behind the cross into the divine mind; they did it, however, on the basis of law and righteousness rather than a historical scheme. They too had "figured God out" in their own way and could develop a theory about the atonement as the satisfaction of the divine wrath. Even though the scheme was different the results were similar, for a wrath which can and in fact has been "bought off" can hardly be taken very seriously. A forgiveness which has been "earned" and a divine "love" which could stage such a "show" is not very persuasive. Furthermore, the objection raised against Hofmann that Jesus did not *personally* suffer the divine wrath could with equal justice be made against the orthodox view. For the orthodox Jesus too must be one who suffered with full knowledge of the end which such suffering would accomplish. He knew that he was the God-man and that his suffering would satisfy the divine wrath; he knew, therefore, that it would all "come out well" in the end. If Hofmann's Jesus died the death of a good *heilsgeschichtliche* theologian, the orthodox Jesus dies the death of a good orthodox theologian. In either case the outcome was assured by the system, and Jesus was protected from the full consequences of death and defeat. The orthodox structure too is one which threatens the real historical nature of the cross event. The theologizing about the event leads one to focus attention on a theory or doctrine *about* the event rather than to trust *in* the event itself.

Thus the underlying similarity of the two systems is exposed in spite of differences. *Both* attempted to understand the atonement in terms of a *theory* which threatened to rob the event of the cross and resurrection of its historical actuality. The orthodox operated with a theory about an eternal law whose demands could be vicariously satisfied by proper payment. Hofmann operated with a theory about a divine love-will which realized itself in a historical process—a view of history borrowed from German Idealism.[2] In the one instance, law provided the eternal standard for understanding the atonement; in the other law is simply replaced by a historical scheme. But in *either* case one ends up with a system which robs the cross of its historical actuality. This is demonstrated by the inescapable element of docetism that remains in both views. Jesus is "protected" from the full consequences of his death because he "knows the system."

We have reached a point here where something of the complexity of the problem of the place of law in the theological system is revealed. If our analysis to this point is correct, some conclusions can be drawn.

On the one hand, law cannot be understood merely in a static-ontological sense, as a *lex aeterna* according to which God can be "bought off." On the other hand, law cannot be treated merely as though it were part of a historical dispensation superseded by a dispensation of love. For in either case one runs into difficulties and detracts from the seriousness of the cross event itself. One draws attention away from the event to a speculative scheme "behind" the event.

But what then is to be the place of law in the theological system? How is one to think theologically about law? This is a question which we are not yet prepared to answer, for it is the subject of the discussion which continued after Hofmann's time. Perhaps we can just say in anticipation that it must be a view of law—and of wrath—which is more existentially real than either the orthodox or Hofmann could admit, so that the event of the cross becomes for the believer a real deliverance. It must be so conceived that faith for the believer is not merely belief in a theory *about* the cross, but a real *participation* in the event of deliverance itself.

This is a subtle and elusive distinction but nevertheless an exceedingly important one for the understanding of law. Perhaps I can illustrate what I mean with the problems which we have discovered in both views of the atonement, the significance of Christ's death for himself. If when they came to that point they could have said that Christ actually suffered defeat, that he met his *end*, suffering under all the consequences of sin that historical man encounters *including* the agony of despair and utter desolation, then the full gravity of the event would have become

---

2. See E. W. Wendebourg, "Die Heilsgeschichtliche Theologie J. C. K. v. Hofmanns in ihrem Verhaltnis zur romantischen Weltanschauung," *Zeitschrift für Theologie und Kirche* 52, no. 1 (1955): 64–104.

apparent. For this means that *even in his own consciousness* Jesus would see nothing but dereliction. Then the resurrection would appear in all its eschatological newness as an absolutely new act, not as a foregone conclusion on the basis of the "system." Then there would be no *theory* to lessen the gravity of the event by providing for some kind of continuous transition from death to life, but only the event itself. Resurrection would be an entirely new event, actually snatching victory from defeat.

In this understanding the real significance of the death of Christ as an actual event is intensified because even for Jesus himself there would have been no way around the full consequences of the cross, no protection from real suffering and death, no theory or system to provide an escape. The death of Jesus Christ itself would then have been the ultimate proclamation of "the law.' Christ's death is then the final proclamation that there is for the sinner no convenient alternative of "believing a system" but only the person of Christ himself and the event of death and resurrection.

Such a view of law could result in an ultimate and existential conviction, for if the sinner wanted to inherit the hope of the resurrection, he would have to "die with Christ in order to be raised with him." He could not merely accept a theory about the cross, for in such a view there is no theory about the event which could remove the necessity of participation in the event. In other words, the paradigm for faith is not an act of cognition, the acceptance of a theory, but death and resurrection, participation in the event itself. The life of faith is a life of participation, a life in the "body of Christ."

Such a view of the atonement demands a thinking about law which is much more existential and actual than that of either orthodoxy or Hofmann. It is a type of thinking which seeks to protect and convey more accurately the nature of the cross and resurrection event as an absolute end and a new beginning. It is a type of thinking which confronts the sinner with a theology *of* the cross and not merely a theory *about* the cross. Such thinking presents theology, no doubt, with a subtle and elusive problem, but the subsequent history of the debate shows quite evidently that nothing less than such thinking is demanded by the nature of the case; indeed, the continuing discussion after the atonement controversy can be seen as the struggle to reach that goal.

Before we turn to that discussion, however, it would be well to assess Hofmann's significance in the history of the debate. Does Hofmann's theology represent an advance or a retreat? In a recent study, Robert Schultz judged that Hofmann's attack on the concept of vicarious satisfaction was basically destructive for Lutheran theology.[3] What was at stake, he argued, was the problem of law and gospel; in this he is certainly correct. But he maintains that Hofmann's reconstruction in terms of salvation history brought about a neglect of this problem which left Lutheran theology illprepared to cope with subsequent developments such as Ritschlianism and historicism.

There is no doubt some truth to this charge. Insofar as Hofmann sought to solve the problem of law and gospel by shifting the emphasis to history he is responsible for some of the confusion which resulted. But Schultz does not seem to appreciate the nature of the difficulty which confronted Lutheran theology at this time. The attack against legalism was open and widespread, and the demand for a reorientation persistent. Orthodoxy could protect itself against Hofmann only by returning to a concept of wrath and law which was beset with difficulties. As long as Lutheranism remained bound to this scheme it would be doomed to theological insignificance. Hofmann's great importance lies in the fact that he challenged this system and criticized it cogently. Because of this challenge he presented a severe crisis for orthodox Lutheran theology, a crisis which had to come if there was to be any advance beyond a covert repristination of 17th century theology. It may be true that not everything which resulted from this crisis was entirely fortunate, but it was only because of Hofmann's kind of attack that discussion over law and gospel could begin anew. This is apparent from the subsequent history of the debate. It is not, after all, simply accidental that theology today has returned to a discussion of the problem of law and gospel; it is a result of the discussions set in motion by the attack which Hofmann made.

In spite of the criticisms we have made of Hofmann's theology, there are many points at which he made contributions of great value. His was a creative attempt to restate the theology of the Reformation in terms of the emerging historical worldview. His project of "thinking in" the situation of faith may have led him to overstep somewhat the boundaries of such thinking, but nevertheless he directed our attention to the proper starting point for theological reflection. His battle against all forms of legalism, especially in theological thinking and doctrinal form, can only be applauded. His reassertion of the concept of divine love as the deepest creative ground in God rescued a fundamental theological insight from its relative oblivion in the orthodox scheme. His attempt to understand the atonement as the victory of this divine love placed him considerably

---

3. Robert Schultz, *Gesetz und Evangelium in der Lutherischen Theologie des 19. Jahrhunderts* (Berlin: Lutherisches Verlagshaus, 1958), 110. I am indebted to Schultz's book for many helpful suggestions and insights but find myself in some disagreement over final conclusions.

ahead of his time. Both in his Luther research and in his own thinking he anticipated present-day views.

Perhaps Hofmann's most important contribution, however, is his concept of the new humanity in Christ. His view of the church as the new humanity is an attempt to overcome both the individualism and the subjectivism of earlier views. As such this attempt to think in terms of the new was an attempt to find a real theological place for the "new age" in the theological system. Instead of thinking only in terms of a static ontological scheme, Hofmann introduced the concept of a transition from the old to the new. Due to his *heilsgeschichtliche* scheme the nature of this transition remained somewhat problematical, but in introducing this "two age" scheme he had returned to a fundamental biblical motif. Eschatology is no longer just the "doctrine of the last things" as it was for orthodoxy, but it now permeates the entire system.

Nevertheless, despite those fruitful beginnings Hofmann bequeathed to subsequent generations a complex problem. In effect he substituted an idea of historical progress for the static-ontological concept of law as the main structure of his system. This meant that he attempted to understand the Christ event in terms of a more-or-less continuous process, the self-realization of the divine love. According to the important study on *Heilsgeschichte* by Gustav Weth, this is the point at which the basic difficulty of every *Heilsgeschichte* intrudes.[4] In the shift from the legalistic scheme of orthodoxy to a scheme based on historical process, the continuity or idea of progress accomplishes the same function as law in the system of orthodoxy—it provides the structure for understanding the Christ event. But when the event is understood as part of a continuous scheme, it is inevitably robbed of its newness. It does not represent a radical break, an end and a beginning in man's history. It is simply a part of a necessary process. In other words, the eschatological nature of the event itself is threatened. *Heilsgeschichte* as a system obscures the eschatological newness of the Christ event just as the old system of law had done. As we shall see, it took subsequent generations considerable time to sort out the problems involved in Hofmann's reconstruction. Perhaps the most immediate effect of it all was that in shifting from the system of law to the system of the realization of the divine love-will, Hofmann changed the emphasis in the theological system from wrath to love. Consequently it was in this form—the argument about wrath and love—that the debate about law and gospel was prosecuted in the years after Hofmann's work.

---

4. Gustav Weth, *Die Heilsgeschichte* (München: Chr. Kaiser Verlag, 1931), 134ff.

Theodosius Harnack

In the context of the atonement controversy, the most important feature of Harnack's interpretation of Luther was his use of the concept of the natural knowledge of God as the basis for the doctrine of wrath. Such natural knowledge helps to secure the dialectic of wrath and love. Hofmann, it is to be remembered, rejected all thought of a natural knowledge of God; he claimed that it was on the basis of such knowledge that a faulty doctrine of the atonement was constructed. Harnack, on the contrary, claimed that there is such a thing as a natural knowledge of God in Luther, and that such knowledge forms a necessary part of his theology.

Most significant, however, was Harnack's insistence that on the basis of this natural knowledge of God through the law, Luther taught a doctrine of vicarious satisfaction. Harnack believed that for Luther the law was an independent and objectively valid expression of the divine will for man, and that as such its demands had to be satisfied if man were to be released from the threat of punishment and death. The concept of the natural knowledge of God is, according to Harnack, the basis for Luther's teaching on the law, and consequently the basis for the doctrine of vicarious satisfaction.[1]

Here Harnack encountered a certain difficulty. He was well aware that Luther could alternately praise and damn the law.[2] The problem for Harnack lay in determining how Luther's ambiguous attitude toward the law corresponded with the idea that the law is an expression of God's eternal will, a "way" of salvation which can serve as the structure for the doctrine of vicarious satisfaction. How can the law be both a benefactor and at the same time placed among the despicable tyrants that assail man? Harnack answered that Luther made a basic distinction in the doc-

---

1. Theodosius Harnack, *Luthers Theologie: Mit besonderer Beziehung auf seine Versöhnungs- und Erlösungslehre*, new edition, 2 vols. (Munich: Chr. Kaiser Verlag, 1927), 1:365–68.
2. Harnack, *Luthers Theologie*, 1:368–83.

trine of law between "essence" and "office" (*Wesen und Amt*).³ The law in its essence is eternal, irrevocable, and good. In the office it has to carry out among sinful men, however, it is the instrument of wrath, an accusing tyrant which destroys. By means of this basic distinction, Harnack claimed, Luther left the law intact as an objective juridical scheme in "essence," while the "office" it performs against sin is overcome through the atonement. Because of this interpretation of the law, Luther could both praise the law as good, see it as providing the necessity for a doctrine of vicarious satisfaction, and also condemn it as a tyrant whose power must be overcome.⁴

But even when the problem of law is thus "settled" there are further difficulties in connection with Luther's view of the atonement. Harnack is well aware that Luther expressly rejected any "theological apriorism" which constructed a doctrine of God from rational premises in order constantly to determine what God must do to redeem the world.⁵ Here we face again the question of the necessity for the atonement. In a section entitled "The relative necessity for the sacrifice of the Son" Harnack pointed out that Luther held no thought of an absolute necessity from God's point of view.⁶ Love was not first made possible by a vicarious satisfaction. Harnack even quoted those passages in which Luther suggested that perhaps God could have given the Son in a different manner. But Harnack was inclined to regard these as vestiges of nominalism which had not been fully overcome.⁷ Harnack insisted that even if Luther rejected the idea of necessity, he also rejected the concept of an arbitrary God. Luther, Harnack said, placed himself solely under the revelation in the Word; from that vantage point for Luther the atonement "must" happen in the way it did happen. Thus the atonement in this form was "relatively necessary." It was not an absolute necessity for God, but given the situation it was the necessary form for the manifestation and realization of his love among men. It was, one might say, the necessary sign and seal of the divine love; as such it was the actual real-

---

3. Harnack, *Luthers Theologie*, 1:368–40 .
4. Harnack's interpretation of the "essence" / "office" distinction has been questioned, partly because one of the main passages Harnack uses to support his case is critically suspect. Robert Schultz points out that one of the passages Harnack uses does not clearly bear Harnack's interpretation and the other is a faulty translation of Luther's original statement. Schultz further contends that the essence-office distinction is one which Harnack got from his earlier teachers and imposed upon his Luther study. Robert Schultz, *Gesetz und Evangelium in der Lutherischen Theologie des 19. Jahrhunderts,* 142.
5. Harnack, *Luthers Theologie*, 2:82.
6. Harnack, *Luthers Theologie*, 2:75–85.
7. Harnack, *Luthers Theologie*, 2:83.

ization of that love and not merely a proclamation of a love that could be taken for granted.

Here there could be no thought of an abstract *a priori* system which set up a scheme according to which the necessity of the atonement could be developed. God did not need to be atoned before he could be loving. He is loving *in* Christ, and one is not faced with the "before" or "after" alternative. Harnack's interpretation, though, became considerably more confused when he followed this section with a section entitled "The absolute necessity of atoning God."[8] Before he came to this section Harnack had given considerable attention to Luther's "dramatic-dualistic" imagery in treating the atonement. Harnack did not obscure the fact that Luther put a great deal of his emphasis upon such imagery. He admitted that orthodoxy had not creatively developed this aspect of Luther's thought. But Harnack seemed to regard this simply as an evidence of the "richness" and "profundity" of Luther's spirituality. Luther, he said, was not content to expound atonement merely in external and theoretical terms, but described it in terms of its "full, profound and immeasurable ethical significance." For Luther there had to be an actual redemption of the subject from the tyrannical forces (flesh, world, death, devil, and hell); this could come about only through redemption from a bad conscience.[9]

The dramatic-dualistic element was therefore interpreted in terms of its relation to the release of the individual subject from the tyranny of a bad conscience. But, said Harnack, there is a fundamental distinction between this redemption (*Erlösung*) and objective atonement (*Versöhnung*). Redemption is the release of the captive in the present, but such a redemption is possible only insofar as it is based upon the atonement accomplished once for all in the past. Redemption releases one from the *dominion* of Satan, but this is possible because he has lost his *rights* in the atonement. The rights which he possessed under the sanction of the divine wrath had to be "bought off." This could only have come about by a vicarious satisfaction for man's guilt. God's wrath had to be stilled and his righteousness satisfied. The dualistic-dramatic element in Luther's thought thus did not exclude for Harnack the doctrine of vicarious satisfaction, but rather *required* it.

Thus the stage was set for a return to the basic orthodox doctrine of the atonement. Harnack claimed to find in Luther the idea of "an absolute inner-divine necessity for the sacrifice of the Son."[10] The con-

---

8. Harnack, *Luthers Theologie*, 2:241–50.
9. Harnack, *Luthers Theologie*, 2:250
10. Harnack, *Luthers Theologie*, 2:242.

cept of vicarious satisfaction, Harnack held, was the heart of Luther's view of the atonement.[11] This in turn rested upon an interpretation of law in which a distinction was made between essence and office. One is redeemed from the "office" of the law because the "essential" demand has been satisfied vicariously.

So we have in Harnack's Luther a "relative" and an "absolute" necessity for the sacrifice of the Son. It is difficult to see how these two could be held together. What Harnack seemed to be saying was that for Luther the sacrifice of the Son was not an abstract *a priori* necessity in order for God to be loving, but rather an innerdivine necessity for the divine love to be actually realized among men. God did not have to atone, and no one could dictate from man's point of view the manner in which he would have had to send the Son. But if the love of God was to be realized among men as love, then it must have occurred in the manner in which it did occur. This seems to be the gist of Harnack's interpretation of Luther.

The view of the atonement which Harnack derived from Luther presented a rather confusing picture. Its most distinctive feature was its doctrine of wrath derived from a natural knowledge of God and the law. This knowledge is dialectically opposed to the knowledge of God which comes through the gospel. So there is to be a real dialectic between wrath and love, law and gospel, but how is this dialectic to be conceived? If both wrath and love are of equal status, then one is threatened with a dualism in God. The solution, in this view, was given, apparently, in faith. In faith one learns that natural knowledge does not yield the ultimate truth about God. It is true that God is wrathful towards sinful men, but this is God as he is only "outside of Christ." "In Christ" and for faith he is different; there he is a God of love. This is the ultimate truth about God.

But what is the nature of this knowledge gained by faith and how does it relate to the natural knowledge? Faith, apparently, is the acceptance of objective atonement, the acceptance that the demands of the law have been satisfied. It seems therefore to be a propositional truth of the same type that one derives from the natural knowledge. But the propositions "God is wrathful" and "God is loving" cannot both be equally true. One must therefore be relativized. One is *more true* than the other. Wrath, though it is asserted in no uncertain terms, must be relativized if love is to be maintained.

There was an inner connection for Harnack between the doctrine of the atonement and the manner in which the wrath-love dialectic was

---

11. Harnack, *Luthers Theologie*, 2:250.

stated. Because the atonement was an "objective" vicarious satisfaction, the dialectic ultimately had to be relativized. For then the "knowledge of faith" is a doctrine, a propositional truth which must either compete or be synthesized with the natural knowledge. Both could not be equally true if they contradicted each other, so that one had to be relativized at the expense of the other.

By way of anticipation, it can be asked if there is not another way of understanding the problem. If, for instance, faith is something else, if it consists solely in participation in the death of Christ, then there would be no reason to relativize the divine wrath. If one could say that wrath in its full force is the historical power under which man must meet his end—God's judgment of man—then the atonement could be interpreted as the event in which Christ suffered that end and won the victory. Wrath would be *conquered* in him but not relativized. It would still be in force as the judgment that unless man dies with Christ he shall not be raised with him. Faith would then be understood as participation, not merely as the reception of truths about an "objective" transaction. And there would be no reason for a "knowledge of faith" to compete on the same level with a natural knowledge. In such a view it could even be said that the knowledge of faith was the "true" knowledge of God, whereas natural knowledge is not ultimate truth; but in doing so one would be saying it in a different setting and it would mean something quite different. In such a view it could be said that knowledge of God derived from the law leads only to *idolatria* and that it was a *falsum figmentum*, or the devil's instrument. This would not mean that one was relativizing it but only *exposing its terrible power*. In short, in such a view all of the same terminology could be used, but it would mean something quite different; the atonement would be understood against the background of an entirely different systematic structure, and some of Harnack's inadequacies could be avoided.

The view of the atonement which Harnack derived from Luther had the same shortcomings that we found in the orthodox view and in Hofmann's view. Whether Harnack's interpretation was true to Luther is an open question. One can hardly avoid the impression that there was a real "tug of war" in Harnack's interpretation between Luther's view and the orthodox view. Harnack himself pointed out that Luther often polemicized against the concept of satisfaction because he felt it "too weak, not descriptive enough or comprehensive enough, and too easily leading to a superficial juridical view."[12] It is difficult to see how Luther could make

---

12. Harnack, *Luthers Theologie*, 2:270.

such criticism and at the same time hold that a juridical view of vicarious satisfaction was the most basic interpretation of the atonement.

Nevertheless, Harnack made some important contributions to the continuing discussion. He showed, certainly, that there is more to Luther's view than Hofmann was willing to realize. He demonstrated that there was a place in Luther's thought for such a thing as a "natural knowledge of God" and that such natural knowledge was intimately connected with Luther's understanding of law and wrath. Harnack also showed that Luther used the terminology of the vicarious satisfaction view side by side with the dramatic-dualistic terminology, and that Luther did not seem to be aware of any contradiction between them.

Perhaps Harnack's greatest contribution, however, was his discovery of Luther's dialectical concept of God. This stood in sharp contrast to the monistic tendencies in Hofmann and Ritschl and the entire 19th century. It is for this reason that Harnack's work still enjoys popularity today. The dialectic between God "in Christ" and God "outside of Christ" injected new possibilities into the discussion of the atonement. Whether Harnack himself fully understood and accurately reproduced Luther's own thought on all these matters, however, will also be a part of the continuing discussion.

For our purposes, though, Harnack's work is important as one extreme in the field of the various reactions to Hofmann. The important fact is that he tried to establish a more dialectical understanding of God in relation to man and that he did this by insisting on a "natural knowledge" as the dialectical opposite of revealed knowledge. He maintained the dialectic by holding law, wrath, and hiddenness *outside* of Christ in a strict separation. Law remained outside the revelation in Christ and provided eventually a structure for understanding the atonement. The construction is faulty, however, because to avoid a dualism Harnack had to relativize one pole; this led ultimately to the same sort of speculative synthesis between wrath and love which was present in orthodoxy. Clearly the idea of a natural knowledge which is equated with law and wrath needed closer attention.

Thus the controversy which began as a debate over the doctrine of the atonement came to focus increasingly on the issues of law, wrath, and love—the problem of the doctrine of God. For this reason, direct debate about the atonement receded into the background for some time; it came to the fore again only in later Luther studies. Since atonement ceased to occupy a central position in the discussion, we shall attempt in what follows to trace the debate as it developed and then return to the question of atonement when it is raised again.

Gospel as the End of the Law

The current interpretation of law among Lutheran theologians is a result, mainly, of Luther research. Since the debate began with an argument about Luther's theology, this is a quite natural development. The argument, of course, is still continuing, since Luther interpreters do not all agree. It need not be our purpose here to discuss all the variant interpretations; many of them reflect positions we have already encountered in the course of the debate. Rather I shall select some representative interpreters who seem to me to set forth a definite advance in the debate about law. My main interest is in those men who claim to find in Luther an interpretation of law which runs counter to the interpretation we have found in the development from Hofmann through Ritschl to Barth. My concern here will be to point out a general development without dwelling on individual differences which may exist between these interpreters. Perhaps the best place to begin is with the problem of Luther's relationship to orthodox Lutheranism, since this has been one of the major questions throughout the discussion. Clarification of this issue would also help to answer Barth's question of how the concept of law espoused by his Lutheran critics differs from the "natural law" he finds so destructive.

The Finnish Reformation scholar Lauri Haikola has devoted considerable attention to this question; his work represents the fruit of much contemporary Luther research, especially that done by Swedish scholars.[1] Haikola finds that the major difference between Luther and later orthodoxy lies precisely in the understanding of law.[2] In later Lutheran ortho-

---

1. Laurel Haikola, *Gesetz und Evangelium bei M. Flacius* (Lund: C. W. K. Gleerup, 1952). *Studien zu Luther und zum Luthertum*, Uppsala Universitets Aarsskrift, no. 2 (Uppsala: A. B. Lundquistika Bokhandeln, 1958), cited hereafter as *Studien*; *Usus Legis*, Uppsala Universitets Aarsskrift, no. 3 (Uppsala: A. B. Lundquistika Bokhandeln, 1958).

2. Haikola, *Studien*, 9–12, 106–7.

doxy law was understood as an eternal, objective order, a *lex aeterna*, which described the ideal to which human life must aspire.[3] Law in this sense was defined as an objective scheme of demands and prohibitions which must be fulfilled. Since law was understood in this way, it was quite easy to conceive of the atonement as a substitutionary fulfillment, provided one did not press the logic too far.

Luther, on the other hand, says Haikola, understood law quite differently.[4] The proper relationship between man and God could not, in Luther's view, be understood in terms of an objective legal order. Luther's view, Haikola says, is quite different from the *lex aeterna* doctrine of later orthodoxy, even though Luther does on occasion use the term.[5] At no time, according to Luther, does man possess full knowledge of the divine will, but only a knowledge of the law appropriate to his actual historical situation. This is true both of man in his original state and in his fallen state. The prohibition of eating from the tree of knowledge, for instance, Luther takes as an indication that God has not revealed his absolute will to man even in paradise. The will of God is not made known to man in once-for-all fashion, least of all can man capture this will in the form of eternal principles. Rather man must learn to know God's will anew in each new situation. God's command and God's continuing creation belong together. Law remains, in view of its potentially changing appearance, in a certain sense hidden. Its content will depend upon the concrete situation in creation at a given time; man cannot have it in the form of eternal principles in advance of any concrete situation.[6]

This means that for Luther law does not constitute, as it does for orthodoxy, a fixed scheme according to which God and his revelation can be "figured out." Rather law is a term for the manner in which the divine will confronts sinful man in his existence, in every concrete situation. Gerhard Ebeling concurs with Haikola:

> For Luther, law is not a revealed statutory norm to which man relates himself thus and so, but law is an existential category in which the entire theological interpretation of man's actual existence is comprehended. Law is

---

3. Haikola, *Studien*, 9.
4. Haikola, *Studien*, 10ff.
5. Haikola points here to Heckel's study, *Lex Charitatis,* where it is maintained that the term *lex aeterna* means something quite different for Luther than it did for Aquinas. Haikola, *Studien*, 10n8. Heckel says that for Luther divine law is in itself, to be sure, unchangeable and eternal, but in its working upon man it alters itself incessantly depending upon man's relationship to God at the moment and consequently appears as the most changeable thing conceivable. Johannes Heckel, *Lex Charitatis*, Abhandlungen der Bayrischen Akademie der Wissenschaften, Neue Folge 36 (München: Verlag der Bayrischen Akademie der Wissenschaften, 1953), 54.
6. Haikola, *Studien*, 12.

not therefore an idea or a collection of propositions but the reality of fallen humanity.[7]

Law, according to this interpretation of Luther, is to be understood in terms of its immediate effect upon sinful man. Theologically, this means that it is understood as that which attacks and accuses man in his self-sufficiency. This means that law, for Luther, cannot be *identified* with any set of propositions or prescriptions, be it the decalogue or any other code. Law is *anything* which frightens and accuses "the conscience." The bolt of lightning, the rustling of a dry leaf on a dark night, the decalogue, the "natural law" of the philosopher, or even (or perhaps most particularly) the preaching of the cross itself—all or any of these can and do become the voice of the law.[8]

This means in relation to the discussion with Barth that it would be quite impossible to reverse the law-gospel order, or to penetrate beyond it to some kind of self-evident unity. Law cannot be dismissed simply as something "misunderstood" or erased, as one erases a code or group of propositions. Such attempts are purely theoretical exercises which may remove certain laws but which do not and cannot remove *the* law as Luther defined it. It is impossible to dispose of *the* law in that manner because the law is an existential category. It designates the manner in which God confronts sinful man in judgment. This confrontation in judgment must always and necessarily *precede* the gospel.

This argument can be illustrated by a significant passage from Luther's "*Wider die Antinomer.*"[9] The Antinomians of Luther's time, like Ritschl, insisted that repentance arises from the gospel; from this they drew the conclusion that the law should be removed from preaching. This affords an interesting parallel to the contemporary argument because here Luther is forced to define more carefully the place and function of the law. Whereas against the Roman Catholic position he argued against the law, here he had to argue for it. The manner in which he did this is very significant. To those who attempt to remove the law from preaching he replied:

> Who would know what Christ is and why Christ suffered for us if no one knew what sin or law was? Therefore the law must be preached if one wants

---

7. Gerhard Ebeling, *Wort und Glaube* (Tübingen: J. C. B. Mohr [Paul Siebeck], 1960), 65.
8. See Ebeling, *Wort und Glaube,* 288–91. Cf. Gerhard Rost, "Der Zorn Gottes in Luthers Theologie," *Lutherischer Rundblick* 9, no. 1 (1961): 15–16n29a.
9. The writings of Luther against the Antinomians represent an important and relatively untapped source for Luther's view of the law. Ebeling has apparently recognized this and has promised a study of the disputes (*Wort und Glaube*, 65n64, 68), but to my knowledge it has not yet appeared.

to preach Christ, even if one refuses to call the law by name. For the conscience will nevertheless be frightened by the law when the sermon declares that Christ had so dearly to fulfil the law for us. Why then should one want to remove it *when it cannot be removed, indeed, when it is even more deeply entrenched through the removal?* For the law terrifies even more frightfully when I hear that Christ, God's Son, had to bear it for me, than if it were preached to me outside of Christ merely as a threat without such great torture of the Son of God.[10]

Here it is quite apparent that when Luther speaks of law, he does not mean merely a *code of laws*, but rather that which terrifies the conscience. The statement that Christ by his death fulfilled the law—a statement which ordinarily would be considered gospel—here is accorded the function of law because it threatens the sinner in his self-sufficiency. Law, in this sense, is not something which can be removed or placed after the gospel by some sort of theoretical rearrangement. Law will do its work first, prior to the gospel, regardless of what men may attempt to do with it in their theologies.

Those who attempt to get rid of the law by a theoretical construction, Luther says, "do nothing more than throw out these poor letters, 'L-A-W,' but nevertheless establish the wrath of God which is indicated and understood through these letters."[11] To speak about law means not merely to speak about it "technically or materially . . . or grammatically . . . , but as it is and sounds in your heart, exhorting, piercing the heart and the conscience until you do not know where to turn."[12] Law is a power which threatens man because of sin, and remains a power until death. The following theses from Luther's disputes against the Antinomians point this out clearly:

1. The law has dominion over man as long as he lives.
2. But he is freed from the law when he dies.
3. Necessarily, therefore, man must die if he would be freed from the law.
. . .
7. These three, law, sin and death, are inseparable.[13]

---

10. H. H. Börcherdt and George Merz, eds., *Martin Luther, Ausgewählte Werke* (München: Chr. Kaiser Verlag, 1957), 4:196 (italics mine). (Cited hereafter as *München Ausgabe*.)
11. Luther, *München Ausgabe*, 4:198.
12. WA 39/1:455.
13. WA 39/1:354.

The "end" of the law, consequently, comes only in the death of the sinner in Christ and in participation in his resurrection:

10. Indeed, in Christ the law is fulfilled, sin abolished and death destroyed.
11. That is, when through faith we are crucified and have died in Christ, such things [law fulfilled, sin abolished, death destroyed] are also true in us.
. . .
36. To one raised in Christ there is certainly no more sin, no death, no law—things to which he was subject while living.
. . .
40. Now, in so far as Christ is raised in us, in so far are we without law, sin and death.[14]

It is therefore impossible to remove the law by some sort of "theological erasure":

14. Necessarily, therefore, in as far as they are under death, they are still also under the law and sin.
15. They are altogether ignorant and deceivers of souls who endeavor to abolish the law from the Church.
16. For that is not only stupid and impious, but *absolutely impossible*.
17. For if you want to remove the law, it is necessary at the same time to remove sin and death.[15]

The question which arises at this point is one which we have already encountered in Theodosius Harnack's interpretation of Luther. What Haikola, Ebeling, and others point to as the existential character of the law Harnack would have referred to as the "office" of the law in relation to sinful man. But is there not also a sense in which Luther speaks of the eternal "essence" of the law, the unchanging content of the divine will, as Harnack maintained? This question, to my knowledge, has not really been answered satisfactorily.

Closely related is the problem of the "third use" of the law. The idea of law as an eternal ideal and the "third use" of the law go hand in hand. For if the law is the eternal ideal, it stands to reason that this must be man's guide even after justification. If the foregoing analysis is correct, however, it would seem that law can never be taken merely as an abstract

14. WA 39/1:355–56.
15. WA 39/1:354.

ideal which man can isolate and fix in his "system." Taken in its absolute seriousness, law is always an accuser from which man cannot escape on his own. It is always law in this existential sense which concerns Luther. What he seeks is *actual* deliverance from the threat of the law.

In the face of the concrete existential situation, the question about a distinction between essence and office is beside the point. The point is that "under the law" man cannot escape the accusation; the "essence of the law" for the sinner is that it always accuses. The sinner cannot dispose of the law by making theoretical distinctions. He cannot "break through" by means of some theoretical tour de force to a position where he can recognize an abstract will of God which does not threaten him. The problem is not that of a distinction between essence and office, but whether a man hears the will of God as law or as gospel. The will of God is indeed eternal, but the question is how man as sinner hears the will of God as it confronts him in the Word. For man "under the law" a distinction between essence and office is impossible, and for man "under the gospel" it is unnecessary.

This conclusion can be documented by some further passages from the disputations against the Antinomians. In the second set of theses for disputation, the question was whether law, like circumcision, was only temporal and thus came to an end after Christ: that is, whether one can dispose of law by means of a *heilsgeschichtliche* scheme. Luther states in his theses that this is not so, that the law remains to all eternity because it discloses sin and must be fulfilled:

45. For the law as it was before Christ did indeed accuse us; but under Christ it is placated through the forgiveness of sins, and thereafter it is to be fulfilled in the Spirit.
46. Accordingly after Christ, in the future life, [law] will remain, having been fulfilled, and then the new creature himself will be what [law] in the meantime demanded.
47. Therefore the law will never in all eternity be abolished but will remain either to be fulfilled by the damned, or already fulfilled in the blessed.
48. These pupils of the devil, however, seem to think that the law is temporal only, ceasing under Christ just as did circumcision.[16]

Here it would seem that Luther is arguing for law as an eternal ideal, but it is important to see the sense in which this is meant. The Antinomians had argued that if the effect of a thing ceased, then the cause of

---

16. WA 39/1:349–50.

that effect ceases. Since the effect of the law ceases in Christ, as Luther seems to have said previously, then the law itself ceases and must consequently be abolished.[17]

It would appear, then, that the Antinomians argued just as Luther did. If the law is defined in terms of its effect, then law would surely cease when the effect ceases. Indeed, Luther begins by conceding the point,[18] but he goes on to make some important qualifications:

> Where sin ceases, there law ceases, and to that degree that sin ceases, to that degree law ceases, so that in the future life the law ought completely to cease, because then it will be fulfilled.[19]

Where sin ceases, there law indeed ceases. But this is an eschatological possibility and can be realized fully only *in the future life*. The end of the law cannot therefore be fixed according to some historical scheme. To do this is not a possibility for man; as long as sin is present, the law will continue to accuse.

But what then does Luther mean when he says that the law is eternal? What does he mean when he says on the one hand that the law will never in all eternity be abolished and on the other that where sin ceases, there law ceases? The reason is the close connection between law, sin, and death. It is not enough to say, as the Antinomians did, that the appearance of Christ at a point in time does away with the law, for the law is a power which can never be erased by an objective theoretical arrangement. This is true to all eternity. The law has its end only where it is fulfilled *in actuality*, and where it is fulfilled, there sin ceases. And where sin ceases, the law also ceases because it ceases to accuse. It is very significant that Luther, whenever he insisted upon the impossibility of removing the law, always based this on the fact that the law is "written on our hearts" and not on a theory about the eternal will of God. The persistence of the law is due to the fact that it is utterly impossible for man to escape it in this life.

Luther's defense of the eternality of the law is thus quite different from Harnack's "essence-office" distinction. The law is eternal because man as sinner cannot escape it. One might say indeed that for man as sinner, the "essence" of the law *is* the "office" precisely because, as sinner, man cannot distinguish between them. As long as sin remains, the law will *always*

---

17. "When the effect ceases then the cause in actuality ceases. The effect of the law ceases. Therefore the law itself ceases and is consequently abolished and removed." WA 39/1:430.
18. WA 39/1:431.4–5.
19. WA 39/1:431.6–7.

accuse; it will never be a neutral "essence." Only when it is fulfilled does it cease.

But does not the fact that law must be fulfilled before it ceases mean that it is "in essence" still in effect and therefore remains in effect throughout eternity? Must not Luther finally make the same distinction that Harnack makes? Luther is finally driven to make a distinction of sorts, but it is important to note the manner in which he conceives of this distinction.[20] One must distinguish, Luther says, between an "empty or quiescent . . . law and a law which accuses us or a decree inscribed in our minds."[21] The distinction Luther makes here is not between the essence and the office of the law, but between an empty or quiescent law and an accusing law written in man's heart or mind. Only the angels and saints in heaven, he says, know the law as empty (*vacua*), because in them it is fulfilled.[22] Eschatologically, therefore, the law ceases because it is empty (*vacua*)—no longer active.

In another instance Luther argued that the law in the sense of the decalogue can be said to be eternal, but only because the reality, the *res*, which is its fulfillment, is eternal. In this case the Antinomians had held that the law, like circumcision, is abolished at a point in time. Luther replied that circumcision, like baptism, is temporal, "but only the decalog is eternal, *in its reality*, however, *not as law*, because in the future life those things which the law demands will be realized."[23] The decalogue remains eternally in the sense that the reality demanded remains, but *not as* law. Here the distinction is between reality (*res*) and law, but not between the essence of law and the office of law. The term "law" applies only to the "office," and not to the *res*.

The point seems to be that Luther did not want to grant eternal status *to* the law as law. Instead, he defined law in its existential sense as that which accuses. Quite naturally he did not allow that such a situation (that of being under accusation) should last eternally. But then how does it end? Certainly not by an abrogation of the divine will, and not by some theoretical cancellation of the law. The law "ends" only when it is fulfilled—when the state which the law demands is realized in actuality. The law ends (the accusation becomes powerless) when the new situation, the *res* to which the law points eschatologically, breaks in. When law no longer accuses, it is emptied of its power and becomes what Luther

---

20. Cf. Ebeling, *Wort und Glaube*, 65.
21. WA 39/1:433.1ff.
22. WA 39/1:433.
23. WA 39/1:413.16ff. Cf. Ebeling, *Wort und Glaube*, 65.

called a *lex vacua*. The fulfillment of the law is the end of the law,[24] and an entirely new situation obtains: man lives under the gospel. By faith man participates in the new situation under the gospel even though as a sinner he still lives in this age and still hears the voice of the law. Only the angels know the law completely as a *lex vacua*.

But is not this really the same as the distinction between essence and office or, at the most, only a quibbling about words? The difference, no doubt, is a subtle one, but still it is exceedingly important, for it reflects one's whole theological approach and thus affects one's entire system. The essence-office distinction can ostensibly provide man with a theoretical scheme according to which he can place himself apart from the law, view it in the abstract, and construct theories about how God's eternal will is satisfied. This allows man to place himself *above* the law and to look at it from God's point of view. The law is therefore disposed of theoretically, and faith consists of man's "understanding" how this has taken place. An eternal static order is posited which is objectively fulfilled; the paradigm for faith is the act of cognition.

To distinguish between a powerless law (*lex vacua*) and an accusing law (*lex accusans*) or between the dialogue as *lex* and as *res*, however, is quite different. To know the *lex* as *vacua* or to participate in the *res* of the decalogue is strictly an eschatological possibility. Man as sinner can never escape the *lex accusans*. He can never place himself above the law. Insofar as he is sinner, he is always under the law. Only actual death and resurrection can deliver him from this predicament. Only, therefore, as he participates in the death and resurrection of Christ in faith and hope is deliverance possible. The paradigm for faith is death and resurrection. In faith and in hope man is free from law. The eschatological possibility is made a present possibility only through faith in Christ.

The theological systems which result from these two ways of defining law are also quite different. In the first instance, law "in its essence" remains the basic structure of the system. It provides an eternal structure for the speculative doctrine of the atonement which we have described in earlier chapters. In the second instance there is a decisive break. The law comes to its *end* in the eschatological event, the *res* which the law demands breaks in and brings the law to an end. This means that in place of a one-membered eternal scheme, a two-membered dialectical scheme governs the system. Only by participation in the eschatological event

---

24. *Qui enim implent Euangelium, non sunt sub lege. Quia iam nulla est super eos, cum earn impleverint et iam ei adequati sunt. Lex enim non dominatur nec est supra eos, qui eam implent. Sed potius ad eam ascendunt et pertingunt ad eam.* ("Impletio legis est mors legis." Rom. 7 *Quamdiu vir vivit.*) WA 3:463.33–37.

does the law come to its end for the believer. This gives the terminology of the system a basically different thrust, even though that terminology may in many instances be the same.

The basic test for this distinction is the doctrine of the atonement. If what modern Luther interpreters have been saying is accurate, then it should be reflected especially in Luther's doctrine of the atonement. There has been some debate over Luther's doctrine of the atonement in recent years especially among Swedish Lutheran interpreters.[25] The question at issue has been whether Luther's manifold statements on atonement can be entirely comprehended under what Aulén has called the "classic" view of the atonement.

This modern debate is in many ways a repetition of the debate precipitated by Hofmann. Several interpreters argue that essential aspects of Luther's view can be understood only from the Anselmic or "Latin" point of view.[26] To support this contention these interpreters point to Luther's repeated assertion that Christ bore the punishment of the law which man deserved, that the wrath of God was appeased through Christ's satisfaction, etc.[27] Once again the decisive question is that of the place of law in the system.[28] Aulén, opposing the Latin theory, insists that however one looks at the matter, one thing is certain: for Luther atonement means the abolition of the judicial order (*Rechtsordnung*), the removal of all legalism from one's relationship to God. Atonement through Christ means the casting off of the religiosity of the judicial order, the setting aside of the power and tyranny of the law. In Luther's view, Aulén admits, the law indeed must be fulfilled, but it is fulfilled in order to be *removed* and *cancelled*, not because it is the eternal standard of justice according to which God *himself* must be satisfied.[29]

It is beyond the scope of this study to attempt a solution to this argument among Luther interpreters. It is important to point out, however, that the decisive issue in the debate is the question of *how* the terminology is used. It is not enough merely to point out that Luther did in fact use much of the terminology of the Anselmic theory. If what the several Luther interpreters we have cited have said about Luther's understanding of the law is correct (and the illustrations cited would seem to bear them

---

25. Edgar Carlson, *The Reinterpretation of Luther* (Philadelphia: Westminster, 1948), 58–77. This is the only instance as far as I can see, where debate about atonement again becomes a substantial part of the discussion. It is important to note that the whole debate now hinges on the interpretation of the nature of the law.

26. Carlson, *Reinterpretation of Luther*, 56.

27. Carlson, *Reinterpretation of Luther*, 56.

28. Carlson, *Reinterpretation of Luther*, 58–70.

29. Aulén, *Das Christliche Gottesbild*, 205.

out), then it is quite possible, indeed probable, that all of the "Anselmic" terminology could be used within a different systematic framework and given quite a different thrust. For if the law is understood in a different way, then it follows that such terms as satisfaction and fulfillment will have to be understood quite differently. This is no doubt what Aulén is attempting to say.

This is also the position taken by Haikola in his comparison of Luther and Lutheran orthodoxy. In his chapter on "Christ's Fulfilling of the Law," Haikola tries to spell this out more completely. He says that the fact that Luther did not understand the law merely as an objective scheme of commands and prohibitions means that fulfillment must be understood differently. It cannot be understood as though the law could be *quantitatively* fulfilled by a "substitute."[30] Rather the entire law is summed up in the First Commandment, which demands a *qualitative* subjection of man to God in faith and love. No quantitatively measurable limits can be set for the fulfillment of such a law. The demand of the law is so understood that every thought of quantitative equivalence or supererogatory merit is excluded. The Anselmic alternative satisfaction or punishment (*satisfactio aut poena*) cannot arise; God is not one who allows himself to be "bought off" by a quantitative fulfillment.[31] The atonement occurs indeed through "fulfillment" and "satisfaction" of the law, indeed even by "placating the wrath of God," but everything depends upon how this is understood. If it is understood in the sense that Christ suffered and died under the absolute qualitative demand and thus bore the "punishment," therein coming to his *absolute end*, then it becomes quite a different matter. Then Christ's "satisfaction" is not the quantitative satisfaction of a "sub-statute" but the qualitative satisfaction of one who totally identified himself with man and died, as Hofmann said, "in our place." Then it is the resurrection which "brings the victory," and at the same time brings law to an "end." This is quite different from the vicarious satisfaction or the fulfillment which leaves law intact as an eternal juridical order. The same terms are used, but they mean

---

30. Haikola, *Studien*, 106–10.
31. Haikola cites Karl Holl, *Gesammelte Aufsätze* (Tübingen: J. C. B. Mohr [Paul Siebeck], 1928), 1:69–70: "One ought not allow himself to be deceived by the fact that Luther for his part also uses the Catholic expressions 'satisfaction' and 'merit' because he assigns to them a different meaning from the Catholic Church. There *satisfactio* means a substitutionary accomplishment, a substitute payment to God. I recall here the Anselmian either/or: either satisfaction or punishment. Anselm rejects the second as impossible. Luther on the other hand finds precisely in it the true meaning of the death of Christ in explicit connection with his stricter conception of God and of sin. Sin is something that can never be made amends for and God is not one who allows himself to be bought off."

something quite different. The terminology taken from the Latin view of the atonement is given basically a different thrust.

This difference in focus comes from a basic difference in the manner in which one approaches theology. The orthodox view, leaning heavily on the Latin theory, is based on a theology which attempts to reconcile divine attributes on God's level.[32] Atonement is an "example of rational justice which expresses God's calculation" rather than the mystery of his immeasurable love. As Haikola says:

> The love which comes to expression in Christ's cross is not an expression of God's own sacrifice but of God's calculation. Since the agreement between righteousness and mercy is thought of as having happened already in eternity, so also that which happens in history becomes merely a demonstration of the eternal atonement. Atonement retains a docetic character in spite of the realistic description of the suffering.[33]

In Haikola's view, such thinking is excluded by Luther's conception of the atonement. Such thinking would mean speculation about God's majesty—a vain enterprise.

> In Luther's theology, all thought, including that which is valid of the atonement, must proceed from the historically given and not from God's eternal attributes. . . . Theology should speak only of the revealed God (*deus revelatus*), of God "*in relatione*." In the historical revelation through his acts and words, God appears as wrath and love. On the plane of history he reveals himself as the one who in his love "conquers" wrath. This historical fact, that God in the cross of Christ actually submits to the might of the powers, of sin, death, the devil, the law, and wrath . . . that is the starting point for thinking about the atonement.[34]

Thus Haikola maintains that the entire outlook on atonement took a different shape for Luther. This can be seen at several crucial points. First, God's wrath against sin retains its character as real wrath. It is not, as in the orthodox scheme, that man knows in an objective factual sense that God's righteousness has already received its "due" by a legal satisfaction. God's wrath is no mere demonstration which can be stilled by "objective" knowledge of a transaction; it is real, and it destroys utterly. Man's only hope is participation in the mystery of Christ's triumph over this wrath through faith.

Second, God's love retains for Luther its character as pure, unfath-

---

32. Haikola, *Studien*, 112.
33. Haikola, *Studien*, 111–12.
34. Haikola, *Studien*, 112.

omable mercy. It is the *power* which in resurrection wins the victory in the actual historical battle on the cross.[35]

Third, in this view atonement retains its perpetually actual character. When wrath, law, death, etc., are understood as actual historical forces, atonement can never be understood merely as an objective transaction completed in the past. For it is not merely some objective, abstract and suprahistorical wrath which is atoned and conquered, but precisely that power which attacks man in his own life situation.[36] Atonement is release for man in his actual historical need. The "subject-object" impasse is avoided. Atonement is a unified action in which the real reunion of the opposed parties occurs. "The 'subjective' reception of redemption (faith) is contained in the objective act of redemption."[37] The "subjective" never occurs without the "objective," and vice versa. There is no "objective" atonement apart from faith, apart from actual participation in the action.[38]

Finally, Luther's insistence upon thinking strictly in terms of the actual historical forces means that the problem of history is more easily handled. Since Christ enters into this world, dies under and wins the victory over the actual historical forces which continue to enslave man as long as he remains in sin, atonement is an ongoing work in history. The Word, the proclamation of Christ's victory, is not merely intellectual information about an objective transaction but is itself the bearer of ongoing atonement. The proclaimed Word is, so to speak, the end and the new beginning wherever and whenever it is heard. It announces *and realizes* the end of the old and the beginning of the new when it is heard in faith.[39] The history of the old has its end when Christ is received in faith. The fulfillment of the law and the stilling of the divine wrath are thought of in terms of end and new beginning, not in terms of a timeless legal structure.

The conclusion of these interpreters, therefore, is that Luther's use of Latin or legal terminology by no means proves that Luther can or even should be understood in terms of the Latin or Anselmic view of the atonement. Rather, they say, the entire nature of Luther's thought excludes this view. The decisive point, especially for Haikola, is the understanding of law in Luther's theology. Law in Luther's thinking, Haikola says, simply does not provide the kind of structure necessary to support a Latin theory of the atonement.

35. Haikola, *Studien*, 113–14.
36. Haikola, *Studien*, 114.
37. Haikola, *Studien*, 108.
38. Haikola, *Studien*, 108.
39. Haikola, *Studien*, 115.

The interpretation of the atonement by these men may be taken as indicative of the present status of the argument about Luther's doctrine that began with Hofmann. Perhaps that argument is not yet over, but it is extremely significant that these men find a view of the atonement which is neither that of the orthodox (vicarious satisfaction), nor, strictly speaking, that of a *Heilsgeschichte* like Hofmann's. That which makes it differ from both of these is the understanding of law. Law is neither an eternal framework for a transaction nor is it merely part of a historical dispensation. Law is an existential power from which man cannot escape without a real deliverance in the present. Atonement is the actual end of the law through faith. The atonement has, as Haikola points out, a more actual character. It is a view which, though critical of previous views, nevertheless attempts to do justice to the legitimate concerns in those views. As Otto Wolff remarks of Aulén's interpretation:

> Here Hofmann's energetic insistence upon understanding God's action exclusively as a line running from above to below comes to its historical fulfillment. The battle cry first taken up by him, in which this insistence found its most manifest expression, becomes here the center of the entire composition. But neither is Harnack's counter-complaint forgotten. God is not pictured in colorless one-sidedness, but the tension of the great polarities of wrath and love, etc., permeate throughout. Also Ritschl's basic concern for an independent thinking about faith which grows from its own roots comes in a happy manner to fruition.[40]

Let me sum up our findings on the understanding of law in Luther's thought among these interpreters: These interpreters point to the fact that law and gospel for Luther must be related eschatologically rather than in terms of a continuous or timeless scheme. We are led to the idea here that the relationship and tension between law and gospel should be understood in terms of the relationship and tension between the old and the new age. Haikola, for instance, says:

> When Luther places these antithetical total judgments on man (judgment and grace), he means at bottom the fact that man belongs to two opposing kingdoms, to two ages, between which there is at present perpetual struggle, but which will finally end with the victory of the one kingdom. The totality of the judgment stems therefore from the fact that the two eschatological entities are so utterly opposed and yet both really penetrate into the life of man and determine it.[41]

---

40. Otto Wolff, *Die Haupttypen der neuen Lutherdeutung* (Stuttgart: W. Kohlhammer, 1938), 394.
41. Haikola, *Usus Legis*, 125.

Likewise Ebeling maintains that the actuality of faith in the present can be maintained only through an eschatological scheme, to the exclusion of both the static-ontological scheme and the *heilsgeschichtliche* scheme. To support this contention he points to Luther and quotes Luther's own words about the distinction between the ages:

> "Christianity is divided into two times: in so far as it is flesh, it is under law; insofar as it is spirit, it is under the gospel." But mark well, with this distinction: "The time of law is not forever . . . the time of grace is to be eternal." "They are utterly distinct times, and nevertheless it is fitting that sin and grace, law and gospel be most closely conjoined."[42]

Others as well, among them Wilfred Joest and Helmut Thielicke, claim this eschatologically oriented understanding to be the key to Luther's view of the law.[43]

For these interpreters, therefore, law is understood as an "existential category" which describes man's actual situation in "this age." It cannot be removed by theological erasure or by theological manipulation, but only by the actual breaking in of the "new age" in Christ through faith. Insofar as man, even in faith, remains a citizen of "this age" the law continues in its "office" as that which constantly drives him to Christ. Existence under the gospel is the new possibility which breaks in in Christ. Faith makes one a participant in the new age. The implication is that all the paired terms in Luther's theology—law-gospel, wrath-love, flesh-spirit, hidden revealed, etc.—are to be understood in terms of this eschatological dialectic.

This eschatological orientation helps to clarify the position of these men in their argument with Barth as well as to shed light on the Lutheran position in general. The question of the order of law and gospel, as well as the problem of the nature and function of law, will be fixed by the eschatological scheme. Just as the old age precedes the new, so also law will precede gospel. Just as the old age comes to its end and *telos* in the new age, so also law has its end in the gospel.

The nature and function of law, consequently, must be defined in terms of an eschatological dialectic. Law is a general term for the manner in which the will of God impinges upon man in the old age, both in nature and in the words of Scripture. It is the demand and the judgment which confront him as a sinner. Even the words about the cross

---

42. Ebeling, *Wort und Glaube*, 292.
43. Cf. Wolfgang Berge, *Gesetz und Evangelium in der Neueren Theologie*, Aufsätze und Vorträge zur Theologie und Religionswissenschaft (Berlin: Evangelische Verlagsanstalt, 1985), 38–42.

will initially be heard as demand, as a threat to his being. It is important to note here that law is defined almost exclusively in terms of its function. Nature and function are taken together. The nature of law is that it terrifies.

The corollary to this definition of law is that in the "old age" there is no really decisive break between "natural" and "revealed" law. Both are *law*, both impinge upon man in the same way. This, no doubt, can be seen as the reason for Luther's apparent haziness on the question of natural law and the fact that he can at times make a rather easy identification between the laws of nature and the decalogue.[44] For Luther, law is "natural" to man in the sense that it represents the way he naturally thinks and reacts; this cannot be escaped apart from faith. The law is "written in the heart." But this does not mean that everyone (or anyone, for that matter) has an innate and accurate knowledge of the divine in the form of a timeless moral code; this is ruled out.[45] Law is, on the one hand, "in its expressly rational character the form of being of the reality of man as a reasonable creature in this world"; it is also the "mask" through which God works.[46] One may have only a dim knowledge of law, or he may have a highly refined ethical system derived from the philosopher. He may even derive his ethical code from the Bible which is *quantitatively* more correct. But whatever it is, his code is still law, and on this level there can only be a question of degrees of correctness at a given time. Hence the decalogue is the best statement of the natural law. If man does not know the law, he must be taught. But on this level, within the old age, it remains, it would seem, only a question of the relative appropriateness of a course of action in a given situation. On this level there is no decisive break between what is natural and what is revealed.

The only really decisive break comes in the transition through faith from law to gospel, from the old age to the new age. The true function of law is seen in the light of this break. Law is limited to the old age. The new age is the age of the gospel. It is not strange, therefore, that our interpreters hold that Luther spoke almost exclusively in terms of the first two uses of the law to the exclusion of the third. In the new age, the reality to which law points is given and law reaches its end. Law is therefore accorded the political use in ordering the life of the old age and the theological use of driving the sinner to Christ. To be sure, the law remains in effect even for the believer, but only because he is still also a sinner; that is, he still lives out his life in the old age. But when law is understood

---

44. Cf. Ernst Wolf, *Peregrinatio* (München: Chr. Kaiser Verlag, 1954), 195.
45. Above, pp. 61–62.
46. Wolf, *Peregrinatio*, 196–97.

in terms of the dialectic between the old and the new age, it makes little sense to attempt to reintroduce it again *after* the gospel. To do so would be to fail to recognize the radical nature of the break between the two ages.

Thus modern Luther interpretation has led to a view of law which differs somewhat from that of Barth. Instead of an increasing particularization of the law, as in the line which began with Hofmann and goes through Ritschl to Barth, here there is an increasing *generalization*. Law is a *general* term for describing the nature of man's existence in this age. It is the command which man meets in society, demanding order, and it is also the judgment of his way of life which drives him to the cross. It is defined in a general sense, as that which afflicts the conscience. Nothing *material* is said about the *content* of law as such; that, apparently, may depend upon concrete circumstances. Since law is defined in this general way, no great point is made about a distinction between a natural or a revealed law. It is simply taken for granted that law is natural for man.

This difference between a particularized and a generalized law is one source of the difficulty in the contemporary debate. It means, for one thing, that when the participants in the debate speak of law, they may be speaking of quite different things. It is not strange that a good deal of confusion has resulted.

This generalized concept of law is the outcome of the second line of development which began in Hofmann's interpretation of Luther's theology. The reinterpretation of Luther's concepts of wrath and hiddenness (which we have traced from Harnack through Ferdinand Kattenbusch and Holl) has reached its completion in a reinterpretation of Luther's understanding of law. Harnack, as we saw, opposed Hofmann and Ritschl with his interpretation of Luther's understanding of wrath. But Harnack based his concept of divine wrath on the idea that God "outside of Christ" was a hidden God—that is, a God of law—and used the distinction between essence and office to reinstate the orthodox concept of natural law. Kattenbusch showed that God's hiddenness did not apply only to the natural revelation outside of Christ but also more precisely to God's revelation *in* Christ. Karl Holl rediscovered the dialectic of God's alien and proper work in Luther's view of the relationship between wrath and love.

As I have pointed out, though, these advances did not come to grips with the real problem of law. The work of the contemporary interpreters has more successfully dealt with the problem of law in Luther, and hence has completed this line of development. For when law is understood as an existential category, many of the difficulties in understanding

Luther can be dealt with more fruitfully. This eschatological understanding of law necessitates a fundamental reorientation at a number of crucial points. First, of course, it means that the orthodox concept of law is displaced. Law cannot be understood as a *lex aeterna* in the sense that the orthodox held—an eternal standard which governs the system. Insofar as this is true, there is agreement with the original contention of Hofmann.

Second, however, law is not displaced merely by an objective historical dispensation. For law remains always as that which afflicts the conscience of sinful man in the old age. Here there is a fundamental criticism of Hofmann's scheme of *Heilsgeschichte*. Law is neither an eternally fixed standard nor merely a part of a limited historical dispensation.

Thirdly, some adjustments must be made in Harnack's interpretation. It is misleading to identify law, as Harnack did, with God's revelation of wrath "outside of Christ." For if law is defined as that which afflicts the conscience, then God's action in Christ (as Luther saw) will become the most powerful manifestation of law to the sinner in the old age. Here there is some justification for the Ritschlian position—that true repentance does, indeed, arise from God's action (not, however, from God's action as *gospel*, but God's action as *law*), and that "the same fact that increased our grief . . . will nevertheless be perceptible to us as a word of God convincing us that he has reached down to us."

Here Harnack's view must be found wanting, for law must be extended to include also God's action in Christ. Law as that which judges and terrifies is not and cannot be limited to a "natural revelation" outside of Christ. When law is defined existentially, it certainly includes the natural, but at the same time it includes more—God's judging action in Christ. In the terms of the eschatological dialectic, what is natural is included in the old age, but it is also in this old age that Christ appears and brings the work of the law to its climax. It belongs to man's naturalness in the old age that he apprehends the divine will in all its manifestations as law.

This means also that Harnack's use of the distinction between the essence and the office of law must be rejected. Man cannot get behind the office of the law to find a neutral essence which could be used as a means for reinstating the orthodox view of the atonement. To do so would mean a return to an abstract objectivity which destroys the reality of the atonement. Saying this, however, does not mean that Harnack's insistence upon the dialectic of wrath and love is denied; instead it is reinforced and given a more actual character than his own understanding would allow.

Fourthly, the Ritschlian approach must be revised. The eschatological understanding of the relationship between law and gospel can more fully realize the essential concerns of Ritschlianism; at the same time it can more adequately deal with the criticism of that position. For the eschatological interpretation of law and gospel stresses actuality, actual atonement, actual renewal in the present through participation in Christ's death and resurrection. The framework is eschatological, so that the Ritschlian attempt to affirm the distinction between theoretical and practical reason, between "nature" and "spirit" is discarded. After all, the actuality of the gospel is assured not by these distinctions but only when it is seen as the power which breaks in and defeats the powers which enslave man in the old age. One cannot rid oneself of the "natural" or the "theoretical" by making a further *theoretical* distinction. The "natural" is accepted as a part of man's existence "under the law." "Under the gospel" man learns to see nature in its proper perspective and to realize that it is both impossible and unnecessary to attempt to exclude nature in the Ritschlian manner. From this point of view the Ritschlian polemic against nature and natural law must be judged as mistaken; one does not serve the gospel by that kind of polemic.

So also with the concept of wrath. Love is not served by attempting to erase wrath from the system. The reality and actuality of the divine love is rather asserted most strongly when it is seen as the power which breaks in and overcomes wrath. When law and gospel are related eschatologically the abstract and theoretical nature of theology (which Ritschl abhorred) is overcome, but the problems with which he was concerned are more adequately solved.

Finally, the work of Kattenbusch and Holl must be appended and modified. The eschatological dialectic of law and gospel provides a more viable systematic structure for Kattenbusch's interpretation of the hidden-revealed dialectic in Luther and also for Holl's interpretation of the alien and proper work of God. The contemporary interpretation has simply completed the work they began and has freed it from Ritschlian presuppositions. Kattenbusch's interpretation of the hidden-revealed dialectic receives a more fixed systematic structure: God is indeed hidden—both in nature and in Christ—because man in the old age experiences him as a God of law and wrath. God is *revealed* in Christ because in faith he is received as the God whose power has overcome and brought about the decisive inbreaking of the new age. The hidden-revealed dialectic, therefore, does not refer merely (as Kattenbusch said) to the mystery of God as "the incomprehensible." It relates more precisely to the eschatological nature of God's action.

Likewise Karl Holl's Ritschlian moralism in his interpretation of

Luther is overcome. "Consciousness of the imperative" may indeed play an important part in Luther's thought, but it is not the basis of his religion. The eschatological dialectic of law and gospel shows that the imperative is overcome by the radical nature of the gospel. It is misleading, therefore, to say that the imperative is the basis for Luther's religion; this only creates the impression that the law is the foundation of the system and that the gospel is merely that which makes the law work. The eschatological dialectic gives the law an entirely different function from the gospel, a function as different from it as death is from life, old age from new age. Likewise it is misleading to say that the command which confronts man is in its basic content nothing other than the gospel. To be sure, if the *res* to which the law points is realized in the gospel, then there is a sense in which this is true. But when the eschatological framework is missing the statement is misleading. The eschatological dialectic cuts through the underlying Ritschlian moralism.

The eschatological dialectic is also able to handle Holl's difficulty with the wrath-love problem more effectively. While it is true, as Holl said, that wrath serves love in the sense that its purpose is to drive the sinner to Christ, it is impossible to seek a unity behind the paradox by neglecting or ignoring the fact that wrath can also lead to eternal death. Man simply cannot remove this possibility by his system, for if wrath does not lead to real death, one returns to the docetic tendencies of Hofmann's interpretation of the atonement; love becomes a foregone conclusion and the eschatological nature of the gospel is lost. Leaving open the possibility of a "stringent wrath" better protects Holl's own assertion that the unity of wrath and love can be held only in *faith*.

To sum up, the concept of law and gospel which emerges from the argument over the interpretation of Luther makes possible a systematic reorientation which can absorb the legitimate concerns of the various participants in the debate from Hofmann down to the present. It is of great significance to note that the debate over Luther's theology has been carried out in living dialogue with the developing demands of systematic theology. This is no doubt the reason why in many Lutheran circles Luther research has been almost a substitute for systematic theology, or at least a determinative factor in it.

One might well ask, I suppose, whether the theologians we have investigated have not read into Luther a theology consonant with their own systematic prejudices. This question can also be asked, no doubt, of the emerging eschatological interpretation in present-day interpreters. Have they not, perhaps, read into Luther a theology which meets the demands of the current emphasis on eschatology? Interesting and important as this question may be, it is beyond the scope of this study to attempt an answer. The point which I seek to make is that Luther *has* been interpreted this way and that this interpretation exerts its pressure on present-day systematic conclusions.

The relation of Luther research to the systematic debate, however, means that this research can best be understood in terms of its contribution to the solution of the problem of law and the act character of revelation. Quite clearly, affirming the eschatological character of the relationship between law and gospel is an attempt to deal with this problem. This is especially evident in the work of a man like Gerhard Ebeling. The act character of revelation is maintained through the idea that the gospel is the eschatological *event* which brings men freedom from the law in the present. Law is a general term which describes man's bondage in the old age and which leads to "death." Gospel is the eschatological advent of freedom and life.[47]

---

47. Ebeling, *Wort und Glaube*, 290–93.

PART II
Death and Resurrection

The Lutheran View of Sanctification

Sanctification, if it is to be spoken of as something other than justification, is perhaps best defined as the art of getting used to the unconditional justification wrought by the grace of God for Jesus' sake. It is what happens when we are grasped by the fact that God alone justifies. It is being made holy, and as such, it is not our work. It is the work of the Spirit who is called Holy. The fact that it is not our work puts the old Adam/Eve (our old self) to death and calls forth a new being in Christ. It is being saved from the sickness unto death and being called to new life.

In German there is a nice play on words that is hard to reproduce in English. Salvation is *das Heil*—which gives the sense both of being healed and of being saved. Sanctification is *die Heiligung*—which would perhaps best be translated as "being salvationed." Sanctification is "being salvationed," the new life arising from the catastrophe suffered by the old upon hearing that God alone saves. It is the pure flower that blossoms in the desert, watered by the unconditional grace of God.

Sanctification is thus simply the art of getting used to justification. It is not something added to justification. It is not the final defense against a justification too liberally granted. It is the justified life. It is what happens when the old being comes up against the end of its self-justifying and self-gratifying ways, however pious. It is life lived in anticipation of the resurrection.

As such, sanctification is likely not the kind of life that we (old beings!) would wish, much as we might prattle piously about it and protest about how necessary it is. For the most part we make the mistake of equating sanctification with what we might call the moral life. As old beings we get nervous when we hear about justification by grace alone, faith alone, and worry that it will lead to moral laxity. So we say we have to "add" sanctification too, or we have to get on to what is really important, living the "sanctified life." And by that we usually mean living morally.

Now, living morally is indeed an important, wise, and good thing. There is no need to knock it. But it should not be equated with sanctification, being made holy. The moral life is the business of the old being in this world. The Reformers called it "civil righteousness." Sanctification is the result of the dying of the old and the rising of the new. The moral life is the result of the old being's struggle to climb to the heights of the law. Sanctification has to do with the descent of the new being into humanity, becoming a neighbor, freely, spontaneously, giving of the self in self-forgetful and uncalculating ways. "But when you give to the needy, do not let your left hand know what your right hand is doing, so that your giving may be in secret. Then your Father, who sees what is done in secret, will reward you" (Matt 6:3–4). Sanctification is God's secret, hidden (perhaps especially!) even from the "sanctified." The last thing the sanctified would do would be to talk about it or make claims about achieving it. One would be more likely, with Paul, to talk about one's weaknesses.

No, sanctification is not the kind of thing we would seek. I expect we do not really want it, and perhaps rarely know when it is happening to us. It is the work of the Holy Spirit, the Lord and giver of life. It is given to us in the buffeting about, the sorrows, the joys, the sufferings, and the tasks of daily life. As Ernest Becker rightly put it in his classic work (that ought to be read by everyone interested in the question of "salvationing" today) *The Denial of Death*, the hardest thing is not even the death, but the rebirth, because it means that for the first time we shall have to be reborn not as gods but as human beings, shorn of all our defenses, projects, and claims.[1] Can flowers bloom in this desert? Can we survive and get used to justification? Can we live as though it were true? That is the question.

THE ARGUMENT

Talk about sanctification is dangerous. It is too seductive for the old being. What seems to have happened in the tradition is that sanctification has been sharply distinguished from justification, and thus separated out as the part of the "salvationing" we are to do. God alone does the justifying simply by declaring the ungodly to be so, for Jesus' sake. Most everyone is willing to concede that, at least in some fashion. But, of course, then comes the question: What happens next? Must not the justified live properly? Must not justification be safeguarded so it will not be abused? So sanctification enters the picture supposedly to rescue the

---

1. Ernest Becker, *The Denial of Death* (New York: Free Press, 1973), 58.

good ship Salvation from shipwreck on the rocks of Grace Alone. Sanctification, it seems, is our part of the bargain. But, of course, once it is looked on that way, we must be careful not to undo God's justifying act in Christ. So sanctification must be absolutely separated from justification. God, it seems, does his part, and then we do ours.

The result of this kind of thinking is generally disastrous. We are driven to make an entirely false distinction between justification and sanctification in order to save the investment the old being has in the moral system. Justification is a kind of obligatory religious preliminary that is rendered largely ineffective while we talk about getting on with the truly "serious" business of becoming "sanctified" according to some moral scheme or other. We become the actors in sanctification. This is entirely false. According to Scripture, God is always the acting subject, even in sanctification. The distinction serves only to leave the old being in control of things under the guise of pious talk.

On the level of human understanding, the problem is that we attempt to combine the unconditional grace of God with our notions of continuously existing and acting under the law. In other words, the old being does not come up against its death, but goes on pursuing its projects, perhaps a little more morally or piously, but still on its own. There is no death of the old and thus no hope for a resurrection of the new. The unconditional grace of God is combined with the wrong theological anthropology. That is always disaster. As we shall see a bit later, justification by faith alone demands that we think in terms of the death of the old subject and the resurrection of a new one, not the continuous existence of the old. Unconditional grace calls forth a new being in Christ. But the old being sees such unconditional grace as dangerous and so protects its continuity by "adding sanctification." It seeks to stave off the death involved by becoming "moral."

Sanctification thus becomes merely another part of its self-defense against grace. Justification is rendered more or less harmless. Talk about sanctification can be dangerous in that it misleads and seduces the old being into thinking it is still in control. We may grudgingly admit we cannot justify ourselves, but then we attempt to make up for that by getting serious about sanctification.

Even under the best of conditions, talk about sanctification in any way apart from justification is dangerous. It has a tendency to become a strictly verbal exercise in which one says obligatory things to show one is "serious about it"—but little comes of the discussion. Perhaps one feels sanctified just by talking impressively about it. The result of such talk is what I like to call "the magnificent hot-air balloon syndrome." One talks impressively about sanctification, and we all get beguiled by the rhetoric and agree. "Yes, of course, we all ought to do that," and the balloon begins to rise into the religious stratosphere solely on the strength of its own hot air. It is something like bragging about prowess in love and sex. It is mostly hot air and rarely accomplishes anything more for the hearers than arousing anxiety or creating the illusion that they somehow can participate vicariously. We got started in that direction even in the above exercise in this thesis when we talked about how sanctification is "spontaneous," "free," "self-forgetful," "self-giving," "uncalculating," and all those nice things. Dangerous talk. Dangerous because, like love, none of those things can actually be produced by us in any way. Theology indeed obligates us to talk about them, to attempt accurate description, but unless we know the dangers and limitations of such descriptions, it leads only to presumption or despair. So let the reader beware!

And so at the very least, we can say that sanctification cannot in any way be separated from justification. It is not merely a logical mistake, but a spiritually devastating one. In fact, the Scriptures rarely, if ever, treat sanctification as a movement distinct from justification. In writing to the Christians at Corinth, for instance, Paul refers to them as "those sanctified in Christ Jesus, called to be saints together with all those who in every place call on the name of our Lord Jesus Christ"; and later, he refers to the God who chooses what is low and despised in the world, even the things that are not, as the source of our life in Christ Jesus, "who became for us wisdom from God, and righteousness and sanctification and redemption," so that whoever boasts should boast in the Lord (1 Cor 1:2, 28–31).

To the Thessalonians Paul writes that they have been chosen by God from the beginning "for salvation through sanctification through the Spirit and through belief in the truth" (2 Thess 2:13). Hebrews says that "we have been sanctified through the offering of the body of Jesus Christ once for all" (Heb 10:10). Sanctification appears in Scripture to be roughly equivalent to other words for the salvation wrought by God in Christ, a phrase that designates another facet or dimension of sanctification, but never calls it something distinct or logically different from justification.

J. K. S. Reid is right when he concludes, "It is tempting for the sake of logical neatness to make a clean division between the two [justification and sanctification] but the temptation must be resisted, if in fact the division is absent from Holy Scripture."[2]

---

2. Alan Richardson, ed., *A Theological Wordbook of the Bible* (New York: Macmillan, 1960), 218.

It is difficult to escape the suspicion that the distinction between justification and sanctification is strictly a dogmatic one made because people got nervous about what would happen when unconditional grace was preached, especially in Reformation times. "Does justification not do away with good works? Who will be good if they hear about justification by faith alone?" So the anxious questions went. Sanctification was "added" as something distinct in order to save the enterprise from supposed disaster. But dogmatic distinctions do not save us from disaster. More likely than not, they only make matters worse.

JUSTIFICATION BY FAITH ALONE

It becomes clear, then, that we cannot talk about sanctification without first saying something about justification. The difficulty we have arises because justification by faith alone, without the deeds of the law, is a mighty breakup of the ordinary scheme of morality and religion; a mighty attack, we should say, on the theology of the old being. The fact that we are justified before God—the eternal Judge, Creator, and Preserver of all life—unconditionally for Jesus' sake and by faith alone, simply shatters the old being's entire system of values and calculations.

As old beings we do not know what to do with an unconditional gift or promise. Virtually our entire existence in this world is shaped, determined, and controlled by conditional promises and calculations. We are brought up on conditional promises. We live by them. Our future is determined by them. Conditional promises always have an "if-then" form.[3] If you eat your spinach, then you get your pudding. If you are a good girl, then you can go to the movies. If you do your schoolwork, then you will pass the course. If you do your job, then you will get your pay. If you prove yourself, then you will get a promotion. And so on and so on, endlessly until at last we die of it, wondering if we had only done this or that differently, perhaps then . . . Though such conditional promises are often burdensome and even oppressive, they are nevertheless enticing and even comforting in their own way because they give life its structure and seem to grant us a measure of control. If we fulfill the conditions, then we have a claim on what is promised. We have what we call "rights," and we can control our future, at least to a certain extent.

So, as old beings, we hang rather tenaciously onto these conditional promises. As a matter of fact, that is what largely characterizes our being

---

3. Eric Gritsch and Robert Jenson, *Lutheranism: The Theological Movement and Its Confessional Writings* (Philadelphia: Fortress, 1976), 8, 42.

in this world as old. We hang desperately onto the conditional promises, hoping to control our own destiny. We live "under the law" and cannot get out—because we really do not want to. We prefer to go our own way even up to the last barrier: death. And there we must either hope that the conditionality ends and all account books simply close, or perhaps we make the fatal mistake of thinking that we can extend our control under the conditional promise even into the beyond. We think we have a claim on heaven itself if the proper conditions are met. Religion is most often just the attempt to extend this conditionality into eternity and to gain a certain measure of control even over the eternal itself.

But the saving act of God in Jesus Christ—comprehended in justification by faith alone—is an unconditional promise. Unconditional promises have a "because-therefore" form. Because Jesus has overcome the world and all enemies by his death and resurrection, therefore (and only for that reason) you shall be saved. Because Jesus died and rose, therefore God here and now declares you just for Jesus' sake (not even for your sake, but for Jesus' sake). Because Jesus has borne the sin of the whole world in his body unto death and yet conquered, therefore God declares the forgiveness of our sins.

Now, of course, as old beings we have a desperately difficult time with such an unconditional promise. It knocks everything out of kilter. We simply do not know how to cope with it, so we are thrown into confusion. Is it really true? Can one announce it just like that? No strings attached? Do we not have to be more careful about to whom we say such things? It appears wild and dangerous and reckless to us, just as it did to Jesus' contemporaries. The best we can do is to try to draw it back into our conditional understanding—so all the questions and protests come pouring out. But surely we have to do something, do we not? Do we not at least have to make our decision to accept? Isn't faith, after all, a condition? Or repentance? Isn't the idea of an unconditional promise terribly dangerous? Who will be good? Won't it lead perhaps to universalism, libertinism, license, and sundry disasters? Do we not need to insist on sanctification to prevent the whole from collapsing into cheap grace? Does the Bible not follow the declaration of grace with certain exhortations and imperatives? So the protestations go, for the most part designed to reimpose at least a minimal conditionality on the promise.

It is crucial to see that here we have arrived at the decisive point which will entirely determine how we look at what we call sanctification. It is true, you see, that as old beings we simply cannot understand or cope with the unconditional promise of justification pronounced in the name of Jesus. What we do not see is that what the unconditional promise is calling forth is a new being. The justification of God promised in Jesus is not an "offer" made to us as old beings; it is our end, our death. We are, quite literally, through as old beings. To use the vernacular, we have "had it." All the questions and protests that we raise are really just the death rattle of the old Adam and Eve who sense that their kingdom is under radical and final attack. No doubt that is why the defense is so desperate, and why it even quite innocently takes such pious and well-meaning forms.

But isn't the unconditional promise dangerous? Of course it is! After all, look what happened to Jesus! It is the death of us one way or another. Either we stick in our conditionality and go to that death which is eternal, or we are put to death to be raised to new and eternal life in the one who lives eternally. The point is that when we come up against the danger and radicality of the unconditional promise, the solution is not to fall back on conditionality but simply to be drawn into the death and resurrection of Jesus. The old being cannot survive the promise, the promise that makes new beings out of nothing. God is the one who calls into being that which is from that which is not. The new being finds its center now not in itself, but in Jesus.

One has only to follow out the argument in Romans to see Paul clearly developing this point. The law, the conditional promise, did not stop sin; it only made it worse. As a matter of fact, the law was given to show sin as sinful beyond measure, a bottomless pit, an endless hall of mirrors. But where sin abounded, grace abounded all the more! But is not such argument terribly dangerous? Aren't all the careful barriers built against sin suddenly destroyed? Does one not come perilously close to saying that sin is somehow presupposed by or even necessary for grace? Couldn't one then justly say, "Well then, shall we not sin the more that grace may abound?" It is a serious question and one that has to be raised. As a matter of fact, if the question isn't raised, one probably has not yet grasped the radical *hilaritas*, the joy of grace. No doubt, it is the old being's last question prior to its death. But what is the answer? It does not lie in returning to the law, to conditionality, but rather in the death of the old.

> Should we continue in sin in order that grace may abound? By no means! How can we who died to sin go on living in it? Do you not know that all of us who have been baptized into Christ Jesus were baptized into his death? Therefore we have been buried with him by baptism into death, so that, just as Christ was raised from the dead by the glory of the Father, so we too might walk in newness of life. For if we have been united with him in a death like his, we will certainly be united with him in a resurrection like his. We know that our old self was crucified with him so that the body of sin

might be destroyed, and we might no longer be enslaved to sin. For whoever has died is freed from sin. But if we have died with Christ, we believe that we will also live with him. We know that Christ, being raised from the dead, will never die again; death no longer has dominion over him. The death he died, he died to sin once for all, but the life he lives, he lives to God. So you also must consider yourselves dead to sin and alive to God in Christ Jesus (Rom 6:1–11).

Actually, all evangelical treatment of sanctification should be little more than comment on this passage. The end to sin is death, not following the law, not moral progress, not even "sanctification" as the old Adam or Eve thinks of it. To sin the more that grace may increase is, of course, absurd and impossible precisely because of the death. To do so would mean to will to return to sin in order to get more grace. That would be like a lover desiring to return to the state of unloving in order to experience falling in love again. Quite impossible! How can one who has died to sin still live in it? The movement is simply irreversible if one catches a glimpse of what the grace is all about.

Furthermore, it is crucial to note that Paul does not tell his readers that they have to get busy now and die. He announces the startling and unconditional fact that we have died. It is not a task to be accomplished. All who were baptized into Christ Jesus were baptized into his death, so that out of that death may come newness of life, just like and as sure as the resurrection of Christ. Sin is a slavery from which we escape only through that death. Only one who has died is free from sin. There is no other way. The old self has been crucified so that the sinful body might also be destroyed and we might at last be set free. There is no continuity of the old self to be carried over here. Christ now becomes our life.

Just the sheer and unconditional announcement "You have died!"—the uncompromising insistence that there is nothing to do now, that God has made his last move—just that, and that alone, is what puts the old being to death, precisely because there is nothing for the old being to do. The God who says, "I will have mercy on whom I will have mercy," has decided to do just that through the death and resurrection of Jesus. There is no way for the old being to do anything about such grace. The unconditional justification, the grace itself, slays the old self and destroys its "body of sin" so as to fashion a new one. It is all over! Christ being raised from the dead will never die again. One cannot go back and repeat it. He died to sin once for all, and now he lives to God. Conclusion? You can now only consider yourself dead to sin and alive to God in Christ Jesus!

So, when we come to the decisive and crucial point about justification and the unconditional promise of grace, it is imperative to see that God is at work making new beings through this (to us) shocking act. The answer to all our questions, to the "death rattle" questions of the old Adam or Eve, lies not in falling back on conditionality, but in learning to cope with death and resurrection. All the questions must therefore be answered with a confident yes.

Do you mean to say we do not have to do anything? Yes! Just listen! Do you mean to say that even faith is not a condition, nor is making our decision, nor repentance? Yes! Faith is a gift. It comes by hearing. It is the Spirit's work. It is a being grasped by the unconditional promise, a being caught by the sheer newness and joy of it, a being carried by the Word of Grace. But is not such unconditional promise dangerous? Yes, I suppose it is in this evil age. After all, Jesus got killed for it! But God has apparently decided to take the risk and sealed it by raising Jesus from the dead. "Sleeper, awake! Rise from the dead, and Christ will shine on you" (Eph 5:14).

But do you mean to say we cannot say no? That kind of question is, of course, the trickiest of the old Adam or Eve. But in spite of everything, it must be answered with a confident yes—from the point of view of the new being. The old Adam or Eve will, of course, only say no, can really only say no. The old Adam or Eve wants to remain in control of the matter and so says no even while wanting to say yes.

So saying no is not an option? Perhaps the best answer would be, "What do you want to do that for?" It would be like arriving at the altar for the wedding and answering the big question. "Do you take . . ." with, "Do you mean to say I cannot say no?" If we see at all what is going on, we would see that even here the answer finally has got to be yes: "Yes, I do not see how you can say no!" The new being by definition is one who says yes. One is not forced here, one is made new, saved—heart, soul, mind. One is sanctified in the truth of the unconditional promise of God. The answer to the persistent questions of the old Adam or Eve is therefore always yes, yes, yes until at last we die of it and begin to whisper, "Amen! So be it Lord!" Sanctification is a matter of being grasped by the unconditional grace of God and having now to live in that light. It is a matter of getting used to justification.

SIMULTANEOUSLY JUST AND SINNER

But now we must look a bit closer at how the unconditional promise—justification by faith alone—works in our lives if we are to arrive at an appropriate understanding of what we might call sanctification. The first thing to grasp is, of course, that the unconditional promise works quite differently from a conditional one. The unconditional promise, the divine decree of justification, grants everything all at once to the faith it creates. We are simply declared just for Jesus' sake. But that means simultaneously that we are revealed to ourselves as sinners. The sin revealed is not just a misdeed, but it is precisely our lack of faith and trust over against the incredible goodness of God. The sin to be ultimately expelled is our lack of trust, our unbelief. All our impetuous questions are shown for what they are: unbelief, our reservations over against the God of grace, our fear of being made new.

And still we ask, Do we not have to do something? You see, that is all we really planned to do—just a little something! We hadn't counted on being made new! Just that, you see, is the sin exposed! Nevertheless, God simply declares us to be just for Jesus' sake because that is the only thing that will help. That act of God itself finally exposes us as sinners, desperately in need of saving. So then, for the time being, we are, as Martin Luther said, *simul justus et peccator*, simultaneously just and sinner. It is the unconditional grace of God that makes us so. In that, we see the truth. And it is in the truth that we are sanctified. The first step on the way of sanctification is to realize that.

This is radically different from our usual, conditional thinking. Conditional thinking is wedded to the schemes of law and progress characteristic of this age. Sin is understood primarily as misdeed or transgression of such a scheme. "Sanctification" is the business of making progress in cutting down on sin according to the scheme. Holiness or righteousness could not be said to exist simultaneously with sin in the same scheme. Righteousness and sin would simply exclude each other. The more righteousness one gains, the less sin there would be. This would be measured by what one does or does not do. It would be a matter of works. Grace would then have to be understood as the power to do such works, to achieve such righteousness. The logic would then be that with the help of grace one progressively gains more and more righteousness and thus sins less and less. One strives toward perfection until, theoretically, one would need less and less grace or perhaps finally no more grace at all.

But such conditional schemes pose all sorts of problems for one who wants to think and believe "in the fashion of Scripture," as Luther called it.[4] In the first place, it does not fit with the divine act of justification by grace alone, by faith alone. There is no real place for justification in the

---

4. Martin Luther, *Lectures on Romans*, trans. and ed. Wilhelm Pauck, The Library of Christian Classics, vol. 15 (Philadelphia: Westminster, 1961), 128.

scheme. If it comes at the beginning of the scheme, it makes the subsequent progress unnecessary. Why work at becoming just if you are already declared to be so? On the other hand, if justification comes at the end of the scheme, it becomes unnecessary. You do not have to be declared just if you have already become so.

The systematic problem is that both justification by faith alone without the deeds of the law and such a scheme of sanctification cannot possibly coexist together. The tradition no doubt recognized this when it insisted on making a sharp and complete distinction between the two, at least in theory. In actual practice, however, one or the other of them generally comes to be regarded as more or less fictional or dispensable. And more likely than not, it will be justification that is so regarded. It comes to be looked upon as a decree contrary to actual fact, a kind of "as if" theology. We are regarded "as if" we were just. Or perhaps it is a kind of "temporary loan" granted until we actually earn our way. Sanctification according to this scheme takes over the center of the stage as the real and practical business of the Christian.

But this leads only to a further, more personal problem in the life of faith if one becomes honest before God. What if the scheme just does not seem to work? This is the much-celebrated problem of the "anxious conscience" that bothered Martin Luther. What if one is honest enough to see that one is not actually making the kind of progress the scheme proposes? I am told that grace gives the power to improve, to gain righteousness and overcome sin. I am told, furthermore, that grace is absolutely free. But what if I go to church to "get grace" and then get up the next morning and see the same old sinner, perhaps even a little bit worse, staring back at me through the mirror? What then? I am told that grace is free, and that there is nothing wrong with the "delivery system." Not even a bad priest, minister, or a faulty church can frustrate or limit the grace of God. But I do not seem to get better. If I am in any way serious, I can only become more and more anxious. I am told that grace gives one the power to love God. But as a matter of fact, I only become more and more resentful of a God who sets up such systems and makes such demands. I do not seem to grow in love of God. I begin to hate him! The magnificent hot-air balloon bursts.

Now I face the really desperate question: Whose fault is it if the scheme does not work? There are two possibilities. Either I have not properly responded to or cooperated with the free divine grace, or most frightening of all, the God of election who presides over such grace has decided, in my case, not to give it. The scheme leaves me either depending on my own abilities to respond, to remove all obstacles to grace, to "let myself go," and so forth, or it leaves me with the terrors of predestination. Usually, of course, we recoil in horror from the very thought of predestination. We piously would not want to lay the blame on God—and besides, we would then lose all control of the matter!

So all things considered, we would rather take the blame for the breakdown of the scheme on ourselves. If it did not work, it must be because we did not do something right. We did not repent sincerely enough; we did not really and truly seek him; we did not wholly give our hearts to Jesus; and so on. But in that case, the more we talk about "free grace" the worse it gets. When the system does not work, "grace is free" turns out to mean that there is no way we can put the blame on grace. But then no matter how much we talk about the grace of God, absolutely everything then depends on us, on our sincerity, our truthfulness, the depth of our feeling, the wholeheartedness of our confession, and so on. The system simply turns against us. While we live as old beings in this age, we simply cannot escape the law.

So it is impossible to put God's unconditional act of justifying sinners for Jesus' sake alone together with our ideas of progress based on conditions. It does not work either logically or in the life of faith. That is why Martin Luther came to see that we must take a radically different approach. In place of all ordinary understandings of progress and sanctification, the true Christian life begins when we see the simultaneity of sin and righteousness. God begins with us simply by declaring us to be righteous because of Jesus. We begin to see the truth of the situation when we realize that because God had to do that, we must have been at the same time sinners. God would be wasting his breath declaring people to be righteous if they were not actually and wholly sinners! Indeed, as Paul put it, "if justification comes through the law, then Christ died for nothing" (Gal 2:21).

And there can be no cheating here. Since the declaration of God is total and depends totally on what Jesus has accomplished for us, the sin simultaneously exposed is total. All the dreams, schemes, and pretensions of the old Adam or Eve are unmasked in their totality. Sin, as a total state, can only be fought by faith in the total and unconditionally given righteousness. Anything other than that would lead only to hypocrisy or despair. If there is to be anything like true sanctification, it must begin with these considerations.

If our righteousness depends totally on Jesus and is appropriated only in the relationship of trust (faith), then we can begin to see that God has two problems with us. The relationship can be broken in two ways.

The first would be by our failure, our immorality, our vices. Since we lack faith and hope in God's cause, the relationship is threatened or broken; we go our own way. That problem is usually quite obvious. But the second problem is not so obvious. It is precisely our supposed success, even our "morality," our virtues—the relationship with God is broken to the degree that we think we do not need the unconditional justification, or perhaps even to the degree that we think we are going to use God to achieve our own ideas of sanctity. The relationship is broken precisely because we think it is our holiness.

The first problem, our failure and immorality, is usually most easily recognized and generally condemned because it has consequences, both personally and socially. But the second problem, while generally approved in human eyes because it is advantageous and socially useful, is more dangerous before God (*coram deo*, as Luther put it) precisely because it is praised and sought after. It is the kind of hypocrisy Jesus criticized so vehemently in the Gospels: "like whitewashed tombs, which on the outside look beautiful but inside they are full of the bones of the dead and of all kinds of filth" (Matt 23:27). No matter how good and useful such virtue is in the world (and we must not fail to see that it is really so and does have its place), it cannot be counted as sanctification. Those who blow their own horns when they give alms so as to be seen and admired by the public do indeed have their reward: the praise of others. But that is all they get. True sanctification is God's secret (Matt 6:2-4).

So the first step on the way to sanctification is to see that, before the judgment of God as it comes through the crucified and risen Jesus, we are rendered totally just at the same time as we are exposed totally as sinners. Sanctification is thus included in justification as a total state. True sanctification is at the outset simply to believe that God has taken charge of the matter. Where can there be more holiness than where God is revered and worshiped as the only Holy One? But God is revered as the only Holy One where the sinner, the real and total sinner, stands still and listens to God. There the sinner must realize that his or her ways are at an end. The final assault is under way. There the sinner begins to realize that neither virtue nor vice, morality nor immorality, neither circumcision nor uncircumcision counts for anything before God, but what matters is the new creation (Gal 6:15). Sanctification is not a repair job. God is after something new. He wants his creation back as new as when it came from his hand.

PROGRESS IN SANCTIFICATION: THE INVASION OF THE NEW

But is there not such a thing as growth in sanctification, progress in the Christian life? No doubt there is a sense in which we can and even should speak in such fashion. But when we do, we must take care, if everything we have been saying up to this point is true. If justification by faith alone rejects all ordinary schemes of progress and renders us simultaneously just and sinners, we have to look at growth and progress in quite a different light.

That brings us back to our thesis: sanctification is the art of getting used to justification. There is a kind of growth and progress, it is to be hoped, but it is growth in grace—a growth in coming to be captivated more and more, if we can so speak, by the totality, the unconditionality, of the grace of God. It is a matter of getting used to the fact that if we are to be saved it will have to be by grace alone. We should make no mistake about it: sin is to be conquered and expelled. But if we see that sin is the total state of standing against the unconditional grace and goodness of God, if sin is our very incredulity, unbelief, mistrust, our insistence on falling back on our self and maintaining control, then it is only through the total grace of God that sin comes under attack, and only through faith in that total grace that sin is defeated. To repeat: sin is not defeated by a repair job, but by dying and being raised new.

So it is always as a totality that unconditional grace attacks sin. That is why total sanctification and justification are in essence the same thing. The total sinner comes under the attack of the total gift. That is how the battle begins. How then can we talk about the progress of the battle—the transition, let us call it—from sin to righteousness, old to new?

There are, I believe, two aspects of this transition we need to talk about. The first is that since we always are confronted and given grace as a totality, we find ourselves always starting fresh. As Luther put it, "To progress is always to begin again."[5] In this life, we never quite get over grace, we never entirely grasp it, we never really learn it. It always takes us by surprise. Again and again we have to be conquered and captivated by its totality. The transition will never be completed this side of the grave. The Christian can never presume to be on the glory road, nor to reach a stage that now forms the basis for the next stage, which can be left behind. The Christian who is grasped by the totality of grace always discovers the miracle anew. One is always at a new beginning. Grace is new every day. Like the manna in the wilderness, it can never be bottled

---

5. Luther, *Lectures on Romans*, 370.

or stored. Yesterday's grace turns to poison. By the same token, however, the Christian never has an endless process of sanctification to traverse. Since the totality is given, one knows that one has arrived. Christ carries the Christian totally.

Looked at from Luther's point of view of "always beginning again," the transition is therefore not a continuous or steady progress of the sort we could recognize. It is rather more like an oscillation between beginning and end in which both are always equally near. The end, the total gift, is constantly and steadily given. But to grasp that we have constantly to begin again—we never can get over it! It is like lovers who just cannot get over the miracle of the gift of love and so are constantly saying it over and over again as though it were completely new and previously unheard of! And so it constantly begins again.

The second aspect of the transition of the Christian from old to new, death to life, is that all our ordinary views of progress and growth are turned upside down. It is not that we are somehow moving toward the goal, but rather that the goal is moving closer and closer to us. This corresponds to the eschatological nature of the New Testament message. It is the coming of the Kingdom upon us, not our coming closer to or building up the Kingdom. That is why it is a growth in grace, not a growth in our own virtue or morality. The progress, if one can call it that, is that we are being shaped more and more by the totality of the grace coming to us. The progress is due to the steady invasion of the new. That means that we are being taken more and more off our own hands, more and more away from self, and getting used to the idea of being saved by the grace of God alone. Our sanctification consists merely in being shaped by, or getting used to, justification.

Getting used to justification means that the old Adam or Eve is being put to death, and thus, as Paul put it, "being freed from sin." How might we conceive of this? Here we must be careful lest in our attempts to describe the matter we once again get seduced into inflating the magnificent hot-air balloon. Being freed from sin by the unconditional promise means that the totality of it begins to overwhelm and destroy our fundamental skepticism and incredulity, our unbelief. "Lord, I believe; help my unbelief!" (Mark 9:24) becomes our prayer. We can see light at the end of the tunnel. We begin to trust God rather than ourselves. When Martin Luther talked about these things, he began to talk more about our actual affections than lists of pious things to do.

Under the pressure of the total gift, we might actually begin to love God as God, our God, and to hate sin. Think of it: We might actually begin to dislike sin and to hope for its eventual removal. Ordinarily we feel guilty about our sins and fear their consequences, but we are far from hating them. I expect we do them, in spite of all fears and anxieties, because we like them. Sanctification under the invasion of the new, however, holds out the possibility of actually coming to hate sin, and to love God and his creation, or at least to make that little beginning. It is not that sin is taken away from us, but rather that we are to be taken away from sin—heart, soul, and mind, as Luther put it.[6] In that manner, the law of God is to be fulfilled in us precisely by the uncompromising totality and unconditionality of the grace given.

Sanctification always comes from the whole, the totality. Whether it takes place in little steps, in isolated actions against particular sins, in those tender beginnings, it is always because of the invasion of the new. Always the totality is intensively there—the total crisis, the entire transition, the dying and becoming new. What is the result of this? It should lead, I expect, to something of a reversal in our view of the Christian life. Instead of viewing ourselves on some kind of journey upward toward heaven, virtue, and morality, our sanctification would be viewed more in terms of our journey back down to earth, the business of becoming human, the kind of creature God made. Our problem is that we have succumbed to the serpent's temptation, "You shall not die, you shall be as gods." Creation is not good enough for us; we are always on our way somewhere else. So we even look on sanctification in that light—our "progress" toward being "gods" of some sort. If what we have been saying is true, however, our salvation, our sanctification, consists in turning about and going the other way, getting back down to earth. The trouble we have is that it is a long way back for us. To get there we must learn to trust God, to be grasped by the totality of his grace, to become a creature, to become human.

What might that look like? When I think about such sanctification, I think about several things: spontaneity, taking care, vocation, and attaining a certain elusive kind of truthfulness and lucidity about oneself. Perhaps I can end by saying a few words about these things.

SPONTANEITY

What is a truly good work, one that might qualify as the fruit of sanctification? One, I think, that is free, uncalculating, genuine, spontaneous. It would be like a mother who runs to pick up her child when it is hurt. There is no calculation, no wondering about progress, morality, or virtue. There is just the doing of it, and then it is completely forgotten.

---

6. Luther, *Lectures on Romans*, 194.

The right hand does not know what the left is doing. Good works in God's eyes are quite likely to be all those things we have forgotten! True sanctification is God's secret.

TAKING CARE

If we are turned around to get back down to earth by grace, then it would seem that true sanctification would show itself in taking care of our neighbor and God's creation, not exploiting and destroying either for our own ends, religious or otherwise. It would mean concern for the neighbor and society, caring for the other for the time being. Here one should talk about the place of morality and virtue and such things. Although we do not accept them as the means by which we are sanctified, they are the means by which and through which we care for the world and for the other. This is what the Reformers meant when they insisted that good works were to be done, but one was not to depend on them for salvation.

VOCATION

How does the one who has died and is being made new, the one who has been taken off his or her own hands, enter into the battle in this world? The answer comes in the concept of carrying out one's vocation as a Christian in the tasks and occupations of daily life. We always get nervous about what we are to do, it seems. The magnificent hot-air balloon syndrome seduces us into thinking our sanctification consists in following lists of pious dos and do nots. That always seems more holy. But it is in the nitty gritty of daily life and its tasks that our sanctification is hammered out.

Precisely because of the totality of the gift, the new being knows that there is nothing to do to gain heaven. Thus the Christian is called to the tasks of daily life in this world, for the time being. Students, for instance, are sometimes very pious and idealistic about "doing something," and so get caught up in this or that movement "for good." It never seems to dawn on them that perhaps for the time being, at least, their calling is simply to be a good student! It is not particularly in acts of piety that we are sanctified, but in our call to live and act as Christians.

TRUTHFULNESS AND LUCIDITY

In many ways, this essay has been an appeal for more truthfulness in our talk about the Christian life and sanctification. I think that should be the mark of sanctification as well. As Paul put it, we are not to think of ourselves more highly than we ought (Rom 12:3).

The talk of progress and growth we usually indulge in leads us all too often to do just that. But if we are saved and sanctified only by the unconditional grace of God, we ought to be able to become more truthful and lucid about the way things really are with us. Am I making progress? If I am really honest it seems to me that the question is odd, even a little ridiculous. As I get older and death draws nearer, it does not seem to get any easier. I get a little more impatient, a little more anxious about having perhaps missed what this life has to offer, a little slower, harder to move, a little more sedentary and set in my ways. It seems more and more unjust to me that now that I have spent a good part of my life "getting to the top," and I seem just about to have made it, I am already slowing down, already on the way out. A skiing injury from when I was sixteen years old acts up if I overexert myself. I am too heavy, the doctors tell me, but it is so hard to lose weight! Am I making progress? Well, maybe it seems as though I sin less, but that may only be because I'm getting tired! It's just too hard to keep indulging the lusts of youth. Is that sanctification? I would not think so! One should not, I expect, mistake encroaching senility for sanctification!

But can it be, perhaps, that it is precisely the unconditional gift of grace that helps me to see and admit all that? I hope so. The grace of God should lead us to see the truth about ourselves, and to gain a certain lucidity, a certain sense of humor, a certain down-to-earthness. When we come to realize that if we are going to be saved, it shall have to be absolutely by grace alone, then we shall be sanctified. God will have his way with us at last.

Two Ways of Being a Theologian

The two stories, the glory story and the cross story, join in mortal combat over which shall define and determine our destiny. The cross itself is the place where the combat is joined. When the cross conquers, it becomes clear to us that there is a quite different way of being a theologian. We become a theologian of the cross. Just as there are two basic stories, there are two ways of being a theologian. We are either a theologian of glory or a theologian of the cross.

Before we delve into that either/or, a digression to say a word about the business of theology may be useful. We should not worry about talk of "being a theologian." We are not speaking here about being a "professional" theologian. Indeed, being a theologian of the cross has no automatic connection to what might be called "academic theology." Luther liked to say that what makes a theologian is the ability properly to distinguish between law and gospel, not ability and prowess in scholarly pursuits. Of course, it is to be hoped that the two abilities do come together in reflective Christians, especially in pastors and teachers of theology. Unfortunately, that is not always the case. But becoming a theologian of the cross is a different matter. As we shall see, it means being turned to seek out "the real" in a quite different fashion. Becoming a theologian of the cross involves turning to face the problems, joys, and sorrows of everyday life. To be sure, for some that will include being professors and academics, and the theology of the cross should affect the way they do that. It should also affect all of life in its own way. That will no doubt become clear as we look at the Heidelberg Disputation.

Suffice it to say for now, though, that all of us are theologians in one way or another. Being a theologian just means thinking and speaking about God. True, we may not do much of that. We might go for days and weeks without a thought of God entering our heads, but that is usually impossible. Things happen. Accidents. Tragedies. Deaths and funerals. Natural disasters. Illness. Loss. Suffering. Disappointment. Wrongdoing. And so on and on. There is also good fortune. Perhaps unexpected success or escape from danger or certain disaster. Experience of great beauty or pleasure. Sheer grace. Chance encounters that determine our lives. Love. We begin to wonder. God pops into our thinking and conversation. We may cry out in agony, "Why God?" or in relief, "Thank God!" Or we may just use God's name in cursing. Sooner or later we are likely to get thinking about God and wondering if there is some logic to it all in our lives, or some injustice. We become theologians.

Becoming a theologian is not a matter to be taken lightly. We can be blessed by it if we "get it right," as well as cursed by it if we don't. Nevertheless, the task, especially for believers, is inescapable. I always remember a wise professor's warning, "Those who take up the task of theology sometimes come a-cropper, but those who refuse the task altogether will most certainly do so." With such words in mind, it should be worth our while to spend some time thinking on the logic of God and the task of becoming theologians—and what kind of theologians we ought to be. This little book is an invitation to such thinking. It invites us to the kind of thinking shaped by the cross. It is about becoming a theologian of the cross.[1]

Returning to our either/or, it is evident that, since the two stories, the glory story and the cross story, actually determine how we think about ourselves, they quite consequently also determine what kind of theologian we are going to be. Once again we emphasize that the issue here is not the more abstract one of talking or writing *about theology* but the more difficult and concrete matter of *being theologians*. In the more famous and decisive theses of the Heidelberg Disputation (19-22) Luther does not talk about theology in the abstract but rather about the two different kinds of theologians and what they do, the way they operate. The question we have to try to deal with is what kind of theologian the two stories make out of us. The answer will be given more completely as we move through the Heidelberg Disputation. Here we only anticipate by means of hasty sketch to alert us

The Disputation is set up quite consistently as a series of sharp contrasts—or better, antitheses—between the two ways of being theologians and the stories that lie behind them. The antitheses focus on basic issues of salvation: the question of law and works; the power of the human will; the attempt to "see" God; the task of speaking the truth in these

---

1. Gerhard Forde, *On Being a Theologian of the Cross: Reflections on Luther's Heidelberg Disputation* (Grand Rapids: Eerdmans, 1997).

matters; faith; and ultimately of the love of God, which creates its own object. The argument proceeds by constantly setting the way of glory over against the way of the cross. In every instance all loopholes are closed so that the believer will in the end simply be cast on that creative love of God, which makes the object of its love out of the nothing to which the sinner has been reduced.

The Disputation itself, one might say, illustrates the manner in which theologians of the cross operate. Claimed, that is to say killed and made alive by the cross alone as *the* story, theologians of the cross attack the way of glory, the way of law, human works, and free will, because the way of glory simply operates as a defense mechanism against the cross. Theologians of glory operate with fundamentally different presuppositions about how one comes to know God. They think one can see *through* the created world and the act of God to the invisible realm of glory beyond it, and they must think this because for the system to work there must be a "glory road," a way of law, which the fallen creature can traverse by willing and working and thus gain the necessary merit eventually to arrive at glory.

The cross too is transparent. The theologian of glory *sees* through the cross so as to fit it into the scheme of works. The cross "makes up" for failures along the glory road. The upshot of it all is a fundamental misreading of reality. The theologian of glory ends by calling evil good and good evil. Works are good and suffering is evil. The God who presides over this enterprise must therefore be excused from all blame for what was termed "evil." The theology of glory ends in a simplistic understanding of God. God, according to philosophers like Plato, is not the cause of all things but only what we might call "good."[2] It is hard to see how such a god could even be involved in the cross.

Theologians of the cross, however, "say what a thing is." That is, a characteristic mark of theologians of the cross is that they learn to call a spade a spade. Since the cross story alone is their story, they are not driven by the attempt to see through it but are drawn into the story. They know that faith means to live in the Christ of the story. Likewise they do not believe that we come to proper knowledge of God by attempting to see through the created world to the "invisible things of God."[3] So theologians of the cross look on all things "through suffering and the

---

2. "Then God, if he be good, is not the author of all things, as the many assert, but he is the cause of a few things only, and not of most things that occur to men. For few are the goods of human life, and many are the evils, and the good is to be attributed to God alone; of the evils the causes are to be sought elsewhere, and not in him." Plato, *Republic* 2.379.
3. Page 233–37 below, Heidelberg Disputation, thesis 19.

cross."[4] They, in other words, are led by the cross to look at the trials, the sufferings, the pangs of conscience, the troubles—and joys—of daily life as God's doing and do not try to see through them as mere accidental problems to be solved by metaphysical adjustment. They are not driven to simplistic theodicies because with St. Paul they believe that God justifies himself precisely in the cross and resurrection of Jesus. They know that, dying to the old, the believer lives in Christ and looks forward to being raised with him.

Theologians of the cross therefore come to understand that the only move left is to the proclamation that issues from the story. The final task is to *do* the story to the hearers in such a way that they are incorporated into the story itself, killed and made alive by the hearing of it. The hearers are to be claimed by the story. Thus theologians of the cross will be compelled to theologize on the story that there are no escape hatches, no loopholes. They are constrained to rule out the attempt to see through creation or the cross to some supposed secret behind it. There is no secret passage to glory. They insist that there is no other place to look but to the cross story itself. This means that a certain suspicion and polemical edge is usually evident. Theologians of the cross know the temptations of a theology of glory well and are concerned to counter them at every turn. In essence, that is what comes to expression in Luther's Heidelberg Disputation. It is a thoroughgoing exposition and refutation of a theology of glory. A passage from Luther's *Work on the Psalms* from the same period as the Heidelberg Disputation makes all this quite explicit:

> In the kingdom of his humanity and his flesh, in which we live by faith, he makes us of the same form as himself and crucifies us by making us true humans instead of unhappy and proud Gods: humans, that is, in their misery and their sin. Because in Adam we mounted up towards equality with God, he descended to be like us, to bring us back to knowledge of himself. That is the sacrament of the incarnation. That is the kingdom of faith in which the cross of Christ holds sway, which sets at naught the divinity for which we perversely strive and restores the despised weakness of the flesh which we have perversely abandoned.[5]

The passage well illustrates how the cross story becomes our story. It must not be forgotten, however, that the crucifixion is not the end of the story. The passage goes on to speak of the final hope:

---

4. Page 237–39 below, Heidelberg Disputation, thesis 20
5. WA 5:128.31–5:129.4. Martin Luther, *Luther's Commentary on the First Twenty-two Psalms*, vol. 1, trans. John Nicholas Lenker (Sunbury, PA: Lutherans in All Lands, 1903), 204.

But in the kingdom of his divinity and glory he will make us like unto his glorious body, where we shall be like him and shall be no longer sinners, no longer weak, but shall ourselves be kings, the sons of God, and as the angels that are in heaven. Then we shall say "my God" in real possession, which now we say only in hope.[6]

To sum up, the two stories with the two resultant ways of being a theologian are indicative of two quite different perceptions of Christian faith and life. The theologian of glory searches endlessly for escape hatches, for a way to glory enticing enough to attract the free will (or what is left of it) of the seeker. I use the analogy of addiction throughout the book in the attempt to demonstrate the difference between the theologian of glory and the theologian of the cross. The theologian of glory is like one who considers curing addiction by optimistic exhortation. The theologian of the cross knows that the cure is much more drastic. Luther virtually invites this analogy of addiction in the proof for thesis 22 of the Disputation, when he likens the theology of glory to the thirst for money, or wisdom, or power, and so forth and declares that the soul's insatiable "thirst for glory is not ended by satisfying it but rather by extinguishing it."[7] A theologian of glory attempts to cure those addicted to glory by optimistic appeals, that is, by the law. But what happens thereby is only a reinforcement of one's illusions about oneself. The supposed optimism of the theology of glory turns against itself. When the addict discovers the impossibility of quitting, self-esteem plummets.

---

6. It goes without saying, perhaps, that "glory" here means something quite different from the glory in a theology of glory. The glory of God comes by God's grace and power. The glory of the theology of glory is made, sought, and appropriated by fallen creatures in the attempt to usurp divine glory.

7. LW 31:54. See the discussion below, pp. 108–9. There is an enlightening treatment of the relation between sin and addiction by Linda A. Mercadante, "Sin, Addiction, and Freedom," in Rebecca S. Chopp and Mark Lewis Taylor, eds., *Reconstructing Christian Theology* (Minneapolis: Augsburg/Fortress, 1994), 220–44. Mercadante maintains that while addiction does illuminate aspects of the Christian understanding of sin, it cannot replace it. I quite agree. My use of addiction here is strictly as an analogy to illuminate differences between the operation of a theologian of glory and that of a theologian of the cross. I am quite conscious of the fact that more would have to be said to overcome some of the limitations and work out the ramifications of the analogy. For instance, it is clear from the discussion in the Heidelberg Disputation that sin as "addiction" to self can go one of two ways, addiction either to "baser lusts" or to higher pretensions of self-righteousness and glory. Luther uses it in this treatise in the latter sense. The "addiction" of most concern to the theologian of the cross is the attempt to bypass the cross on the strength of one's own works. The addict, likewise, may be addicted either to the substance in question or to his own obsession with quitting and become a "dry drunk." One might also ask whether the optimistic approach may not work at least in some cases. But as we shall see later, this objection will not work in the case of a theology of the cross for it is not finally doctrines about sin that convince the sinner, but precisely the cross itself. The cross makes all superficial optimism impossible.

The addict tries to hide the addiction and puts on a false front. Superficial optimism breeds ultimate despair.

A theology of glory works like that. It operates on the assumption that what we need, is optimistic encouragement, some flattery, some positive thinking, some support to build our self-esteem. Theologically speaking it operates on the assumption that we are not seriously addicted to sin, and that our improvement is both necessary and possible. We need a little boost in our desire to do good works. Of course our theologian of glory may well grant that we need the help of grace. The only dispute, usually, will be about the degree of grace needed. If we are a "liberal," we will opt for less grace and tend to define it as some kind of moral persuasion or spiritual encouragement. If we are more "conservative" and speak even of the depth of human sin, we will tend to escalate the degree of grace needed to the utmost. But the hallmark of a theology of glory is that it will always consider grace as something of a supplement to whatever is left of human will and power. It will always, in the end, hold out for some free will. Theology then becomes the business of making theological explanations attractive to the will. Sooner or later a disastrous erosion of the language sets in. It must constantly be adjusted to be made appealing. Gradually it sinks to the level of maudlin sentimentality.

Theologians of the cross, however, operate quite differently. They operate on the assumption that there must be—to use the language of treatment for addicts—a "bottoming out" or an "intervention." That is to say, there is no cure for the addict on his own. In theological terms, we must come to confess that we are addicted to sin, addicted to self, whatever form that may take, pious or impious. So theologians of the cross know that we can't be helped by optimistic appeals to glory, strength, wisdom, positive thinking, and so forth because those things are themselves the problem. The truth must be spoken. To repeat Luther again, the thirst for glory or power or wisdom is never satisfied even by the acquisition of it. We always want more—precisely so that we can declare independence from God. The thirst is for the absolute independence of the self, and that is sin. Thus again Luther's statement of the radical cure in his proof for thesis 22: "The remedy for curing desire does not lie in satisfying it, but in extinguishing it."[8] The cross does the extinguishing. The cross is the death of sin, and the sinner. The cross does the "bottoming out." The cross is the "intervention." The addict/sinner is not coddled by false optimism but is put to death so that a new life can begin. The theologian of the cross "says what a thing is" (thesis 21). The theologian of the cross preaches to convict of sin. The addict is not deceived

---

8. LW 31:54.

by theological marshmallows but is told the truth so that he might at last learn to confess, to say, "I am an addict," "I am an alcoholic," and never to stop saying it. Theologically and more universally all must learn to say, "I am a sinner," and likewise never to stop saying it until Christ's return makes it no longer true.

The theology of the cross is the true and ultimate source of human optimism because it always presupposes the resurrection.[9] We should always bear in mind in pondering texts like the Heidelberg Disputation that resurrection is always taken together with the cross. The fundamental question of the Disputation is how to arrive at that righteousness that will enable us to stand before God. It is about resurrection, finally, even when the word is not explicitly spoken. Indeed, it is not possible to have a theology of the cross without resurrection. The powerful attacks launched against even the best of human works that put the sinner to death would simply not be possible if the resurrection were not presupposed. Some theologians of the cross seem afraid to bring in talk of resurrection because they apparently fear it will mitigate the unrelieved "tragedy" of the cross and its attack.[10] But the opposite is the case. Without the resurrection theologians will always be tempted to tone down the attack in order to leave room for at least some optimism, some hope for the survival of the old self. They end by telling sweet lies, calling the bad good and the good bad. Without the resurrection theologians cannot speak the truth about the human condition, and without hearing and confessing such truth we have no hope, no resurrection. For a resurrection to happen, there must first be a death. The truth must be heard and confessed; then there is hope. A new life can begin, and with it a new sense of self-worth can blossom. That is the ultimate aim of the Heidel-

---

9. James Nestingen has made the point well in his essay, "Luther's Heidelberg Disputation: An Analysis of the Argument," in *All Things New, Essays in Honor of Roy A. Harrisville*, ed. Arland J. Hultgren et al., Word and World Supplement Series, no. 1 (St. Paul: Luther Seminary, 1992), 147–48. Nestingen criticizes Jos E. Vercruysse ("Gesetz und Liebe, Die Struktur der 'Heidelberg Disputation' Luthers [1518]," *Lutherjahrbuch* 48 [1981]), to whose analysis I am indebted considerably here, for failing to see the Disputation in the light of Luther's apocalyptic view, thus missing the note of resurrection. Nestingen would like to see theses 1–18 interpreted as the cross side of the argument, and theses 19–24 as the resurrection side. That is certainly quite possible. However, I find it also important to regard the resurrection as a presupposition for the entire argument. The devastating attack launched in theses 1–18 against even the best of our works, which puts the sinner to death, is simply not possible where there is no resurrection. A theology of glory is a theology premised on what Ernest Becker called "the denial of death." A theology of the cross sees that we must go through death to receive the gift of new life.

10. This is one of the questions I have about the work of Douglas John Hall, especially in its earlier stages (see, e.g., *Lighten Our Darkness*). One almost gets the impression Hall is afraid to turn to the resurrection for fear it will mitigate the unrelieved negativity of the cross vis-à-vis the "official optimism" of North America.

berg Disputation. For in the end we arrive, as we shall see, at the love of God, which creates anew out of nothing.

PART III
The Bondage of the Will

The Argument about God

This gouty foot laughs at your doctoring.
—LW 33:53

The Bondage of the Will arouses much incredulity, dismay, anxiety, and outright anger when we hear what Luther has to say about God. God rules all things by immutable necessity. So says Luther. To be sure, Luther did not like the philosophical and scholastic terminology in which the argument was couched, particularly words like "necessity," "immutability," "fate," "force," "foreknowledge," and so forth. In ordinary parlance such words imply that we are like puppets being jerked around against our wills by a malevolent master puppeteer. Nevertheless, Luther sails steadfastly into the maelstrom brought on by the actual words and the doctrine of God the argument engenders. We shall look at Luther's argument a bit later. First, we need to look briefly at the Erasmian position regarding God.

Erasmus' position reflects at bottom the same dreary moralism touted by everyone from the lowliest neophyte to the most learned professor. People worry endlessly, in countless subtle ways and often with touching piety, that grace is going to upset the moral applecart, or perhaps that they will lose control over their destiny. The differences among them are merely matters of degree. In other words, Erasmus' view on free choice is the common stock of virtually everyone who thinks on the matter, from believer to unbeliever, saint to sinner, theologian to philosopher. Indeed, Luther even tried to excuse himself for not replying to Erasmus right away by claiming that Erasmus had said nothing new! If God rules all things by immutable necessity, so the argument goes, both morality and theodicy are undercut. Who would lead a moral life? Who would reform his life? How could our works be meritorious? Who could love such a God with all her heart, a God who condones and apparently wills the suffering of the innocent?

Furthermore, and perhaps of most gravity for Erasmus' method, he held that there were some things that were better reserved for the learned and dispassionate discussion of the schools and universities. They ought not be published where they would vex and trouble the "common herd" (Erasmus' own words).[1] Thus, for Erasmus, even if it were true that God rules all things by immutable necessity, it would be better not to let the "common herd" in on such lofty and dangerous academic secrets. It would only cause violence, upheaval, war, and bloodshed. Some diseases, Erasmus opined, are better borne than their cure. A wise physician will know how best to moderate the proper cure.

Luther was infuriated by such exegetical imperialism that allowed Erasmus to persist in his opinion that the doctrine of the bondage of the will was among those doctrines that ought not be put on public display before the unlearned. Erasmus persisted in his opinion that the doctrine of the bondage of the will was among those doctrines that ought not be put on public display before the unlearned. For Luther, Erasmus once again plays the role of the zealous and pious preacher who holds back on grace to make sure that morality will be served! This was of fundamental importance for Luther. In fact, he called the proper knowledge of what God does in relation to human free will a good one-half of the Christian "summa" (system of Christian dogma).

Some of the argumentation is worth repeating to get a feeling for the flavor and urgency of the debate. When Erasmus holds that it is unnecessary, irreverent, inquisitive, and superfluous for the "average" person to be bothered about the bondage of the will, Luther is enraged. The Erasmian position simply persists in its view that the first concern is morality rather than larger issues of faith, reverence before God, and the deeper dimensions of the Christian life under the cross. The laity can concern themselves with moral reform while the professors debate abstract theological issues—a familiar procedure in the life of the church, alas, even down to the present day. Luther's fury was heightened by Erasmus' statement on the "sum" of the Christian life:

> So in my opinion, as far as free choice is concerned, what we have learnt from Holy Writ is this: if we are in the way of true religion we should eagerly press on to better things, forgetting the things that are behind; if we are entangled in sins, we should strive with all our might, have recourse to the remedy of penitence and entreat by all means the mercy of the Lord, without which no human will or endeavor is effective; and whatever is evil

1. Found in LW 33:45.

in us, let us impute to ourselves, whatever is good let us ascribe wholly to the divine benevolence, to which we owe our very being; then for the rest, let us believe that whatever befalls us in this life, whether joyful or sad, it has been sent by God for our salvation, and that no wrong can be done to anyone by him, who by nature is just, even if some things happen that we feel we have not deserved, nor should anyone despair of forgiveness from a God who is by nature most merciful.[2]

These are, of course, very pious, high-sounding, and appealing words. But Luther found them shockingly vacuous as a description of Christian faith. Why? Because there is nothing particularly Christian about them! There is no mention of Christ's distinctive work, nor is there mention of the Spirit. It is a draft of the Christian faith, Luther says, "which any Jew or Gentile totally ignorant of Christ could certainly draw up with ease."[3] Hence, they are for Luther, Christless, Spiritless words, chillier than ice.[4] Erasmus replied that he was giving only what should be enough for "ordinary people" in contrast to the highly debatable and almost inexplicable problems that beset the subject of free choice.[5] Erasmus doesn't seem to realize that that is precisely the problem! Theologians don't "fix" the God problem by a remodeling job or by whisking him away behind the walls of academia. The attempt to do so only makes matters worse. If Jesus and the Spirit are taken out of the picture the only possible means of divine approach is undercut. A gospel preacher has no common ground with such a procedure.

So we begin to see the point of Luther's pithy saying, "this gouty foot laughs at your doctoring."[6] Gout was an excruciatingly painful, and in those days virtually incurable, affliction. It was a disease that just would not yield to the doctors' manipulations. The more the doctors attempted to do something about it, the worse it got.

And so it was for Luther with Erasmus' proposed "treatment" of the problem of free choice versus immutable necessity. Erasmus counsels avoiding the matter. He claimed it to be too difficult and upsetting—indeed irreverent, useless, inquisitive, and superfluous—for the "common herd." He finally concluded, "What is above us does not concern us." In Luther's view, that was Erasmus' solace for the sufferers. We shall see later that Luther too could use the adage but in a radically different sense. Erasmus used it as a defense of free will and the claims of the

2. LW 33:30–32n27.
3. LW 33:29.
4. *Martin Luther on the Bondage of the Will*, trans. J. I. Packer and O. R. Johnston (Westwood, NJ: Revell, 1957), 75.
5. Luther, *Bondage of the Will*, 76.
6. LW 33:53.

moral life. One could safely ignore that which is above to concentrate on moral perfection and more "practical" matters. Luther used the adage as a consequence of the God revealed in the preaching of the gospel. Protecting the place of the moral life does not help the stricken conscience. The gouty foot mocks such advice. The desperate pain of guilt, failure, and emptiness remains unhealed.

In effect, Luther's reply to Erasmus' stratagem (which remains basically the same today: ignore the problem!) is to point out that the "common herd" knows all about it already. In the vernacular, Luther's reply to Erasmus was, "Who are you kidding, Erasmus? Everybody knows already, or at least fears or even resents the God who rules all things by necessity and foreknows nothing contingently! The pain of God cannot be removed by theological doctoring. The problem is to get this God off our backs!" The question is, how this is to be done? How is the gouty foot to be healed? One thing is for certain. It is not done by redoing God's "job description." That only makes matters worse.

Before turning to the basic argument in the God-question, Luther asks some subsidiary questions. Why is it, he wants to know, that Christians have so much trouble with the doctrine of God when pagan poets, philosophers, and even common folk have no problems? From this we can see, Luther maintains,

> that the knowledge of God's predestination and foreknowledge remained with the common people no less than the awareness of his existence itself. But those who wished to appear wise went so far astray in their reasonings that their hearts were darkened, and they became fools (Rom. 1[:21–22]) and denied or explained away the things that the poets and common people, and even their own conscience, regarded as entirely familiar, certain and true.[7]

Luther was adamant about the importance of knowing what power free choice has over against the immutability and foreknowledge of God. This, he could say, was "the cardinal issue." For if God is God it follows that all we do must be subordinate to his will and happen by his necessity. This, for Luther, is the thunderbolt that knocks free will flat and utterly shatters it.[8] At this point the argument for Luther is a matter of straightforward and hard-nosed logic. If God is asserted to be just and kind must he not be immutably so? All scholastic attempts to make distinctions to ameliorate the crisis of the encounter with almighty God are cast aside.

---

7. LW 33:41.
8. LW 33:263.

For instance, consider the distinction between the immutability of God's will over against his foreknowledge. Erasmus apparently wanted to insist on the idea that God's will is immutable but not his foreknowledge. This might give Erasmus room to say that though God's will is immutable, a changeable foreknowledge affords room for change with regard to the future. Luther will have none of it. "God's . . . will is eternal and changeless, because His nature is so." Then Luther simply follows out the logic:

> From which it follows, by resistless logic, that all we do, however it may appear to us to be done mutably and contingently, is in reality done necessarily and immutably in respect of God's will. For the will of God is effective and cannot be impeded, since power belongs to God's nature; and His wisdom is such that He cannot be deceived.[9]

Thus Luther moves to plug every loophole that would give free choice a place to assert itself, and answers Erasmus' charge that openly teaching the bondage of the will would yield terrible chaos and devastating warfare:

> Let me tell you, therefore—and I beg you to let this sink deep into your mind—I hold that a solemn and vital truth, of eternal consequence, is at stake in this discussion; one so crucial and fundamental that it ought to be maintained and defended even at the cost of life, though as a result the whole world should be, not just thrown into turmoil and uproar, but shattered in chaos and reduced to nothingness.[10]

The best-known and heftiest battle was (and still is?) around the problem of necessity. Scholastic theologians tried to work with the distinction between the "necessity of consequence" and "the necessity of the thing consequent." If God wills something to come to pass, the necessary consequence is that it come to pass. There is a kind of necessity involved. But it is not a necessity of the thing consequent; that is, God is under no necessity to bring it to pass. Were there such necessity, it would be a necessity of the thing consequent. If God, that is, wills to create a world, then it necessarily comes to be. But God is under no absolute necessity to create that world. That would be determinism. But the distinction intends to allow for a kind of necessity at the same time as it makes room for a little bit of free choice. Luther dismisses the distinction as being patently ridiculous. All it establishes is that the thing consequent is not

---

9. Luther, *Bondage of the Will*, 80.
10. Luther, *Bondage of the Will*, 90.

god! And that we knew already. The gouty foot is not healed by scholastic distinctions.

To be sure, Luther does have some reservations about the use of the word "necessity" in the discussion of free choice. He wishes there were a better word. Necessity carries with it too much the notion of compulsion and is inappropriate to describe willing, either in God or humans. "For neither the divine nor the human will does what it does, whether good or evil, under any compulsion but from sheer pleasure or desire, as with true freedom; and yet the will of God is immutable and infallible and it governs our mutable will."[11] An exceedingly important text! We shall have to return to it later. For now it is enough to note that it shows clearly that the bondage of the will in question is not, for Luther, a matter of force or determinism. No one is forced. It is something more like an addiction. We all do what we want to do! That is precisely our bondage. We are not jerked around by a transcendent puppeteer. Luther appeals to the reader's intelligence to supply what the word "necessity" ought to convey:

> The reader's intelligence must therefore supply what the word "necessity" does not express, by understanding it to mean what you might call the immutability of the will of God and the impotence of our evil will, or what some have called the necessity of immutability, though this is not very good either grammatically or theologically.[12]

Having dispensed with some typical attempts to find loopholes in divine necessity we turn to Luther's main argument. Why, we might well ask, does Luther insist so adamantly on the immutability of God when it seems to undermine both faith and morals? As Erasmus asked, "Who will be good? Who will change his life?" and so forth. Reflected in the Erasmian position is evidence of more concern for the morals of the "common herd" than anything else. Luther was of a completely different mind:

> Who will take pains to correct his life? I answer: No man will and no man can, for God cares nothing for your correctors without the Spirit, since they are hypocrites. But the elect and the godly will be corrected by the Holy Spirit, while the rest perish uncorrected. Augustine does not say that no man's or all men's good works are crowned, but that some men's are. So there will be some who correct their life.
>
> Who will believe, you say, that he is loved by God? I answer: No man

---

11. LW 33:39.
12. LW 33:39.

will or can believe this; but the elect will believe while the rest perish in unbelief, indignant, and blaspheming as you are here. So some will believe.

As to your saying that a window is opened for impiety by these dogmas, let it be so; such people belong to the above-mentioned leprosy of evil that must be endured. Nevertheless, by these same dogmas there is opened at the same time a door to righteousness, an entrance to heaven and a way to God for the godly and the elect.[13]

What can Luther mean by these strange and offensive words? Careful attention must be paid because they indicate once again that Luther thinks about these matters in quite a different fashion from that of Erasmus and the vast majority of interpreters down to the present day. For Erasmus the fact that God "runs the show" according to his immutable foreknowledge is destructive of faith and morals. God becomes a frightening ogre who must be brought to heel, made "nice" by the interpreter. As Luther put it to Erasmus,

> To talk as you do, one must imagine the Living God to be nothing but a kind of shallow and rather ignorant ranter declaiming from some platform, whose words you can if you wish interpret in any direction you like, and accept or reject them accordingly as ungodly men are seen to be moved or affected by them. And: it was here you should have put your finger to your lips in reverence for what lay hidden, and adoring the secret counsels of the majesty you should have cried with Paul: "O man, who art thou that contendest with God?"[14]

For one who thinks as Erasmus does, the immutability of God which seems to cancel out "free choice" is detrimental to faith and morals. Indeed, it makes them impossible. For Luther the matter is just the opposite. The divine immutability is what makes faith possible. How, after all, can we be certain of salvation? If God does not rule by his immutable necessity, who, Luther asks, will believe his promises? Luther, that is, goes directly to the divine immutability as the basis for faith's certainty. How do we know? Faith is grasped, captivated by the revealed God. In baptism, for instance, God has promised! It has happened! It is revealed! And God does not lie. His promises are immutable. Faith is created and sustained by the promises of God, not by the efforts of free choice. This is a matter of highest importance for faith. As Luther put it:

> I go farther and say, not only how true these things are . . . but also how religious, devout and necessary a thing it is to know them. For if these things are not known there can be neither faith nor any worship of God.

13. LW 33:60–61.
14. LW 33:60.

> For that would indeed be ignorance of God, and where there is such ignorance there cannot be salvation as we know. For if you doubt or disdain to know that God foreknows all things, not contingently, but necessarily and immutably, how can you believe his promises and place a sure trust and reliance on them? For when he promises anything, you ought to be certain that he knows and is able and willing to perform what he promises; otherwise you will regard him as neither truthful nor faithful, and that is impiety and a denial of the Most High God. But how will you be certain and sure unless you know that he knows and wills and will do what he promises, certainly, infallibly, immutably, and necessarily? And we ought not only to be certain that God wills and will act necessarily and immutably, but also to glory in the fact, as Paul says in Romans 3[:4]: "Let God be true though every man be false."[15]

Luther's claim is that if the divine action in, say, baptism is not a carrying out in history of the immutable will of God, it loses its object and thus its certainty. It could be just an "accident" or a matter of social custom, or perhaps just the wish of Grandma! All such contingencies will no doubt be at work, but God does all things by immutable necessity, in spite of all the contingencies that appear to be at work. Luther insists that the act, the promise, is the deed of the immutable God. For that is precisely the Christian faith: to believe and trust in the promises of the immutable God, no matter what that may entail, no matter how many contingencies and difficulties may afflict. The immutability of God is the guarantee, the "backup" for the preaching of the gospel. If it happens, it is the will of God! That is the only cure for the gouty foot! If one attempts to effect a "cure" by redoing God, erasing the divine immutability, one simply tears God out of the picture and leaves the believer helpless and hopeless. As Luther put it,

> Christian Faith is entirely extinguished, the promises of God and the whole gospel are completely destroyed if we teach and believe that it is not for us to know the necessary foreknowledge of God and the necessity of the things that are to come to pass. For this is the one supreme consolation of Christians in all adversities, to know that God does not lie, but does all things immutably, and that his will can neither be resisted nor changed nor hindered.[16]

We are approaching here Luther's doctrine of the hidden God. We shall have to deal with this more fully later. For the present it is enough to note that Luther sees trust in the revealed God as inherent to faith itself and the only "solution" to the "problem of God." The revealed God is the

15. LW 33:42.
16. LW 33:43.

God of the immutable promise. Thus it bids us stop before the supreme majesty of the hidden God. There seems to be a conundrum when we come to this point. On the one hand Luther insists on the givenness of the hidden God and that it is entirely necessary for faith to grapple with that God. As it is often put, we must know the "what" of the hidden God. But at the same time we cannot know the "why." We must know that God is the immutable one who elects and rejects. We are not running the show. But we cannot know why one and not the other is among the elect. If we knew that we would turn it into a legal system and it would destroy us! Faith in the word of proclamation is the only way. What the revelation tells us is that we cannot know the hidden God. We cannot even know that God is hidden. Hiddenness is, paradoxically, a revealed truth! This should be apparent to us in the cross.

There is considerable confusion about this among theologians of Erasmus' stripe. Erasmus thought the hiddenness involved was mere secrecy, something that could easily be brought into the light of day—like the mysterious Corycian cavern of fame in Greek myth and religion. From the vantage point of that understanding of hiddenness, Luther is often criticized for knowing too much about the hidden God. The talk of immutability and necessity, for instance, is often taken in this light. The reason for such criticism, however, is patent. The critic seeks holes in the hiddenness so as to insert ideas of human sovereignty and "works righteousness." If the criticism can unseat divine immutability, it can force room for the self to become the subject of all sentences granting salvation. The "I" becomes the lead (and ultimately the only) actor in the story of salvation. One need only listen to today's sermons to see the result of that!

So the picture begins to emerge. Jesus comes into this world only to evoke and reveal hiddenness. No one knows who he is. In Mark's Gospel only the demons recognize him. So he is crucified for his claims. So why this torturous "road to salvation when," as Luther is well aware, "so many evils appear to proceed from them?" Luther begins in his usual fashion by simply asserting that God has willed it and that that ought to be good enough reason for those who fear God. Nevertheless, Luther does not stop there but goes on to mention two considerations which demand that such things (and now note carefully!) should be preached. The preaching holds the key, not dogmatic arguments attempting to break through to the hidden majesty and remove what appear to be scandalous offenses. The first consideration is "the humbling of our pride and knowledge of the grace of God, and the second is the nature of Christian faith itself."[17]

The humbling of our pride! Luther lays great stress on this throughout *The Bondage of the Will* as well as throughout the rest of his theology. It is our pride over against God that makes us think we can "re-do" God and break in upon him in his hidden majesty to discover why he acts as he does and criticize his actions "Why," Luther asks Erasmus, "do you not restrain yourself and deter others from prying into things that God has willed to be hidden from us, and has not set forth in the Scriptures?" Humility guards the door to the knowledge of God. With the Augustinian tradition anchored in 1 Peter 5:5 Luther holds that God has "assuredly promised his grace to the humble, those who lament and despair of themselves."[18] Such humility, however, goes beyond the Augustinian type because it has its root in justification by faith alone. True humility comes only when one knows that salvation is utterly beyond one's own powers, devices, endeavors, will, and works. It depends entirely on the choice, will, and work of another, namely, of God alone. Humility, that is, is rooted in the *sola gratia*. "When a man has no doubt that everything depends on the will of God, then he completely despairs of himself and chooses nothing for himself, but waits for God to work; then he has come close to grace, and can be saved."[19]

Why should these offensive words be published? Remember Erasmus maintained that they should not be published because he feared they would undermine human striving for virtue. But Luther saw otherwise. Virtue established on human striving does not impress God. The word on humility is to be spoken for the sake of the elect, to make and keep them humble so they can be saved. One cannot put on humility as one would put on a fancy garment. One can be made humble only by the act of grace! So God's action alone is what makes salvation possible. It has become a fashion in churchly circles these days to disparage the teaching of such despair. But Luther has some words that fit directly into the modern temper:

> It is thus for the sake of the elect that these things are published, in order that being humbled and brought back to nothingness by this means they may be saved. The rest resist this humiliation, indeed they condemn this teaching of self-despair wishing for something, however little, to be left for them to do themselves; so they remain secretly proud and enemies of the grace of

---

17. LW 33:61.
18. LW 33:61.
19. LW 33:62.

God. This I say is one reason, namely, that the godly, being humbled, may recognize, call upon and receive the grace of God.[20]

The second reason why these things should be preached comes to light in Luther's famous and perplexing statement about the very nature of faith itself. Faith, Luther insists, has to do with things not seen. In order that there be room for faith, therefore, it is necessary that everything that is to be believed should be hidden. And the deepest form of hiddenness is when it is hidden under its opposite. We have already encountered the doctrine that hiddenness is a revealed truth, not a deduction from observation. If it were the result of our observation, we would take it under our control and water God down according to our ideas of what God ought to be. Here the doctrine is expanded into the understanding of a revelation under the form of opposites. That which is hidden cannot be hidden more deeply than under the form of its opposite. Thus when God makes alive he does so by killing, when he justifies he does so by making us guilty, when he exalts to heaven he does so by bringing down to hell, and so on. So, Luther says, the Scripture speaks: "The Lord kills and brings to life, He brings down to Sheol and raises up (1 Sam 2[:6])."

Humility is not highly regarded in contemporary church and public life. But when it is rejected and God is remodeled to fit human devices the result is the loss of Christian freedom. Here the argument takes a devastating turn. Suddenly it is the very Luther who insists upon the bondage of the will who now becomes the champion of freedom! That is inevitable, of course, since a thinker like Erasmus has such a heavy investment in moral reform. Such reformers will usually end by suspecting the gospel to be the cause of immorality and by proposing various types of law as a remedy (for example, the "third use"). Luther's penetrating analysis of Erasmus' remarks about private confession is a good example of how the argument goes. Erasmus admitted that there was little or no support for private confession in either Scripture or the Fathers. Yet he suggested that it was better to keep such practices because they help to keep people moral! Luther was livid at such a procedure. "Is that the way to teach theology," he thundered, "to bind souls by laws and, as Ezekiel says [Ezek 13:18f.], to slay them, when they are not bound by God?" This manner of "teaching theology" brings down upon us "the whole tyranny of Papal laws."[21]

Here we see clearly that the argument takes a flip-flop. Luther is finally the champion of freedom in the debate! The moralist cannot, will not, give up. The blame for immorality must be attributed to the gospel!

20. LW 33:62.
21. LW 33:49.

The "average lay person" cannot be trusted with freedom. Such thinking Luther referred to as part of the "temporal leprosy" that has to be borne, as he put it to Erasmus.

> As to your fear that many who are inclined to wickedness will abuse this freedom, this should be reckoned as one of the said tumults, part of that temporal leprosy that has to be endured and that evil which has to be borne. Such people should not be considered so important that in order to prevent their abusing it the Word of God must be taken away. If all cannot be saved, yet some are saved and it is for their sake the Word of God comes. These love the more fervently and are the more inviolably in concord. For what evil did ungodly men not do even before, when there was no Word? Or rather what good did they do? ... But now the coming of the gospel begins to be blamed for the fact that the world is wicked, whereas the truth is that the good light of the gospel reveals how the world was when it lived in its own darkness without the gospel. In a similar way the uneducated find fault with education because their ignorance is shown up where education flourishes. That is the gratitude we show for the Word of life and salvation.[22]

In other words, why blame the gospel for the wickedness and immorality of the world? The failure of such theological thinking and method is evident: If one starts from the premise and defense of freedom of the will one will end in bondage. The gouty foot laughs at such doctoring. If one starts from the premise of bondage and hears the Word and promise of the gospel of Christ Jesus, salvation breaks, for bondage shall be broken. But what is the nature of such bondage? The answer lies in the argument about our willing.

To sum up the argument in this "one-half of the Christian summa": God rules all things by immutable necessity. The words are harsh and difficult to take, but no amount of theological doctoring can erase or change the matter. The "God disease," if we can refer to it this way, is like the gout. It just does not go away. Another apt image Luther uses is that of the "arrow of conscience" stuck fast in the heart. I heard a rabbi in one of the memorial ceremonies for the destruction of the two World Trade Towers declaim that nothing or no one could convince us that God somehow willed the terrible tragedy with all its attendant suffering and loss of life. But the problem is that such declamations, alas, do not hold. When all is said and done, the pain and sorrow and mourning continue. The cry goes up nevertheless, *Why?* As Luther could put it, "The arrow of conviction remains stuck fast in the human heart."[23] All such declamations accomplish is to throttle the preaching of the gospel. They

---

22. LW 33:55.
23. Luther, *Bondage of the Will*, 218.

substitute lame explanations and shallow comfort where there should be proclamation.

The only solution to this kind of necessity is the proclamation. That is, if God rules all things by absolute necessity, then our only recourse is to attend to what he does do. The solution to the problem of the absolute is absolution! There the immutable God does "what is necessary"! God is "determined" to have us back! But we can see that only in Christ Jesus.

Apart from Jesus we are on our own. Luther could even say that apart from Jesus God is indistinguishable from the devil. And apart from Jesus we have to attempt to redo God more to our liking or do what most moderns do, dispense with him altogether. But the gouty foot laughs at such doctoring.

Luther and Erasmus

Luther recognized that Erasmus put his finger on the heart of the matter. Erasmus wanted to argue that God would not have given us all these commandments if there were no possibility of fulfilling them. Law would then be indirect proof of freedom. The problem is that such indirect, would-be schemes of salvation always lead into a trap. Inferences like Erasmus' always enslave us, especially inferences about the law. So Luther would answer Erasmus "Hold on a minute, the law doesn't prove freedom; it takes freedom away!" Freedom is not a reward that is realized—that thinking takes us right back into the law. Such inferences always begin and end with the law for the person trying to establish the powers of the free will. Use of the law in that way is automatic and deadly. That is the bondage.

The issue is exposed when one comes up against the *deus absconditus*. Erasmus does not really know what kind of a trap he is in. The fallacy of his whole argument is that he is left to infer what God must be like merely from the law, while the Holy Spirit is out making assertions apart from the law concerning the Father's only Son, Jesus Christ. In the middle of the argument Luther breaks out in the confession, "He sent his *Son* to save us." That is the heart and soul of his entire argument. The work of theology is not for making inferences from the law, but for a proclamation that is all about Christ. It is not about human possibilities and limitations, but what the Father is doing in his Son to reconcile the world to himself. Luther simply recognized that if the Father is sending his Son to save us, it is not the law that frees.

The problem of this freedom for Erasmus is that God robs us of all our claims to work salvation by ourselves and sets about to captivate us. God's very Godness then is the problem. But for Luther, God's own way of being God is also the only solution to the conundrum of human freedom precisely because he sent his Son to save us. All other inferred or preferred solutions are bogus, and it is such bogus theology that has been cheating the church ever since.

The preaching of Jesus Christ and him crucified on account of sinners is God's desired way of being God. That means, according to Luther, that preaching must be categorical. In today's jargon that means unconditional. Proclamation that gives forgiveness to sinners on account of Christ alone is the only solution for all our problems with God. The only way to end the threat of the unpreached God is by the preached God. That is the presupposition for all Christian preaching and the reason for this book. Luther is adamant at this point:

> For if you doubt or disdain to know that God foreknows all things, not contingently, but necessarily and immutably, how can you believe his promises and place a sure trust and reliance on them? . . . For this is the one supreme consolation of Christians in all adversities, to know that God does not lie, but does all things immutably, and that his will can neither be resisted nor changed nor hindered.[1]

In this way, only preaching that assumes the bondage of the will for its hearers truly comes to free. Preaching, however, seems to have gotten off the track of late. And when that is the case preaching degenerates into telling cute stories with the preacher taking over as the primary narrator. The preaching then either gives anecdotes or talks about personal experience. Instead, the kind of categorical preaching that Luther describes gives a God who is truly preached. The God whom we discover ourselves is always a hidden God, literally a God not preached. The climax of this hiddenness is that God robs us of all our claims to work salvation by ourselves. Ultimately no preachers can then remain the subjects of their own fantasies. The only way to overcome the problem of the hiddenness of God not preached is by God preached. But that will not happen by attempting to infer God's will from the law. It happens only when the preaching is categorical, unconditional, just as God did not spare his Son but gave him to captivate our bound wills, drawing all to himself.

People sometimes complain that Luther seems to know an awful lot about the hidden God. Luther would simply answer, "Christ crucified draws all these things with him." God sent his Son to save us, and instead of our discovering a hidden God it is God who discovers us. So it is that the Father says, "This is my beloved Son, listen to Him!" (Luke 9:35). God does not lie, "but does all things immutably," especially in the promise of his beloved Son, so "take the saying of Christ in John 6[:44]:

1. LW 33:42–43.

'No one comes to me unless my Father draws him.' What does this leave to free choice?"[2] That is the heart of the matter.

---

2. LW 33:285.

Heidelberg Disputation: Thesis 15

THESIS 15. Nor could free will remain in a state of innocence, much less do good, in an active capacity, but only in its passive capacity.

Scholastic teaching prior to the Reformation tried to rescue some optimism in the understanding of human nature by claiming that at least before the fall there was some active capacity of free will to maintain the self in the state of innocence. This active capacity was apparently not considered potent enough to make progress toward the good, but it was at least strong enough to enable the creature to remain, to stand (*potuit stare*), in a state of innocence by virtue of the grace of creation. If there were not a "little bit" of such active capacity in the will, it was argued, how could Adam be held responsible for the fall? Thesis 15 rejects even this relatively mild attempt to establish some little toehold for free will and its works. Even before the fall Luther insists, free will had no active capacity to remain in the state of innocence, but rather only a passive capacity. That is to say, even before the fall Adam and Eve were upheld in the state of innocence not by their own power but from without. They remained strictly creatures who lived by faith and trusted in their creator and not their own power.

Although it may appear to be an obscure point, thesis 15 indicates clearly the kind of move a theologian of the cross will make when looking at the nature of our existence. The attempt to argue for at least a little bit of freedom in order to maintain human fault for the fall and sin is the telltale sign of the theologian of glory at work. Here that theology takes the form of claiming that at least before the fall Adam had the active capacity to persevere in the state of innocence. But is such a claim sufficient to maintain human responsibility and guilt? The questions tend eventually to rebound on God. Why could not God have given Adam the active capacity not only to stand in the state of innocence but also to progress toward the good? The problem, of course, is that if such an active capacity is ascribed to Adam before the fall, we run head-on into the claims that must also be made on behalf of grace. So the theologian of glory backs off and modestly claims just enough capacity in free will to make one guilty but not enough to do anything toward salvation. The assumption remains always the same. The way of works is the way of salvation. One needs help even before the fall, but more so afterward.

The theologian who "looks at all things through suffering and the cross" however, sees that this is just another instance of calling the bad good and the good bad. For what is the fall? It is precisely the attempt to claim something for the self and its works before God. To understand our relationship to God in terms of a scheme of law is exactly the mark of a fallen creation. To attempt to save even a little bit of such a scheme is simply to call the bad good.

Thus the theologian of the cross moves to close another door on the theology of glory. Even, or perhaps we should say *especially*, before the fall there is no active capacity either to stand or to progress in righteousness. Such an active capacity could only mean that the creature makes a move to be independent of the creator and sets out to create its own goodness. No good is done by the claim that without an active capacity of free will the creature cannot be held responsible because the problem is precisely that the fallen creature is blind to the true state of affairs. The fallen creature projects the scheme of works back before the fall and claims that responsibility can be accorded and measured only according to such a scheme. The theologian of glory then ends by equating what is really fallen existence with the state of innocence. The bad is called good and the good bad once again.

The cross spells the end of all such moves. Before the fall the creature lives by faith, trusting that creation is good and bending all effort toward taking care of it. The creature has only a passive capacity for the good, not an active one. That is, the creature is never meant to stand or operate alone but to be one through whom the creator works. The creature is turned about to take care of creation, to seek the good of the other, not of the self. To fall is precisely to be captivated, bound, seduced, and blinded by another vision, another hope, that of the active capacity of free will and its works. Responsibility for sin is never firmly established by such a scheme because we are blind to the original sin, the sin of independence from God, the sin of unfaithfulness parading as piety. True, we may confess to certain sins thereby but not to SIN. The sins we confess to in such cases are only peccadilloes, misdeeds, and failings according to the letter of the law—mostly the second table. They are, of course, serious enough, the source of guilt and anguish but more or less evident. When it comes to SIN, however, we have a deeper problem. As subsequent theses, particularly 19 and 20, will indicate, we are blind. It takes the cross to shock us, so to speak, into seeing. Only when that occurs will we begin to take responsibility for SIN.

PART IV
Good Works

Heidelberg Disputation: Theses 26–28

THESIS 26. The law says, "do this," and it is never done. Grace says, "believe in this," and everything is already done.

This thesis is quite incomprehensible to the theologian of glory. It seems at best an exaggeration and at worst just plain false. But the fact is that this negative judgment on the futility of the law is made from the vantage point of the theologian of the cross, being quite captivated by the grace of God. Looking back, we see that the law simply cannot bring into being what it commands. Furthermore, we see that whatever the law does bring into being bears no real relationship to what grace inspires. The law says, "Thou shalt love!" It is right; it is "holy, true, good." Yet it can't bring about what it demands. It might impel toward the works of law, the motions of love, but in the end they will become irksome and will all too often lead to hate. If we go up to someone on the street, grab them by the lapels and say, "Look here, you're supposed to love me!" the person may grudgingly admit that we are right, but it won't work. The results will likely be just the opposite from what our "law" demands. Law is indeed right, but it simply cannot realize what it points to. So it works with wrath. It can curse, but it can't bless. In commanding love law can only point helplessly to that which it cannot produce. So we repeat the paradoxical word of Leif Grane, "What the Law requires is freedom from the law."[1] The law says, "Do this!" and it is never done.

This, Luther maintains in his rather short proof, is simply standard Pauline and Augustinian teaching: "The law works wrath and keeps all men under the curse."[2] Likewise, the second part of the thesis, "Grace

---

1. Lief Grane, *The Augsburg Confession: A Commentary*, trans. John H. Rasmussen (Minneapolis: Augsburg, 1987), 67–68.
2. LW 31:56.

says, 'believe in this,' and everything is already done," is straightforward Pauline and Augustinian fare. To extend the analogy of love, grace, instead of demanding love, simply gives it unconditionally. It is simply the "I love you." Faith justifies. Faith is the righteousness God wants and aims to get. Faith is what Adam and Eve lost, and faith is restored by grace alone. Luther backs this up by reference to St. Augustine: "'And the law (says St. Augustine) commands what faith obtains.' For through faith Christ is in us, indeed, one with us. Christ is just and has fulfilled all the commands of God, wherefore we also fulfill everything through him since he was made ours through faith."[3]

We should note that there is a certain exuberance in the language here. "Faith obtains" what law commands. Through faith Christ is in us. We fulfill everything through him since he was made ours through faith. The theologian of the cross simply will not back off from this and, when challenged, drives it home all the harder. To the theologian of glory the language seems utterly hyperbolic at best and at worst quite dangerous. What will happen to moral earnestness if people get wind of the claim that through faith all has been fulfilled in Christ? The temptation is always to fall back on the law, either in its original sense or perhaps in some new sense, like a "third use." But the theologian of the cross knows that there is no way back. So Luther here pushes the language to the limit and will not back off. He knows that if there is faltering here, all will be lost. This is expressed nicely in a passage from Luther's 1519–21 *Operationes in Psalmos*:

> Wherefore, let this be your standard rule: wherever the holy scriptures command good works to be done, understand that it forbids you to do any good work by yourself, because you cannot, but to keep a holy Sabbath unto God, that is, a rest from all your works, and that you become dead and buried and permit God to work in you. Unto this you will never attain, except by faith, hope, and love; that is, by a total mortification of yourself (Col 3:5) and all your own works.[4]

The insistence that only those works are truly good that are done spontaneously and joyously out of faith, hope, and love belongs to the very heart and soul of Luther's Reformation. That is why he can make the claim that faith doesn't have to be prompted to do good works because in faith everything is already done. This seems a preposterous claim. It is based, however, not on any claim we can make about ourselves

---

3. LW 31:56.

4. Martin Luther, *Luther's Commentary on the First Twenty-two Psalms*, vol. 1, trans. John Nicholas Lenker (Sunbury, PA: Lutherans in All Lands, 1903), 277; WA 5:169.14–19.

but on the fact that the Christ who creates faith has fulfilled all things. Indeed, one should not miss the spectacular nature of the claim here. The believer is not being exhorted to do works on the basis of faith in order to catch up with what is demanded. Rather, the announcement is made that because the Christ who has fulfilled all things dwells within the person of faith, everything has *already* been done! There is simply nothing to do!

Here is a drastic parting of the ways with a theology of glory. The Christ of the cross *takes away* the possibility of doing something. The theologian of glory might be able to follow to the point of accepting the truth that Christ has fulfilled all things, but then that will have to be used as motivational fuel to make sure the law gets its due. The point is precisely that the power to do good comes only out of this wild claim that everything has *already* been done. The language has to break out into preaching. Never mind that when we look to ourselves we find no sign of good works. Never mind our fears and anxieties. We are looking in the wrong place. Look to Christ! He has done it all. Nothing will be gained by trying to shore up the Old Adam. Christ leaves nothing for the Old Adam and Eve to do. The old can only be killed by the law, not given artificial respiration by recourse to it. That is the point of the language here and its exuberance. To the theologian of the cross the language of grace and faith must be pushed absolutely to this length—until it kills the old and raises the new. Nothing at all will ever be gained by backing down. We will only fall back into law where the demand continues endlessly and nothing is ever finally done. So we can only let the language of grace sound forth. Grace says, "believe it" and everything—EVERYTHING!—is already done. It is the creative Word of God. If that doesn't work then nothing will. The Disputation is moving inexorably to its concluding assertion about the creative love of God.

> **THESIS 27.** Rightly speaking, therefore, the work of Christ should be called the operative power, and our work, the operation; so our operation is pleasing to God by the grace of the operative power.

Thesis 27 spells out more directly what has been developed to this point. It is an attempt to describe how it all works for the life of faith. The real operative power in all works that can be called good is the work of Christ, that outrageous assertion that in Christ all that God demands has been fulfilled and that this Christ dwells in us by faith. The believer is "aroused" to work through living faith *in Christ's work*, to be "imitators" of God as Ephesians admonishes, "drawn" after Christ. That is the way the proof for this thesis puts it:

Since Christ lives in us through faith, so he moves us to do good works through that living faith in his work, for the works that he does are the fulfillment of the commands of God given us through faith. If we look at them, we are moved to imitate them. For this reason the Apostle says, "Therefore be imitators of God as beloved children" [Eph 5:11]. Thus deeds of mercy are aroused by the works through which he has saved us, as St. Gregory says: "Every act of Christ is instruction for us, indeed, a motivation." If his action is in us, it lives through faith, for it is exceedingly attractive according to the verse, "Draw me after you, let us make haste" [Song 1:4] toward the fragrance "of your anointing oils" [Song 1:3], that is, "your works."[5]

The entire passage deserves close attention. Notable is the fact that it says not one word about law. The impetus to good works comes entirely from being moved, aroused, and motivated by the completed work of the Christ, who dwells in the believer through faith. Christ's work is the complete fulfillment of the commands of God and as such moves the faithful to works. "Deeds of mercy are aroused by the *works through which he has saved us.*" The very action of Christ is in us through faith. It is "exceedingly attractive." The references to the Song of Solomon are not, of course, just incidental. There was, as is well known, a long tradition that interpreted this ancient biblical love song as an allegory of the relationship between Christ and his bride, the church. Without entering into that interpretive quagmire, we can still remark how the language of faith mirrors the language of love. The language of law does not foster truly good works. The language of love is more appropriate. One is "drawn," "attracted" by the very action and saving works of Christ. It is, as pointed out above in the comment on thesis 26, the very claim that all has been fulfilled that draws the faithful to works. The language of love here already points to the final thesis about the creative power of divine love.

Christ is the "operator," the believer is the one "operated upon." The work thus produced is pleasing to God not in and of itself but by virtue of the grace of the operator, Christ. It is interesting and no doubt significant that the language used in this thesis (*opus operans, operatum, operis operantis*) comes from the sacramental vocabulary of medieval theology. Luther is no doubt thinking of the Augustinian insistence that Christ must first be a sacrament for us before he can be an example. So Christ is *operans*, the one doing the operating, and believers who receive his work sacramentally as sheer gift are *operatum*, worked upon. Their work in turn pleases God, not in and of itself, but *gratia operis operantis*, strictly

---

5. LW 31:56–57.

because of the grace of Christ's operation. That is how it all works. This paves the way for the final move to the creative love of God.

> **THESIS 28.** The love of God does not first discover but creates what is pleasing to it. The love of man comes into being through attraction to what pleases it.

Now we have arrived at the opposite side of the great arch described by the Disputation. All else has been shorn away, put to death. What remains is simply the creative love of God. The innermost nature of the operation of the previous thesis is now announced. It is love, the love of God that creates out of nothing, calls into being that which is from that which is not. This love of God that creates its object is contrasted absolutely with the love of humans. Human love is awakened by attraction to what pleases it. It must search to find its object and, one might add, will likely toss it aside when it tires of it.

The proof for this thesis Luther finds simply in the fact that the love of God flows forth to the unlovely:

> The first part [of the thesis] is clear because the love of God that lives in man loves sinners, evil persons, fools, and weaklings in order to make them righteous, good, wise, and strong. Rather than seeking its own good, the love of God flows forth and bestows good. Therefore sinners are attractive because they are loved; they are not loved because they are attractive. For this reason the love of man avoids sinners and evil persons. Thus Christ says: "For I came not to call the righteous but sinners" [Matt 9:13].[6]

All of this flows forth strictly from the cross. It is the outcome of the *theologia crucis*:

> This is the love of the cross, born of the cross, which turns in the direction where it does not find good that it may enjoy, but where it may confer good upon the bad and needy person. "It is more blessed to give than to receive" [Acts 20:35], says the Apostle.[7]

Here we have reached the other side. God is not, as in the theology of glory, one who waits to approve those who have improved themselves, made themselves acceptable, or merited approval, but one who *bestows* good on the bad and needy. The great reversal is complete. Indeed, the final sentences of the proof touch in interesting fashion on a reversal in the very question of being itself:

6. LW 31:57.
7. LW 31:57.

Hence Ps. 41[:1] states, "Blessed is he who considers the poor," for the intellect cannot by nature comprehend an object that does not exist, that is, the poor and needy person, but only a thing that does exist, that is, the true and good. Therefore it judges according to appearances, is a respecter of persons, and judges according to that which can be seen, etc.[8]

The problem is that for a theology of glory, the bad, poor, needy, or lowly cannot really exist. What really exists is the true, the good, and the beautiful, the great abstractions, the "invisible" things of God. Because the theologian of glory is always looking through what is actually given, the bad, poor, needy, and lowly are invisible. They don't show up on the scale of values and are not regarded. "Evil" is nonbeing. God has nothing to do with it. Hence, there is no reason why the Lord of all should condescend to them. But the Psalmist sees it otherwise, "Blessed is he who considers the poor."

Here at last the existential situation of the fallen creature, the sinfulness and need for salvation, is equated with the very question of being itself.[9] We get further insight into what it means to look on all things through suffering and the cross. Whereas the theologian of glory tries to see through the needy, the poor, the lowly, and the "nonexistent," the theologian of the cross knows that the love of God creates precisely out of nothing. Therefore the sinner must be reduced to nothing in order to be saved. The presupposition of the entire Disputation is laid bare. It is the hope of the resurrection. God brings life out of death. He calls into being that which is from that which is not. In order that there be a resurrection, the sinner must die. All presumption must be ended. The truth must be seen. Only the "friends of the cross" who have been reduced to nothing are properly prepared to receive the justifying grace poured out by the creative love of God. All other roads are closed. The theologian of the cross is thus one who finally is turned about to see "the way things are."

---

8. LW 31:57–58.
9. See Jos E. Vercruysse, "Gesetz und Liebe, Die Struktur der 'Heidelberg Disputation' Luthers (1518)," *Lutherjahrbuch* 48 (1981): 41–43, for some of these concluding insights.

Luther's "Ethics"

For Luther, the Christian is called to serve God in the world God has created, and not self, not devil, not vice, not virtue, but the neighbor. This, of course, is Luther's much-neglected doctrine of vocation. Since one is not called to bring in the kingdom of God, one is called for the time being to serve God in creation, in the various dimensions of daily life—family, church, state. The point in saying that one is to serve God is to oppose the devil. People who complain that Luther has no proper doctrine of good works and sanctification or ethics always seem to forget this understanding of the Christian's calling. Perhaps because it is so utterly realistic and unromantic. But virtually everything Luther wants to say about ethics comes back to his doctrine of vocation. One is to serve God in one's occupation, in one's concrete daily life and its duties in the world. When I tell students that this first of all means that they should pay attention to being better students, they are often a little disappointed. They had more romantic things in mind like leading some protest, manning the barricades, joining in some romantic crusade or "social action" commission that sits about and cranks out resolutions on matters such as sex, to send to the synod. It does not occur to them that their first ethical duty is to be good students! Whatever call there might be for more extreme action, it must be remembered that Luther's idea is that first and foremost one serves God by taking care of his creation.

And this new arena for ethical activity, now disclosed as creation, what Luther sometimes referred to as God's left-hand rule, can never be taken simply for granted. Here is where a second mistake is often made. In the usual two-kingdoms doctrine it is assumed that the left-hand kingdom is just there, that it is a given, something much more evident than the kingdom on the right, which can't be seen and thus is more problematic. But that is once again to forget the devil. The devil for Luther, as for the New Testament, is the "prince of this world." Thus the world we see is not, as such, unambiguously the world as God created it. That the world nevertheless is, in spite of its distortion by the devil, God's good creation is grounded in a faith that is granted by grace. It is because one is saved by grace that one believes in creation. Creation as a sphere of ethical action, an arena for Christian vocation, is not simply a given; it is rather a gift. The good person, the one saved, is given creation back again as sheer gift, an arena in which to do the good. This is illustrated by the apparently apocryphal story about Luther's reply to the question of what he would do if he knew the world was going to end the next day. The answer was that he would go out in his garden and plant a tree. The story is well known but the point is usually missed. Since the kingdom of God is coming, there is nothing one can do about that—it's too late for prayers, piety, repentance, or acts of religious sublimation. But one is turned back into the garden so that when the good Lord shows up one might be found doing what God intended: taking care of the creation. Incidentally, he said the same thing about his marriage. The religious sensibilities of all Europe were shocked when right in the middle of the worst upheavals in 1525, i.e., the peasant's revolt, the debate with Erasmus, and the Reformation hanging in the balance, Luther went and got married. What began at the church door ended in bed. But, unperturbed, Luther replied that he had done it because he thought it would make the angels laugh and the devils weep.

Luther was an "*apocalyptiker.*" He thought indeed that the world was about to end. But the effect of that was just the opposite from the usual. He was not led to forsake the creation, as has recently occurred with a sect in Korea, but precisely to turn back into it all the more. So he said of his marriage that when the good Lord comes he was determined to be found doing "what comes naturally," obeying the command to be fruitful and multiply, in spite of all the nonsense perpetrated by popes, princes, peasants, and ethical pundits. All that nonsense, you see, was for Luther the work of the devil, the prince of this world. When the complaint was raised that he was putting the cause of the Reformation in jeopardy, his answer, in effect, was that this was precisely the cause. A good person does good works. Good works are works done freely and joyously for the neighbor, in and for creation.

But such a view cannot be taken for granted. Even our age now applauds the return to creation, but not as an arena for "good works"! It can be held by faith only in the face of great trial and temptation. Our great temptation, the devil's seduction, is always to desert creation, to be as gods. Creation is never good enough. We are always on our way somewhere else, to an idealist heaven where there is no change or decay or flesh or sex or children and all that, or to a utopia, to Solla Salloo, where they never have troubles, or at least very few. Creation is our stepping stone, and (literally) devil take the hindmost. Thus, Luther could say that belief in creation and the creator God is the highest and perhaps most difficult article of faith.

> For without doubt the highest article of faith is that in which we say: I believe in God the Father, almighty creator of heaven and earth, and whoever rightly believes that is already helped and set right and brought back to that from which Adam fell. But those who came to the point of fully believing that he is the God who creates and makes all things are few, because such a person must be dead to all things, to good and evil, death and life, hell and heaven, and must confess from the heart that he can do nothing out of his own strength.[1]

Note once again how this is true only if the ethical tropology has been displaced by the tropology of grace, death, and life!

For Luther, creation is the arena for ethical action. But now, when one enters into the calling in this world, of course, one soon encounters harsh realities. The Creator's sovereignty is disputed all along the line. We encounter that "unholy trinity": the devil, the world, the flesh. In the optimum case, if we were all "good persons," we would do good works freely, joyfully, spontaneously. True faith needs no law, no coercion, no prodding. As Luther put it in the well-known passage from the "Preface to Romans,"

> Faith . . . is a divine work in us which changes us and makes us to be born anew of God, John 1[:12–13]. It kills the old Adam and makes us altogether different men, in heart and spirit and mind and powers, and it brings with it the Holy Spirit. O it is a living, busy, active, mighty thing, this faith. It is impossible for it not to be doing good works incessantly. It does not ask whether good works are to be done, but before the question is asked, it has already done them, and is constantly doing them.[2]

Again the entire thing is premised on a radical change, in tropology!

Ethicists, you can imagine, would charge Luther and the Reformation with hopeless naïveté because of such ecstatic outbursts. It is significant, and an indication of how much they miss the point, that here, for once, Luther the professional pessimist is charged with being just too optimistic about human possibility! Ethicists usually find Luther either too pessimistic or too optimistic. That good works do not make a good per-

---

1. WA 24:18.26–33.
2. WA 24:18.26–33.

son is too pessimistic for most; but that a good person does good works is too optimistic. The contradictory judgments are simply a sign that they do not understand Luther at all. So, two things must be said. First, these statements about spontaneity are indeed seriously meant. They are a statement of the ultimate hope, the end, the goal of the creature, faith in creation. They are the light at the end of the tunnel. If they are not true, then of course there is no salvation for us. We would then be doomed to ethics forever. Heaven itself—frightfully enough—would be something like a meeting of the ethics section of the American Academy of Religion! Luther did indeed believe that faith would arrive somewhere, that the truly good would be done joyously and spontaneously, and ethics would not be needed. That has to be the light at the end of the tunnel. Christ is the end of the law to those who have faith.

Second, Luther was not naïve about this. He knew full well that the Kingdom has not arrived yet, and that our lives are not so driven by grace and faith as they should and eventually will be. He knew better than most that the Creator's sovereignty was disputed for the time being. "For still our ancient foe, doth seek to work us woe, strong mail of craft and power, he weareth in this hour; on earth is not his equal," as we have it in his hymn "A Mighty Fortress." So there must be, for the time being, a second form of divine rule, a left-hand rule, an alien work. This is why it is appropriate to call it God's backup plan. There is the rule of law. There are ethics. As long as they are limited to this age, to their proper time, these can be and are God's blessing, the instruments by which the creation can be preserved and cared for until the Kingdom comes and their time will be over. To put it most positively, the world is held in readiness by the law until the Kingdom comes.

Thus Luther spoke of the "proper uses" of the law. The concept of proper use is always crucial for Luther's theology, whether one is talking about either law or gospel. It is in the use that the Spirit dwells, not in the thing itself. It is commonly agreed that Luther spoke explicitly of only two uses of the law: the political use—perhaps we could call it the ethical use—and the theological use. Again, it is important to get the nuance here. Luther was talking about the way in which the Spirit uses the law. It was not, for him, an ethical theory, but analytical observation. It was simply a statement about the way the law actually works in our lives. Politically speaking out there in the world, for the time being, law preserves order and restrains evil. It tells you to stop; you stop. Of course, you may choose to run the stoplight, but then you have to take your chances with the police and the violations bureau. It could cost you. So it works, most often, by threat, coercion, power, social persuasion and/

or often just shame, that all-conquering threat: What will the neighbors think? H. L. Mencken said conscience is the little voice inside us that tells us someone may be looking! But it can also work by persuasion, conditional promise, by a kind of seduction or bribery. You eat your spinach, you get your pudding. Okay? Okay! You do your work well, you get your bonus! So it works, politically, ethically.

But theologically speaking, it judges us, convicts of sin. It even says: "Where are you, Adam?" It will cause us to reflect on why we think our agenda is so all-fired important as to endanger the lives of others by running the stoplight. It will do that—especially if we actually do harm to someone. This, for Luther, is not theory. This is the way the law actually works. It can't save us. It doesn't increase our faith or improve our disposition. I do not know of anyone who really learns to like to stop gladly at stop signs. But it does preserve us (first use) and awaken us so we can be saved; it keeps the devil, the world, and the flesh from being the ruin of us. As long as the law is not misused as a way of salvation, it functions as God's backup plan for combating the devil. When one enters creation one serves God through the proper use of law.

One must be very careful here, however, because, as we have seen, the minute one uses the law as a means for salvation, it is the "devil's whore," and faith, in Luther's colorful language, "loses its virginity"! However, such misuse of the law or ethics is not limited to the religious or ecclesiastical realm. The devil will see to that. The state or the social order can and most often does make the same mistake. It can set up a particular ideology or political program as the means to political and social salvation: a "thousand-year Reich," a "classless society," or "making the world safe for democracy." The result is the same. The devil wins. The state, for instance, can use the law to see to it that there is no longer Jew or Greek. But we all know what happens then. Whenever the law is used ostensibly to save rather than to take care of creation, tyranny takes over and someone dies. Paul was not indulging in empty talk when he called it the dispensation of death. Once again: the Kingdom comes by grace alone. The distinction between grace and law must be absolute. Only when that is so is law—as Paul put it—"established."

That is why law must be limited to its two proper uses. Although the argument is more subtle and complicated than we can do justice to now, one should be able to see why it is perilous to accommodate Luther's view with a so-called "third use of the law" as a friendly guide for the reborn Christian. There is no way yet into a state where the Christian can use the law in a third way. Such a view rests on presuppositions entirely different from those of Luther and, for that matter, Paul. It makes too many pious assumptions. It assumes, apparently, that the law can really be domesticated so it can be used by us like a friendly pet. Does law actually work that way? It assumes that we are the users of the law. We do not use the law. The Spirit does. And we really have no control over it. Who knows when it is going to rise up and attack with all its fury? Luther knew full well, of course, that in spite of all his piety he could not bring the law to heel. Indeed, even as a Christian, one needs to hear and heed the law—and the law will attack a Christian just as it attacks the non-Christian. One does not have the key to some third use. We do not live in an eschatological vestibule. Christians need the law in the same way non-Christians do. The idea of a third use assumes that the law story simply continues after grace. Grace is just a blip, an episode, on the basic continuum of the law. Luther's contention is that the law story is subordinate to the Jesus story. The law is for Luther, as it was for Paul, an episode in a larger story, not vice versa. It is only grace that can bring the law to heel.

CONCLUSION

So, to conclude, when one is looking for a positive use for law in life and ethics in Luther's thinking, one should look to his understanding of the first use of the law, the political or ethical use, as the means by which the wiles of Satan are to be held in check while we wait for the kingdom of God. It is one of the great misfortunes of contemporary ethical thinking that people seem to know practically nothing any longer of this understanding of the uses of the law. Even in church publications we see all sorts of nonsense about how the gospel is supposed to have something to say about our ethical dilemmas. And the gospel just becomes synonymous with sloppy permissiveness. So sweet Jesus schlock reigns. The gospel does not have anything to say directly about such dilemmas. We must look to the proper uses of the law, and particularly the first use. We have all we need there; we do not need a third use!

How then does one come to know this law? For Luther, the law is natural to humans. It is written on the heart. He was, it could be said, a kind of "natural law" ethicist. But he was a nominalist, not a realist. That is, Luther did not believe that natural law was just a mimetic copy or imitative reflection of eternal law. In Luther's day most people who theorized about natural law really meant supernatural law, a built-in eternal and unchangeable order to things. For Luther, law is natural in the sense that it was built into the creation, simply a statement of the minimal requirements of daily life, a faithful and practical consideration of what works and preserves human society against the wiles of the devil. Faith frees you to use your head in the battle. The natural law, in that sense, was for Luther "written on the heart." To be sure, such law may be obscured by the fall. But in any case, for Luther, we have a restatement of such natural law in the scriptures, preeminently in the laws of Moses. Luther assumed, it seems, that since the Creator and the author of the scriptures, the Spirit, are one, there should be no fundamental difference between natural law and the law found in scripture. The touchstone for Luther's understanding of what is natural is therefore not a theory of natural analogy, but rather the Holy Scripture and the doctrine of creation. One cannot trust unaided reason without qualification. But where law is understood within and limited by the story of salvation, there it is, so to speak, naturalized. Indeed, the command to love God and the neighbor with all one's heart was for Luther natural law, as was also the Sermon on the Mount. The law is simply a statement of what created life should naturally be. If we don't know what that is, due to our fallenness, we must search the scriptures.

So, for Luther, if one is looking for answers to the question what should we do, for the time being, we will not be directed to our own feelings, or the art of learning how to affirm ourselves or one another in our chosen lifestyle, or whatever it may be. One of the things Luther polemicized against most regularly was the idea of self-chosen works—be they ever so pious. Rather, one must look to the commandments of God. The commandments of God are not given to make us pious, Luther insisted, but to lead us into the world of the neighbor to take care of it as creation for the time being. In this regard, we must realize that the law was made for humanity, not humanity for the law. Even if it happens, as it often does in this twisted world, that one should have to break one commandment for the sake of another, Luther's counsel would be to sin boldly, but trust in the mercy of God all the more bravely! In other words, go ahead and plant a tree in the garden of hope!

PART V
Controversies Concerning the Law

Law and Sexual Behavior

This is an essay about the function of law as it confronts sexual behavior. Therefore the first thing that needs saying is that it cannot be a paper about compassion. To be sure, Christians, not to say human beings in general, are called upon to act with compassion and care toward all, particularly those who suffer, whatever the cause. Since we are enjoined to visit those in prison it is to be assumed that compassion is to encompass even those who have fallen under the punishment of the law. We are indeed also called upon to apply law with compassion. But this essay is not about that. This disclaimer needs to be entered because the vast majority of discussions about sexual behavior, especially of homosexual behavior, become arguments about compassion. Discussants relate tragic and agonizing stories about failures in compassion. Those who wish to talk more "objectively" about law and ethics are faulted for lacking compassion. But we get nowhere arguing about who is more compassionate than whom. Is compassion to be exercised at the expense of law? Toward whom is one then acting compassionately? Of course we are to act compassionately toward those who are caught in the immense web of tragedy that problems of sexual identity and practice have spun about us today. Of course we are to act justly and compassionately toward those who suffer from AIDS or whose civil rights are violated. Let us assume that from the outset. But this is a discussion about law and sexual behavior, not about compassion. And a major dimension of the problem, mostly obscured or forgotten, is that law has no compassion. As the Apology to the Augsburg Confession insists several times over, "Law always accuses."[1]

The second thing to be noted is that the basic concern here is with law as it relates to sexual behavior not to "orientation" or "sexuality." This disclaimer needs to be entered for at least two reasons. First, the major

---

1. BC-T 112:38; 125:128; 130:167.

focus here will be on what the Lutheran tradition has called the civil or political use of the law, later—no doubt misleadingly—termed the "first" use of the law.[2] In its civil use, the law directs itself toward behavior and actual practice, not orientation. I tend to agree with James Burtness when he insists that behavior not orientation is the issue.[3]

The second reason for talking about behavior rather than orientation is that claims made about "sexual orientation" and "sexuality" are both too inconclusive and even largely beside the point for our discussion here. Human sexual drives, passions, and obsessions are many and varied—in all of us, no doubt. We are told that there is a broad spectrum of desire, sometimes in one and the same person, such that it would be inaccurate to pin us down to a single "orientation." The notion that we have something called a "sexuality" of a particular sort within us determining our being that can be discovered scientifically and must be obeyed if we are to be honest with and true to ourselves is a modern invention that seems particularly pernicious.[4] To be sure, such notions have peculiar power and cast us into states and predicaments that are real enough. No doubt it is one of the ways in which law knows no compassion. But our question here is not directly about all of that. Our question is about how we are called to behave in our sexual relations with others under law, particularly in its civil use, whatever our "orientations."

2. Even though Luther generally mentions the civil use of law first, he apparently never adopted the practice of numbering the uses of the law, no doubt for good reason. Numbering gives the impression that there is a kind of succession or order in which the first, as a kind of general or "non-Christian" use, precedes the second, and then of course the third comes as the final step. The practice of numbering arises only when one wants to set apart and advocate a "third" and distinctively "Christian" use. Distinction in the uses of the law then becomes the outline of a progress from "civil" to "Christian" life and eventually a paradigm for the "process" of salvation history. Luther's original view is simply an account of the way law actually and always works—and is supposed to work in this life. Law restrains evil in civil and political life. Theologically it accuses of sin. The distinction between the civil and theological uses of law is an analytical move. The uses are not temporally distinguishable functions but an analytical account from the point of view of faith of what law actually does. See Lauri Haikola, *Usus Legis*, Uppsala Uniterstets Aarsskrift 3 (Wiesbaden: Otto Harrassowitz, 1958), 30n13, and Gustav Wingren, *Creation and Law*, trans. Ross MacKenzie (Philadelphia: Muhlenberg, 1961), 149–50. Wingren's chapters on the uses of the law (149–97) as well as Haikola's book on the subject are exceedingly important and helpful.

3. James Burtness, "Is Orientation the Issue?," *Word and World* 14, no. 3 (1994): 233–38.

4. At present I find the "constructionist" interpretation of sexual behavior like that of David Halperin in *One Hundred Years of Homosexuality and Other Essays on Greek Love* (New York: Routledge 1990), 15–53, most persuasive. The best way to account for the great variations in sexual behavior and preference throughout history and across cultural lines is to postulate that they are the product of social constructs. Categories like "homosexuality" and "heterosexuality" are constructs of very recent vintage. To hold that they are social constructs, however, is not to say that the conditions that result from them are unreal or merely illusory. Social constructs construct social realities. It is precisely this to which we have to attend and about which we have to make critical judgments. That is where law in its civil use enters the picture.

THE END AND ESTABLISHMENT OF LAW

Before becoming more specific we must make some more general observations about the way law works from a theological perspective. Scriptural passages about sexual behavior provide a good illustration. First off, one who takes those passages with any degree of seriousness should soon become terrified. This is particularly true of passages about sexual behavior such as Rom 1:16–32 where Paul concludes his announcement of the revelation of the wrath of God with the frightening words, "They know God's decree that those who practice such things deserve to die, yet they not only do them but even applaud others who practice them." The most appropriate response to law in the first instance would no doubt be something like that of Paul in Rom 7:24: Who will deliver us? If what the Scripture says is true, how shall we escape? The only real answer of course is Christ. Christ and Christ alone is the end of the law to faith (Rom 10:4). But if Christ is the end of the law to faith does that mean that law is now "overthrown" as Paul puts it in Rom 3:31? Is the law rendered useless? By no means, Paul replies. Rather the law is "upheld" or "established," set in its rightful place. As I have argued elsewhere,[5] the proper Christian understanding of law therefore "resonates," to borrow an image from chemistry, between two poles. The first is the gospel declaration that Christ is the end of the law that everyone who has faith may be justified (Rom 10:4). The second is a question posed for us: "Do we then overthrow the law by this faith?" To which the reply is, "By no means! On the contrary, we uphold the law." Faith in the end, that is, does not impatiently try to abrogate the law, but puts it in its proper place (Rom 3:31).

We need to look at this "resonance" more closely. Christ is the end of the law that those who have faith may be justified. That is the first and most crucial pole in the resonance. One cannot begin to understand the place of law in theology unless one is absolutely clear that in Christ it is all over, done with. This is simply another way to say that law is not the way of salvation. There is no way one can buy salvation by the doing of the law. The issue before us is not directly one of salvation. Proper behavior does not merit salvation. Salvation begins not when law begins but when law ends. In Christ we are free from the law. Legalism is over as and to the degree that one is in Christ. But it must be noted carefully that *only* Christ is the end of the law, nothing else, no one else. Human beings have just two possibilities in this regard. We

---

5. Gerhard Forde, "The Normative Character of Scripture for Matters of Faith and Life: Human Sexuality in Light of Romans 1:16–32," *Word and World* 14, no. 3 (1994): 305–14.

can live either "under the law" or "in Christ." And for the time being, of course, since we are simultaneously just by faith and sinners in actuality, we live under both. But only Christ is the end of the law and only when Christ conquers all does law stop. One must be grasped firmly by this, particularly with regard to sexual behavior, because when we come up against laws that call our behavior into question, we usually attempt by one means or another to erase, discredit, or change the laws. We become antinomians. If we don't like the law we seek to remove or abolish it by exegetical circumlocution, appeals to progress, to genetics, to the authority of ecclesiastical task-force pronouncements, or perhaps just the assurance that "things have changed." But all of these moves are not the end of the law. It is folly to believe they are. As Luther put it, this is a drama played in an empty theater.[6] Law just changes its form and comes back at us—usually worse than before. Law is authoritative ultimately not because it is written in law books or even in the Bible, but rather because it is written "in the heart." So only one who is stronger can end it. That is Christ, the bringer of the new age and a new "heart." Christ, as Luther insisted, must reign in the conscience.[7] That is easily talked about, he constantly warned, but hard to hold in actual experience.

But Christ the end of the law is only one pole of the resonance. The second comes in the question, "Do we then by this faith render the law of no effect?" Is the law then useless? "Absolutely not!" says Paul. On the contrary precisely by faith in Christ we uphold the law; we establish it in its rightful place. How are we to understand this? How is law established by a faith that believes its end? There is truly a "resonance" here. A faith that knows of the true end of law in the double sense of goal and cessation will at the same time "establish the law," that is, allow the law to stand just as it is. In the light of the end one can gain some understanding of how God puts the law to its proper uses. Indeed, knowing the end, faith supports the law until the end is given. If the end is given and assured, there is no need to try to "make the law of no effect." That happens only when faith is lost Without faith, that is, there is no hope. There is no end in sight. Law just goes on forever. Since I know of no end, I lose trust. Then I must fend for myself. Reduced to my own resources, I have no recourse but to exercise the antinomian option. I must bring the law to an end somehow, explain it away, reduce it to a size I can manage, or erase it entirely. When faith is gone the self arro-

---

6. WA 39/1:355.
7. LW 26:120 et passim. WA 40/1:213.9–214.7 et passim.

gates to itself mastery over the law. But that of course is a futile game. Law has no compassion. It does not end at our say-so.

THE USES OF THE LAW

The proper establishment of the law through faith in Christ means that in Christ the law comes up against its real limit. Only then can we begin to see what it is truly for. Law, according to Luther, has two uses, the civil and the theological use.[8] But we must take some care here. The doctrine is often wrongly taken to mean that the two uses could easily be separated and assigned, perhaps, to different spheres of operation, the civil having to do with politics and the natural, perhaps, and the theological with "religion" and the sacred. It is no doubt true that in the two uses we do face, so to speak, in different directions—toward the world of the neighbor and the civil realm on the one hand and toward our relation to God on the other—but the separation cannot be rigidly maintained in practice. That would be much too simplistic and could lead to a superficial reading of our situation, especially in matters of sexual behavior. The doctrine of the uses of the law is simply an attempt analytically to discern what law actually does. Law does two things to us, come what may. It sets limits to sinful and destructive behavior, usually by some sort of persuasion or coercion—ultimately by death itself—and it accuses of sin.[9] That is simply what it does. We have no choice in the matter. It works that way. To be noted also in this is what law does not do and cannot do. Law does not save. It is not a way of salvation. Nor is law a remedy for sin. In its civil use law insists upon and promotes moral behavior but it does not stop sin thereby. As a matter of fact, as more astute interpreters like Paul knew, precisely in coercing morality law only makes sin worse (Cf. Romans 7).

THE CIVIL USE OF LAW AND SEXUAL BEHAVIOR

Since we do not, in matters of sexual behavior, have to do directly with the question of salvation, we are concerned first and foremost with the

---

8. Discussion about a "third use" is beyond the scope of this paper.
9. Many will object that this is far too negative a view of law and try to spell out a more "positive" use. Perhaps that can be done. However, all too often what results is simply a kind of covert antinomianism. The law is "tamed" and its coercive and accusing function forgotten. This leads to wholesale ignorance of the way law works. One does not need to apologize for the law, nor does it work to "tame" it. Law will not become a domestic house pet in any case. Furthermore, is it not a "good" and "positive" thing to restrain evil and preserve society from self-destruction?

question of the civil use of law. The civil use of law ushers us into a strange and exciting new world, the world of the neighbor. Talk of the end of the law is unfortunately often taken to imply that the door is suddenly open to a certain relaxation and permissiveness. To think so, however, would be a fatal mistake. What the end of the law opens the door to is the world of the neighbor, the world in which the self is turned outward toward the other. As Luther put it in "The Freedom of the Christian," the believer who is "free lord of all, subject to none" is at the same time "the perfectly dutiful servant of all, subject to all."[10] Being in Christ means being set free from self for the neighbor. Thus the purpose of the civil use of law is to take care of God's creation and God's creatures. To be sure, law is not therefore to be imposed as an absolute which must be obeyed for its own sake. "The sabbath was made for humankind not humankind for the sabbath." In its civil use, law is rather to be applied so as best to exercise the care demanded in particular situations.

But here considerable caution must be invoked particularly in the case of sexual behavior lest we take the antinomian turn. The pressure to set the law aside by reinterpretation, accommodation, declaring it obsolete (e.g., on the ground that biblical writers were not aware of current understandings of sexual "orientation"), and so forth, is immense. Such attempts to circumvent the law usually proceed by appealing to the supposed adaptability of the civil use of law. This is perhaps *the* neuralgic point in the discussion. The argument from compassion takes center stage. Would it not be more "caring" and more gracious for the Christian church simply to go the route of accommodation? Should the church not relax the conditions for entrance to the estate of marriage enough to welcome loving and committed homosexual couples or at least devise a parallel or related form of "blessing" for such unions? As the argument usually goes, "What harm is done if it is a relationship between consenting adults?" That is to say, does not our particular situation enjoin a revision in the civil use of law?

To such questions at least two things need to be said. First of all, the widespread notion that the doctrine of the uses of the law gives permission for fundamental changes in the *content* of the law is quite mistaken.[11] The doctrine of the uses of the law is just what it says. It concerns the use and not the content of the law. The idea that law could be so altered in content that the civil use would be somehow milder than or even contrary to the theological use is quite foreign to the doctrine. Law may indeed be *applied* variously according to the situation but the basic con-

---

10. LW 31:344; WA 7:21.1–4.
11. See Haikola, *Usus Legis*, 25ff.

tent remains the same. Some like to point out that we no longer demand the death penalty for sexual misbehavior as was the case in Old Testament times. But that does not mean that what was once prohibited is now suddenly considered acceptable. A change in penalty does not mean change in content. It can also be the case, as Luther insisted, that commands issued to the people of God in Old Testament times do not apply universally. This was particularly true of commands to attack and destroy enemies in specific instances. Some at the time of the Reformation were tempted to use such commands as legitimation for a species of holy war. But this would be a misuse of law. It is not enough just to say that a given command is "The Word of God." We must always be careful to note whether a command applies to us.[12] But even this does not mean that the content is altered. It is simply a matter of whether a given law applies universally or not.

Some in the church like to argue also that since the church has changed its mind on matters like divorce or ordination of women it seems consequent that it could change its stance on sexual behavior as well. But in questions of the civil use of law it is not legitimate to argue that one example of change justifies another. Each case has to be argued individually.[13]

The second thing that needs to be said is that the fundamental concern of the civil use of the law is for the care of the social order. The purpose of laws regulating sexual behavior is to foster healthy, joyous, and socially fruitful sexual relationships and to guard against the social destruction that results from aberrant sexual behavior. The struggle to establish an order within which sexual behavior can be beneficial to society has been a long and arduous one. According to some the very foundation of Western civilization itself rests on the success of this struggle. Dennis Prager, for instance, argues very powerfully that the biblical demand for all sexual activity to be channeled into marriage changed the world. The prohibition of non-marital sex, he insists, "quite simply made the creation of Western civilization possible."[14] When there are no controls on or boundaries to sexual activity, sex dominates both religion

---

12. LW 35:170; WA 16:384.19–386.14.

13. One ought to distinguish carefully among different sorts of change and the various reasons for them. The church may have changed its practice of remarrying and admitting divorced persons, but it has not declared divorce to be a good thing. Or one may change because the original position was not solidly based on biblical teaching or because the biblical teaching itself is not completely clear or consistent. I would argue that to be the case in the question of women's ordination. But it is beyond the scope of this paper to open such questions. For further reference, see the fine discussion by Craig R. Koester, "The Bible and Sexual Boundaries," *Lutheran Quarterly* 7, no. 4 (1993): 375–90.

14. Dennis Prager, "Judaism's Sexual Revolution," *Crisis* (1993): 30.

and social life. Sex is then a means of exercising power and establishing dominance. Advocates for relaxing the traditional Judeo-Christian stand against homosexual behavior often like to argue that such behavior was common and accepted in ancient societies. But a moment's reflection ought to be sufficient to reveal that such arguments can hardly be advantageous to their cause.

Ancients, it seems, were simply not concerned about gender. Boys, women, slaves, could all equally be objects of desire. What was important socially was to dominate, to penetrate rather than be penetrated. Such considerations ought in any case to be sufficient to waken us to the realization that the civil order itself hangs in the balance in this discussion. It is really not sufficient just to lay claim to a little compassion or to muse a bit about "what harm does it do?" What is being harmed is the very social order itself. And that is the concern of the civil use of the law. In its civil use, law has to be concerned about the whole social order itself, not just about individual convenience. A faith which knows the end of the law sees also that the law is established thereby and will be watchful about all attempts to alter its fundamental content.[15]

THE ESTATE OF MARRIAGE

The product of the concern for the social order in Christian tradition is the estate of marriage. Marriage is the publicly acknowledged joining of a man and a woman together. But marriage is not only the public and ceremonial ratification of their mutual consent. That is indeed essential, but it is more than a contract between two people. It involves admittance to and entrance into an *estate*, a civil reality above and beyond the mutual consent and/or even the loving commitment of the man and the woman involved. The tradition has always insisted that the estate of marriage is divinely ordained and thus especially God-pleasing.[16] It is simply not the case that marriage was looked upon as a kind of necessary evil, a hedge against lust. Luther, for instance, used the 1 Cor 7:9 passage that "it is better to marry than to burn" primarily as a criticism of Roman attempts to claim celibacy as a state higher than marriage. It was better to marry

---

15. Wingren appropriately reminds us that entering into the world of the neighbor does, of course, involve entering into a society which we have not created. Simply to disregard the conventions and rules of solidarity in that society is to disregard the forces which check and restrain human tendencies to evil. One may indeed criticize inadequacies but that is not the same as rejection or the attempt to put something entirely new in place. Wingren, *Creation and Law*, 165.

16. For a comprehensive treatment of these matters see William H. Lazareth, *Luther on the Christian Home* (Philadelphia: Muhlenberg, 1960), esp. chaps. 6–7.

than burn under the burden of falsely required vows. The foundation for the idea of marriage as an estate ordained by God, however, is much more positive. It is to be found in such passages as the account of creation in which God blesses the man and the woman and enjoins that they "be fruitful and multiply" (Gen 1:28) and also the subsequent ratification of the creation account by Jesus in Matt 19:4–6, "Have you not read that the one who made them at the beginning made them male and female, and said, 'For this reason a man shall leave his father and mother and be joined to his wife, and the two shall become one flesh'? So they are no longer two but one flesh. Therefore what God has joined together, let no one separate." The estate of marriage has a positive purpose. The two become one flesh, a substantial unity in difference. The estate is to be a blessing to the married couple, to protect against the vagaries of passion, feeling, and sexual waywardness. And, of course, it is concerned to foster a family life conducive to the raising of children. Society has a tremendous stake in this. The law in its civil use is one expression of this concern.

If we are at all concerned to restore some sanity to social life today in an age of rampant sexual irresponsibility and egocentrism we would do well to pay some heed to what the tradition has to say about the estate of marriage as an application of the civil use of law that flows from it. Attacks on marriage are nothing new. It has always been a rather precarious venture and the butt of much ridicule, satire, and cynicism. Luther even in his day notes that "the estate of marriage has universally fallen into ... awful disrepute." Pagan books, he laments, "treat of nothing but the depravity of womankind and the unhappiness of the estate of marriage." Nor will Luther tolerate the idea that women are only a necessary evil to assuage the lust of men. Such ideas Luther insists are "the words of blind heathen, who are ignorant of the fact that man and woman are God's creation." It is blasphemy against God's creation. He even anticipates that if women were to write books they would say the same things about men![17] A passage from Luther's treatise on "The Estate of Marriage" both recognizes the threat to marriage and indicates the protection the estate intends.

> The world says of marriage, "Brief is the joy, lasting the bitterness." Let them say what they please, what God wills and creates is bound to be a laughingstock to them. The kind of joy and pleasure they have outside of wedlock they will be most acutely aware of, I suspect, in their consciences. *To recognize the estate of marriage is something quite different from merely being married. He who is married but does not recognize the estate of marriage cannot*

17. LW 45:36; WA 10/2:293.7–18.

continue in wedlock without bitterness, drudgery, and anguish; he will inevitably complain and blaspheme like the pagans and blind irrational men. But he who recognizes the estate of marriage will find therein delight, love and joy without end.[18]

Indeed, in what will probably seem to us a kind of simplistic naivete, Luther can say that recognition of the estate of marriage as pleasing to God should override even its most difficult trials.

We err in that we judge the work of God according to our own feelings, and regard not his will but our own desire. This is why we are unable to recognize his works and persist in making evil that which is good, and regarding as bitter that which is pleasant. Nothing is so bad, not even death itself, that it does not become sweet and tolerable if only I know and am certain that it is pleasing to God.[19]

Such words may cause moderns to shudder or shake their heads but that is only an indication of how little concern there is about pleasing God—which is quite probably at the root of all our problems to begin with![20]

THE HOMOSEXUAL AND THE USES OF THE LAW

We have now arrived at the most difficult and controverted part of the discussion, the use of law in either approval or disapproval of sexual misbehavior—in this case specifically of genital sexual relations between people of the same gender. The question before the church is whether law in its civil use can under any conditions be extended to approve or condone such behavior. Two things must be said at the outset to get the question in proper focus. First of all, we may take it for granted that the Bible and the Christian tradition following it unambiguously rejects genital sexual relations between people of the same gender as it

18. LW 45:38; WA 10/2:294.18–26. Emphasis mine.
19. LW 45:39; WA 10/2:295.9–15.
20. One cannot help but wonder whether the change of wording in the marriage ceremony in the recent revision of the hymnal of the ELCA (*The Lutheran Book of Worship*—the "green book") does not already reflect a down-playing and weakening of the idea of the estate of marriage. The old *Service Book and Hymnal* (the "red book") began the ceremony forthrightly with the traditional words: "Dearly beloved: Forasmuch as Marriage is a holy estate, ordained of God, and to be held in honor by all, it becometh those who enter therein to weigh, with reverent minds, what the Word of God teacheth concerning it." Then follow the foundational passages. The *Lutheran Book of Worship* however, begins with a prayer that the joy brought by the presence of the Lord at the wedding at Cana might also be present now. There is no reference to the estate of marriage as such even though, to be fair, one must note the repeated acknowledgement that marriage is established by God. But the basic idea that the couple is entering into the estate of marriage seems missing.

was known to them in their day.[21] Any attempt to deny that would be pure sophistry. The argument today thus has to take the form of asserting that new knowledge or insight has fundamentally changed the conditions for judgment and application of the law in its civil use. So the question usually comes down to whether current experience of "homosexuality" as an "orientation" does not call for a change in the church's stance. The Bible, it is usually admitted, condemns homogenital *acts* but ostensibly knows nothing about *orientation*. So, it is said, conditions have changed. The question therefore is whether such argument is sufficient to alter the long-standing biblical tradition.

Second, since in the Christian tradition genital sexual activity is permitted only within the estate of marriage our question must be as specific as possible. Can or should the church modify or expand its understanding of marriage so as to put its blessing on life-long committed relationships between persons of the same gender involving genital sexual activity? If so, on what grounds? What social or moral good would such sexual activity *per se* promote such that the biblical rejection of it could be set aside? Since the church holds that genital sexual activity is *in any case* permissible only within marriage, that must give the question precise form. All such relationships outside of marriage, whether between those of the same or of opposite gender are unacceptable. If genital sexual relations between people of the same gender are to be approved and/or blessed, the only way that could be done would be to bring them within something akin (at least) to the estate of marriage. Can this be done in terms consonant with our understanding of the uses of the law?

The thesis of this paper is that it cannot. Since our primary concern here is with the civil use of law we had best begin with that. Separation of the two uses cannot ultimately be made, so in the end we shall have to say something about the theological use of law as well. But first, about the civil use. As we have seen, the law in its civil use is concerned with the moral and social import and consequences of our actions. As we have already indicated, "orientation" is much too ambiguous both conceptually and in application to be of use as a basis for ethical decisions. Humans apparently can have various "orientations," inborn or otherwise but that is not sufficient ground for ethical approval of what they are "oriented" toward. Indeed, if the doctrine of original sin is still valid, many of our "orientations" would be restrained or opposed by the civil use of the law. That certainly is why law is necessary. The question to be answered, therefore, must be about the social and moral value of genital sex acts

---

21. See the helpful article by Donald H. Juel, "Homosexuality and Church Tradition," *Word and World* 10, no. 2 (1990): 166–69, and again the article by Craig R. Koester.

between people of the same gender. In much of the discussion that follows I lean rather heavily but loosely on the arguments of James P. Hanigan in his helpful book, *Homosexuality: The Test Case for Christian Sexual Ethics*.[22] Hanigan rightly insists that the question must be very specifically focused on the sex act itself.[23] Homosexuals, of course, can and indeed do become intimate friends and have "loving, committed, relationships," and can be mutually supportive and so on. But so can single friends of the same sex who may share living quarters, care and concerns, be sustaining and supportive and even enjoy a common life together but neither have nor desire sexual relations with one another. Life-long loving and committed relationships are in themselves not sufficient to justify genital activity. We have many such relationships in which genital sexual activity either plays no part or would even be harmful and destructive—most obviously, as we are tragically aware today, relationships with children. Therefore the question we cannot get around is what social or moral value would same-gender genital sexual acts add even for the most loving and committed couples such that they should be recognized as valuable by society or blessed by the church? It is no doubt true that the genital sexual activity of homosexuals has personal and private significance for them. But our question has to be about the social and moral import. In what way does it build up the community, or preserve its unity, or perpetuate it? Why should it be recognized or promoted as a "life-style"?

Some might like to argue that societal legitimization for committed homosexual couples can serve to heal the wounds of society and/or assuage the personal agony and suffering of homosexuals, curb the spread of AIDS and so forth. But that is hardly an argument for the social value of such genital relations. It would seem rather to be an indication of social danger. It is of course true that our mutual experience of having to care for and about one another in the midst of crises like these can teach us vital social lessons. But that is not to say that there is social value in what causes the crisis.

When it is held that society and/or the church ought to "bless" committed homosexual unions what inevitably results is a kind of double standard. Homosexual unions come to be looked upon as something less

22. James P. Hanigan, *Homosexuality: The Test Case for Christian Sexual Ethics* (New York: Paulist Press, 1988), esp. chaps. 3–4, pp. 59–112. We can only briefly recount parts of Hanigan's much more comprehensive argument here and may thereby do him an injustice. Readers are directed to his book for the full picture. To be sure, Hanigan is Roman Catholic. But his arguments can stand on their own account. Roman Catholic moral theologians who have rejected simple obeisance to authoritarianism are often much cleaner and straightforward in the kind of argument needed to support the civil use of law than their Protestant counterparts.

23. Hanigan, *Homosexuality*, 77.

than ideal, less than marriages between man and woman.[24] They are permissible for the satisfaction of the individuals involved as a kind of defensive and protective measure to forestall greater discomfort or tragedy. They are permitted and thus apparently justified morally out of sympathy simply because that appears to be the only way sexual satisfaction can be realized. The end (sexual satisfaction) justifies the means ("blessing the union"). We succumb to the prevailing assumption that everyone has a basic right to "life, liberty, and the pursuit of sexual satisfaction." But there is no such positive right to sexual satisfaction and the means one uses to achieve it are not justified just because it is the only way satisfaction can be realized. "The goodness of what is desired as a means must be established as worthy of moral choice by something other than the end they may or may not realize in and through this choice."[25] There can be no double standard. If homosexual unions are to be blessed by church or society it would have to be on the same ground and for the same reasons that marriages of persons of opposite sexes are blessed.[26] Nor is there an unquestionable right to marriage.[27] Society has always claimed the right to refuse marriage in some cases (incest, for instance) and to see to the fulfillment of legitimate social and personal responsibilities. Hence society also rules on the permissibility of dissolving marriages.

Focusing attention on the moral and social value of the genital sex act itself as we have done here quite naturally requires deeper reflection on the kind of value sex is. Why, finally, should the genital sexual activity of a married man and woman be of value morally and socially where that of persons of the same gender is not? That is the question. What kind of value is sex? As Hanigan points out, sex can be and has been variously valued. It can be valued as a means to an end: a means to earn a living (prostitution), a way to manipulate and control others, to enhance one's self-esteem, to gain attention, to be popular, feel alive. But if it is only a means to an end one treats others only as means, the occasion for one's enrichment, or "self-fulfillment."[28] Such a valuing would, of course, be quite contrary to the law in its proper civil use. The law is there to see to it that we serve the neighbor, not use him or her merely as occasions for self-fulfillment.

But the attempt can also be made to value sex simply for its own intrinsic worth as a physical experience. But where that is the case, technique takes over. The most moral sex is the most physically pleasurable

24. Hanigan, *Homosexuality*, 72–73.
25. Hanigan, *Homosexuality*, 72.
26. Hanigan, *Homosexuality*, 73.
27. Hanigan, *Homosexuality*, 71.
28. Hanigan, *Homosexuality*, 75.

and the sexual virtuoso the most virtuous. While concern for technique has its rightful place, valuing sex in this manner is completely to individualize it. The other is treated once again just as an occasion for one's self-gratification. One need not even have a sexual companion since masturbation or even a machine would do just as well, perhaps better.[29]

But if genital sexual activity cannot be properly valued only as a means to an end or simply for its own intrinsic worth that means it can find proper value only within a higher purpose. It can only signal participation in larger reality.

Its true value consists in the fact that it is a symbolic activity.[30] One should say, I believe, that it is a symbolic activity in Paul Tillich's sense of symbol as participating in the reality which it symbolizes. The sexual activity itself symbolizes and participates in the great mystery of unity encompassed by the biblical calling that the "two shall become one flesh." It is even said to be a unity akin, to that between Christ and the church (Eph 5:31–32). Participating in that gift of unity as a symbolic act, it focuses, celebrates, expresses and enhances the meaning of all substantive activities and relationships.[31] The most significant aspect of these relationships, no doubt, is the personal relationship, love and care, between the sexual partners. But it is more even than that. The sexual act itself is a participation in the mystery of unity. But could this not be said to be the case between homosexual partners as well? It is difficult if not impossible to see how it could be. If the genital sexual act is symbolic as we have suggested, what does such an act between homosexuals symbolize? In what reality does it participate? It is not enough just to say that it symbolizes "committed, interpersonal love." As already pointed out, genital sexual activity is in no way necessary to such love and in many instances would be destructive of it. Committed relationships do not justify just any sort of sexual behavior. If they did why should not those "oriented" toward "bisexuality" be justified in having both male and female as permanent partners? Once again we are thrown back on the question of what specific value homosexual genital intercourse adds such that it should be blessed.

If marriage is to be understood as entry into an estate under the civil use of law, then it should be the case that genital sexual activity involved must itself be seen in the light of one's vocation to serve God and the neighbor through a life of love in the world. "The heart of the mat-

---

29. Hanigan, *Homosexuality*, 76.

30. Hanigan, *Homosexuality*, 89–90. Hanigan speaks of it as a symbolic or ritual activity. However, I have several questions about his understanding of the nature of ritual activity, so I prefer to limit the discussion here to the value of sexual intercourse as a symbolic activity.

31. Hanigan, *Homosexuality*, 77.

ter rests with the claim that the sexual activity itself must be an essential aspect of the exercise and realization of [one's] vocational calling and have social as well as personal import."[32]

Same-gender sexual relations cannot fulfill this vocational calling. In the first place, the calling is that in sexual activity the "two shall become one flesh." This is not possible for persons of the same sex.[33] The most obvious outcome and instance of two becoming one flesh is in their children. Homosexual sexual intercourse obviously cannot do that. Furthermore, persons of the same gender cannot become one flesh in the sense of a shared life of love as a unity in difference. They cannot become one out of two in the sexual act itself.[34] At best the sexual activity of homosexuals can only imitate but not participate in what the act symbolizes.

In the estate of marriage, however, sexual intercourse participates in the reality symbolized. Hanigan puts it well.

> When married couples engage in sexual intercourse and realize the substantial goods of their actions, they are exercising and realizing both the personal and social meaning of their calling, to be for one another . . . and thereby to establish and secure that center of life and love around which family develops and grows and serves society. Their sexual relationship is fundamentally essential to carrying out the vocation.[35]

This is quite obviously not to say that sexual intercourse has meaning and is justified only in relation to procreation. That should be clear from the manner in which the symbolic nature of the sex act has been maintained. Thus even couples who for one reason cannot have children participate in the reality symbolized and carry out their particular vocations in that light. It is to say, however, that the relation between sexual intercourse within the estate of marriage and procreation ought not to be broken or denied. Procreation is not, indeed, the *only* justification for sexual intercourse, but it is part of the reality being symbolized. In reacting against stricter "natural law" views and possessing the means to sever the relation between intercourse and procreation altogether society today has too readily succumbed to making sex simply a means of self-gratification. Society has always had and must take a vital interest in its children and must pay attention to them today. Children all too often are the victims sacrificed on the altar of sexual self-gratification. This too is the concern of the civil use of law.

32. Hanigan, *Homosexuality*, 99.
33. Hanigan, *Homosexuality*, 99.
34. Hanigan, *Homosexuality*, 100.
35. Hanigan, *Homosexuality*, 103.

To bring this section of the paper to a close we set again the question with which we began. Should the civil use of law be so extended as to allow the church, or even society itself, to bless committed same-gender relationships? Shall such relationships be taken within something akin to the estate of marriage? The civil use of law is concerned with moral and social good. So in the end we are left with our question: What social and moral good is created specifically by the genital sexual activity of persons of the same gender? The conclusion of this paper is that no such social or moral good can be discovered. There appears to be no good reason why church or society should alter its understanding of the estate of marriage to include or bless same-gender genital sexual activity. Indeed, to do so is to put society itself at great risk.

CONCLUDING OBSERVATIONS ON THE THEOLOGICAL USE OF LAW

The argument pursued in this paper is not likely to be of much comfort to anyone. Those who consider themselves "homosexuals," should they read it, will no doubt be angered, hurt, perhaps depressed. Many whose sexual "preferences" are otherwise may also feel themselves put off or offended. They might even sense that their own sexual autonomy is under attack. They would, of course, be right. Or one might, as I do, find considerable sadness in the fact that words such as these have to be written. There is no joy in this, or in the writing of it. But that is simply a result of the fact that law has no compassion and, indeed, always turns to accuse and to worm its way into the conscience. As Gustav Wingren could put it, the civil use of law always passes over into the theological.[36] We cannot stop it. It always accuses because we fail to put it to its proper use. As I have indicated throughout, it is not possible to make a clean or absolute separation between the civil and theological use. In "establishing the law," attempting to set forth the civil use clearly and forthrightly as we have done here, the accusing voice inevitably begins to sound as well. And we should make no mistake about it. It will sound *even if we attempt to silence it by altering or abolishing the laws that attack us.*[37]

36. "The first work of the Law, that of compulsion, is continually passing into the second work of the Law, that of accusation. It exercises both of these functions at the same time. It differs only in the mode of its reception. At one time I am forced to look outwards to the world which is purer than I am, and which has a right to my services. At another time I am forced to look inwards to myself, but I am less pure than the world, and remain so whatever I may do. The first and the second uses of the Law coincide." Wingren, *Creation and Law*, 181.

37. Frederick Gaiser ("A New Word on Homosexuality? Isaiah 56:1–8 as Case Study," *Word and World* 14, no. 3 [1994]: 280–93) uses a case of prophetic abrogation of the Torah's law for-

We need to understand this if we are at all to comprehend the nature of the crisis that confronts us. Appeal is repeatedly made to society and church today to make laws in regard to sexual behavior more permissive. Anyone who writes on the subject no doubt feels the pressure of such appeal. But we cannot offer false comfort. To succumb to the pressure is to take the antinomian turn, to think one can wish the problem away by the simple expedient of erasure. It may, of course, be true that many laws concerning sexual behavior ought to be changed. But the problem is deeper, especially when law passes over into its theological use. What used to be called the "natural" law, in the sense of the law "written on the heart," inexorably does its work. What that law enjoins is love of and service to the neighbor. That is its fundamental and ineradicable content. Whenever any form of behavior, sexual or otherwise, becomes solely a means of self-gratification rather than finding its higher reason for being in service the law attacks. Sexual behavior is of course particularly vulnerable here. But it is surely not the only culprit. Hatred, violence, cruelty, and injustice toward those whose sexual behavior is improper under the law comes also under accusation. But if I, thinking to do those who plead for laxity a favor, propose to use whatever authority I have to change or abolish the laws supporting service to the neighbor I will likely only make matters worse. I will only have justified the self-gratification all the more and made the accusation potentially more insistent.

bidding eunuchs entry into the assembly to raise the question whether such prophetic authority could or should be exercised today to abrogate biblical proscription of homogenital sexual acts, thus granting entry and welcome to practicing homosexuals in the church. The argument perhaps needs more attention than can be given here, but from what has already been said the following points can be made. First, the question is not one of abrogating this or that law. In Christ the whole law has been abrogated. Christ is the eschaton, the end of the law to faith. Second, the problem is not one of gaining entry to the "assembly" or the church. Since Christ is the end of the law, the door is open. No one can shut it and as far as I can see, no one is doing so. But it is only as repentant sinners that we all enter through that door. But then the real question begins: "What happens now?" Third, I have tried to argue that abrogation is no simple matter. We *could*, of course, simply declare a given law invalid. Gaiser uses Luther's astonishing freedom in claiming that Christians are now free to write their own decalogue as evidence for this. Nevertheless Gaiser apparently believes that the more difficult question is whether we *should* do so. That is correct as far as it goes. But as this paper argues, beyond the *should* is the troublesome question of whether and to what degree we *can actually succeed* in doing so. Does not the law most of the time have too much "weight" from Bible, tradition, and "nature?" Only Christ can end it, and that eschatologically. To believe is to be grasped by that. So we live for the time being in the "resonance" between the end and the establishment of the law. The Christian, however, is precisely the one freed to enter the world of the neighbor as dutiful servant of all. The Christian, it is to be assumed, will write a new decalogue precisely to establish the law on a more careful basis, not to abrogate it. But this means that for now we are cast back upon the appropriate civil use of the law and the way in which the civil threatens to turn over into the theological use, driving us always to Christ.

This is to say that pastorally the church simply cannot do the rampant sexual misbehavior of our day any good by accommodation or erasure. The law will never go away, as long as sin and death remain. Antinomianism is the one heresy that is theologically impossible. That is why Luther called it a drama played in an empty theater. There is no audience before which it could possibly play. One can erase laws on the civil level, of course, and that will most often be socially debilitating, but theologically the accusation remains. Law has no compassion. It does not go away, it just changes its shape. Can we not see the law taking its revenge today? Is it not tragic that in order to accommodate "sexual preference" society should be divided into camps by "sexuality"—each according to its own "law"? Is it not tragic that human beings should be driven to define their very essence first and foremost in terms of their "sexuality"? Is it not tragic that we come, willy-nilly, to see ourselves as driven by some supposed species of biological fate? That we have to discover or come to some understanding of who we are? The law, it seems, is no longer "in the heart" but somewhere in the genes or the DNA. Is it the case that now at last by appealing to a law written in the genes we have discovered the ultimate protection from the law "written in the heart"? Long ago it was said: "I see in my members another law at war with the law of my mind and making me captive to the law of sin which dwells in my members" (Rom 7:23–24). Has the old battle between the spirit and the flesh now decisively and finally been settled in favor of the flesh—by biology? But are we then at the mercy of the lab technician? When or where will it end? Our supposed protection becomes our prison. Thus does the law work its way among us. There are no loopholes.

Law has no compassion. That is just as it should be. But it is not the end of the matter. Compassion is the business of the gospel. To return to what we said at the outset, there is another pole to the doctrine of the law. Christ is the end of the law to everyone who has faith. Christ is the *only* end. There *is* no other. That is the reason the treatment of law can and must be so uncompromising. For where the law is watered down or jettisoned we come under the most diabolical illusion of all—that there is no longer any need for Christ. We must not take that road. What the church has to offer in these, as in all matters, is not accommodation but absolution and a new life. That is the greatest service to the neighbor we can do. True, many today may find this to be of small comfort. But that may be only because they fail to realize how desperate the battle is.

The Meaning of *Satis Est*

Much of the beauty of the Augsburg Confession (CA) consists in that it means just what it says. In the question before the house in this session it says:

> Our churches also teach that one holy church is to continue forever. The church is the assembly of saints in which the Gospel is taught purely and the sacraments are administered rightly. For the true unity of the church it is enough (*satis est*) to agree concerning the teaching of the Gospel and the administration of the sacraments. It is not necessary that human traditions or rites and ceremonies, instituted by men, should be alike everywhere. It is as Paul says, "One faith, one baptism, one God and Father of us all," etc. (Eph 4:5, 6).[1]

That is the catholic claim of the CA. The meaning is quite plain, and has been so from the beginning of the Lutheran Reformation until now. The *satis est*, especially when taken together with the next sentence stating that it is not necessary that human traditions or rites and ceremonies, instituted by men, should be alike everywhere, is clearly a setting of limits. It states what constitutes the true unity of the church, and limits what can be required of any church in order to be included in that unity. The confession asserts boldly that enough is enough, and that nothing more can be required for the true unity of the church.

We do not need to guess what Article 7 means. The texts are in good shape. We have all the sources any historian could desire. We have the writings of Luther, Melanchthon, and others relevant to the subject. We have the documents used as sources for the CA and plenty of letters. We know the historical context. The churches of the Reformation were accused of schism, breaking the unity of the church, because they had

---

1. Art. 7, translated from the Latin version, BC-T 32.

proceeded without Roman or Imperial institutional approval in undertaking certain reforms, especially in the Saxon Visitations. The CA is their "apology," as they often referred to it, in which they turn back the charge of schism. Even though they have undertaken several necessary steps to reform the church, thus indeed interposing certain discontinuities in existing institutional forms (traditions, rites, ceremonies, instituted by men), they have not broken the true and spiritual unity of the church, the Reformers claimed, because they seek only to proclaim the gospel and administer the sacraments which call that true church into being and give it its unity.

But one should have no illusions about what a drastic step this was for any understanding of the church and social life. It meant a renovation in practically every facet of existence. Just a list of what the "traditions, rites, and ceremonies" devised by men included is enough to indicate that:

> mandatory fasting; auricular confession; the veneration of saints, relics, and images; the buying and selling of indulgences; pilgrimages and shrines; wakes and processions for the dead and dying; endowed masses in memory of the dead; the doctrine of purgatory; Latin Mass and liturgy; traditional ceremonies, festivals, and holidays; monasteries, nunneries, and mendicant orders; the sacramental status of marriage, extreme unction, confirmation, holy orders, and penance; clerical celibacy; clerical immunity from civil taxation and criminal jurisdiction; nonresident benefices; papal excommunication and interdict; canon law; papal and episcopal territorial government; and the traditional scholastic education of clergy.[2]

But if the meaning is quite clear, what is the problem? When questions arise about the meaning of something so clear, our suspicions ought to be aroused. All too often that indicates that a move is afoot to make it mean something other than it has been taken to mean all along. That appears to me to be the case in the current argument over the *satis est*. As is usual in such instances, the question of context is appealed to as the warrant for making the history say something other than what it clearly intends to say. If we wish to get at the question of the meaning of the *satis est* today, I expect we shall have to attend to such argumentation. To use an older distinction which I don't generally espouse but which may be helpful in this instance, the argument about the meaning of the *satis est* is not so much, perhaps, about what it *meant*, but what it *means*. It is not so much, that is, about what it meant back there, though that is inevitably involved, but perhaps more about what it supposedly means

---

2. Steven Ozment, *The Age of Reform 1250–1550* (New Haven: Yale University Press, 1980), 435.

for us today—or even what we would *like* it to mean! It is helpful to distinguish these two things particularly in arguments where one appeals to context. With that in mind, we proceed to the question: What is the meaning of *satis est?*

The standard argument these days is the argument from context. The situation now, so the argument goes, is so different that the *satis est* is supposed to function differently from the way it did back then. This sort of argument has lately been raised to the status of what one supposes is virtual infallibility since it has been accepted as part of the supporting rationale for the ELCA statement on ecumenism at the churchwide assembly.[3] Since this is the voice of authority, we shall treat it as a classic statement of the argument about what the *satis est* means. The historical situation, the voice of the ELCA informs us, is now different from what it was in Reformation days. Then, we are told, the *satis est* was proposed to preserve an existing unity. Now, however, it should function, if at all, apparently, to enable us to move from visible disunity to greater visible unity and "full communion."

Just how the *satis est* is supposed to do that is never very clearly spelled out. Instead we are served a series of statements about the *satis est* that hardly follow from one another and seem virtually contradictory if taken according to their implied meaning. "Today," we are informed, "the *satis est* provides an ecumenical resource to move to levels of fellowship among divided churches." True. But only if the *satis est* is taken as a concept limiting what can be imposed upon churches as institutional requirements for unity. But that clearly is not what the argument is supposed to mean. For the next sentences indicate that the ecumenism statement has something quite other in mind. It moves immediately to try to remove the limits. "Article VII," it announces, "for all its cohesiveness and precision does not present a complete doctrine of the church. It is not in the first instance an expression of a falsely understood ecumenical openness and freedom from church order, customs, and usages in the church." What are such sentences supposed to mean? Clearly the drift seems to be that since CA 7 does not present a complete doctrine of the church and cannot be taken as pointing to a "falsely understood ecumenical openness," i.e., freedom from church order, customs, and usages, then we are called upon now to complete the doctrine of the church and take on, for the sake of visible unity, the orders, customs, and usages that the confessors declared could not be required. Instead, that is, of being a limiting concept, the *satis est* is taken to be something of a minimal

---

3. References are to William G. Rusch, ed., *A Commentary on "Ecumenism": The Vision of the ELCA* (Minneapolis: Augsburg, 1990), 28–29.

requirement for unity, to which a number of other things could freely be added. This, of course, opens up the possibility of accepting the orders, customs, and usages that others may find to be necessary.

But it is hard to see what the next sentences are to mean in this new context. The "primary meaning" of the *satis est*, we are informed next, "is that only those things that convey salvation, justification by grace through faith, are allowed to be signs and constitutive elements of the church." The sentence seems a kind of grudging admission in the midst of the attempts to open things up, that the *satis est* does impose limits which cannot be denied. It seems a contradiction to the argument to this point. Then there is a kind of gratuitous reference to the fact that, unlike the sixteenth century, we must recognize the missionary situation of the church today. Another context is heard from. What that is to mean for the *satis est*, we are not told. Does it mean that in the light of the missionary situation we should be prepared to "loosen up" on the claims of CA 7? If not, why are such statements here? But then the statement returns to the subject by saying, "Yet Article VII of the Augsburg Confession continues to be ecumenically freeing, because of its insistence that agreement in the Gospel suffices for Christian unity." This is taken as warrant for the ecumenical method of bypassing insistence on doctrinal or ecclesiastical uniformity and looking instead to consensus on the gospel. Laudable enough. But what provokes interest is that "yet" with which the paragraph begins. "Yet" CA 7 continues to be ecumenically freeing. Why so, "yet"? Is that a reference back to the fact that the argument for openness, which took the *satis est* to be a minimum to which other things could readily be added, ran into a snag in the fact that "only those things that convey salvation" are allowed to be signs and constitutive elements of the church? So is the *satis est* to be rescued, finally, by a condescending "yet"?

The attempt to answer the question of the meaning of the *satis est* by an appeal to context thus seems to end in confusion. If it is now to function to help restore a lost unity, one can never be quite certain whether it is an enemy or a friend, an open door or a roadblock. If this is the more-or-less official position of the ELCA, we are in trouble. We are left not knowing whether our confessional position is a bane or a blessing. One even hears of snide references these days from highly placed ecumenical leaders, about "*satis est* Lutherans." Like Luther's drunk on horseback, the interpretation of the *satis est* falls off on one side, only to climb back on and fall off on the other. It vacillates back and forth between what it meant and what it supposedly means with no apparent consistency, with the general result that one is quite puzzled as to what it does mean for us today. The argument from context is used, apparently, to demonstrate that it should function differently today, but one is honestly at a loss to divine what that different function is. Perhaps the truth is that the argument actually tries to render the *satis est* irrelevant so it can no longer be an obstacle to our designs.

In what follows, I shall try my hand at expounding the meaning of the *satis est*. To do so, however, one must be considerably more careful about the question of context and therefore with the distinction between what it meant and what it means. It is, of course, a truism to say that matters were different then from what they are now. But then one must try to specify very precisely what those differences are. To begin with, it is doubtful that CA 7 assumes and therefore is designed to preserve an existing visible unity. After all, the confessors were being charged with schism—with having broken the unity of the church. But furthermore, just a little reading around in the writings of Luther indicates that he, and Melanchthon as well, was quite aware of the many ruptures in the visible or physical unity of Christendom. The words of Luther's great confession which stand behind much of the CA bear eloquent testimony to that:

> This [one, holy, Christian Church on earth] exists not only in the realm of the Roman Church or pope, but in all the world, as the prophets foretold. . . . Thus this Christian Church is physically dispersed among pope, Turks, Persians, Tartars, but spiritually gathered in one gospel and faith, under one head, i.e., Jesus Christ. . . . In this Christian Church, wherever it exists, is to be found the forgiveness of sins, i.e., a kingdom of grace and of true pardon. (LW 37:367–68)

One can find many other statements of the same sort in Luther and other reformers.[4] True, the "physical" disunity they see may be somewhat different from that which obtains today. It was not so much a matter of denominations as the church dispersed among different peoples or nations.[5] But differences there were, in traditions, rites, and ceremonies, as they put it, "instituted by men." Therefore, the task they saw was not

---

4. See, for instance, M. Luther, "On the Papacy at Rome," LW 39:55–104, and "The Private Mass and the Consecration of Priests," LW 38:138–14. It is significant that Luther's most ecumenical statements about the unity of all Christendom come in the writings against the papacy!

5. Nevertheless, denominationalism has its roots very early on in the Protestant movement. See the interesting essay by Winthrop Hudson, "Denominationalism as a Basis for Ecumenicity: A Seventeenth Century Conception," *Church History* 24 (1955): 32–50. Hudson points out that seventeenth-century divines found warrant for denominationalism in Calvin. But perhaps they could have found even more direct warrant in Luther's writings against the claims of Rome. See note 4 above. Furthermore, as Hudson points out, denominationalism was not what split the church, but rather an ecumenical strategy to bring it together once again.

that of attempting to preserve an existing physical unity, since that, quite obviously, no longer existed—if it ever had. The task, rather, was that of coming to a deeper understanding of the unity of the church in the face of such physical difference and dispersion. Thus they sought to grasp the *true* unity of the church which persists through all of its physical manifestations. And this true unity of the church could be grasped only in the light of the gospel of justification by faith alone. That is to say, the church and its unity could itself be nothing other than an object of faith, not of sight. The "invisibility" or better, "hiddenness," of such unity was not, therefore, simply a counsel of last resort, a taking refuge in "spiritualization" when all else failed. It was rather a matter of principle. It would make no difference at all to CA 7 whether there were one physical church or several. The true unity would still be an object of faith and not sight. If the church and its unity is to be an object of that same faith that justifies, then it cannot be an object of sight. That was not a counsel of despair. It was part and parcel of the good news itself.

There is a fundamental divide here between the church viewed from the perspective of justification by faith and the perspective of justification by grace-wrought works. Where justification is by works the church must realize and manifest itself by its works in the world. It has, basically, two options. Either it must seek to make the world over and thereby dominate it, via necessary ruling institutions, or it must retreat from the world to its own holy enclave. The genius of Rome, one might say, was that it did some of both—in the papacy and its claims on the one hand and monasticism on the other. To equate the true unity of the church with such visible manifestation was simply to invite and perpetuate tyranny, or, in theological terms, put the Antichrist on the throne.

Where justification is by faith alone, however, the true church is revealed only in acts that set us free from the tyranny of law, sin, and death. So its only visible marks in this world are acts of ultimate liberation, primarily the pure preaching of the gospel and the proper administration of the sacraments, but also, as Luther would sometimes say, in other manifestations of liberation, ministry, bearing the cross, suffering, prayer, and so forth. The true unity of the church is therefore brought about by such acts of liberation from sin, death, and the power of the devil because they call into being a *communio* of those who believe in and hope for the ultimate triumph of this as yet unseen and unseeable "church."

In this light, the *satis est* was not part of an attempt to preserve an already existing unity. It was rather part of an attempt to redefine the true unity of the church in consonance with the gospel of justification by faith. Thus the confessors maintained, in the face of all the apparent physical and visible disunity, that nevertheless the true unity of the church persists by faith alone. Their apology therefore was that they had not destroyed the true unity of the church, and indeed that they could not. Consequently they insisted that for the true unity of the church it is enough to agree on the proper preaching of the gospel and administration of the sacraments. That was a statement of the limit imposed by the nature of justification by faith itself. A line was drawn by the gospel. Whatever traditions, rites, and ceremonies one might propose in addition must take their place this side of the line as strictly of human provenance. The *forms* devised by men to safeguard and deliver the gospel may, and perhaps should, vary. It is enough to agree on the proper doing of it. Enough is enough. That, I believe, is what it *meant*. And one should not serve up contextual hash to obscure that. But that cannot be the end of the story. Just what it *means* for us is, of course, the last, and most difficult question. So we must turn to that question to conclude this exercise.

What does the *satis est* mean today? It goes practically without saying that the context today is different from that of the original text. Critical interpreters are right at least in that. However, as pointed out, the real difference is not to be found on the level of the unity or disunity of ecclesiastical institutions. The major differences we have to attend to are more in the realm of theology and metaphysics. This is hardly the place to go into an exhaustive discussion of such matters, but if one is to draw out the meaning of the *satis est* for today, some judgments of at least a preliminary and suggestive sort will have to be ventured.

Theologically the most important contextual reality for the understanding of the *satis est* as well as ecclesiology in general today is the challenging and breaking up of nineteenth-century liberal and romantic continuities by the recovery of biblical eschatology. To this, Lutherans must also add the recovery of Luther's theology, especially the theology of the cross.[6] It is clear that originally the *satis est* marked an attempt to draw a line in order to protect the very nature of the gospel. To carry this through, the reformers used various distinctions in their thinking about the church: visible versus invisible; physical versus spiritual; sometimes (but all too rarely) hidden versus revealed; and above all, divine versus human institution. These distinctions did not fare well in the eighteenth, nineteenth, and early twentieth centuries. In one way or another, the transcendent (invisible, spiritual, revealed, divine) was col-

---

6. It is well to remember that the phenomenon known as "Luther's Theology" is really pretty much a twentieth-century discovery. The theology of the cross was virtually unknown until W. von Loewenich's book on it in 1929, which was not translated into English until 1976!

lapsed into the immanent (visible, physical, human, moral). A similar fate befell the understanding of the church in both Roman and Protestant camps. The result was what Ernst Wolf characterized as the romanticizing of the church.[7] The church was taken to be a visible reality (a *gemeinschaft*, i.e., a commonality made—*geschaffen*—by human activity) which once—prior to the Reformation—united Europe, but now, because of its physical disunity, fractures it. Such romanticizing spawns a kind of ideology of unity: If we could put the church back together again, and perhaps restore its magisterial integrity, people would return to it. This ideology of unity fires much of the ecumenical pathos in the church today.

But even though the collapsing of the transcendent into the immanent has come under heavy fire in virtually every other theological locus,[8] the doctrine of the church seems to have escaped. Romantic notions of the church have persisted and now take the form of the drive for visible unity, *koinonia*, "full communion" and such grand things. The upshot is that the old distinctions used at the time of the Reformation to protect the gospel come under heavy fire and are often relativized if not rejected outright. Should one not ask whether this relativizing or rejecting is not of a piece with the general slide of the churches into the sociological swamp so vehemently decried elsewhere?

The question before the house, therefore, is whether the *satis est* is to be taken still today in some fashion as a part of our call to faithfulness, or if it is just a piece of historical junk. We will be able to answer that question confidently in the affirmative only if we recognize that it was groping—as were all these Reformation distinctions—for what we today would call an eschatological understanding of the church. The *satis est* pointed towards an understanding of the church that takes account of the eschatological distinction between the ages, this present old age and the future breaking-in in the new. The *satis est* sets an eschatological limit to what can be claimed by the institutional forms of the church in this age. When it asserts that for the true unity of the church it is enough to agree on the right preaching of the gospel and the administration of the sacraments in accordance therewith, it insists that the highest and final exercise of authority in the church is the gospel which sets people free from sin, death, and the power of the devil, thereby inaugurating the new age for faith and hope and granting true unity as a gift. And since

---

7. Ernst Wolf, "Sanctorum Communic. Erwägung zum Problem der Romantisierung des Kirchenbegriffs," *Peregrinatio* (Munich: Chr. Kaiser Verlag, 1954), 279–301.

8. One might hold, of course, that it is not only in the understanding of the church that the theology of the nineteenth century is alive and well. That, of course, is true. But it is also precisely our problem today.

the preaching of the gospel of Jesus Christ, crucified and risen, is the highest exercise of authority in the church, the reformers always insisted, particularly against papal and episcopal claims, that Christ was the head of the church. He is the end of the church and the promise of the new beginning, the new age, the kingdom of God. Whatever the leadership of the church in this age, and however necessary and useful it might be, it was strictly of human arrangement and its forms could not be considered obligatory. The church, that is to say, should be understood strictly as a this-age entity. What comes after the church in this world, that for which the faithful hope, is the kingdom of God. And the kingdom of God comes by God's power alone in God's good time. There will be no church then, thanks be to God! The church lasts until the end of the age, and is its end.[9]

If the *satis est* is taken eschatologically, it means that the eschaton can be carried now only by the preached word and delivered sacrament. The eschatological word can only be, finally, its own warrant. If we grasp what Luther's theology is about, we will see that at stake is a different understanding of how a truly "objective" reality is mediated. The eschatological word draws its objectivity from the fact that it is an "alien" word entirely from without, from God's future which is the end of us. It can live, therefore, only from its own inherent power. It does, indeed, need to be mediated, spoken and administered by humans exercising the office of such speaking and doing. One can even say that such an office is divinely instituted since God, by "providing the gospel and the sacrament," called it into being. But since it is an office announcing the end, it is self-limiting. It can only seek to get out of the way for the eschatological Kingdom. This is what the *satis est* means. It is a self-limiting concept. Therefore one can claim no more than human warrant for the institutional forms coined in this age.

And one should not look upon this self-limiting, pointed to by the *satis est*, as though it were something negative. As always, the eschatological limit saves the institutions of this age precisely by putting them to their proper tasks, making them truly historical. "Do we then overthrow the law by this faith? By no means, we uphold the law" (Rom 3:31). Whenever the church claims something more than that, we have trouble. The trouble is just that law overcomes gospel. Indeed, if one of the churches claims to be the one church we will have nothing but trouble. History bears repeated witness to the fact that the drive towards visible

---

9. CA Article 7 says, of course, that the true church will last forever. However, the Schwabach Articles say it will last only until the end of the age. Here, as elsewhere, the Schwabach articles are better!

unity in one visible church on earth is a dream most detrimental of all to ecumenism. The eschatological limit is transgressed and the figure of the Grand Inquisitor hovers in the wings. When the eschatological line is transgressed, the church begins to claim itself to be the unifying end of history, the fulfillment of history's meaning, and it "seeks to prove the truth of its message by the continuity of its traditions, the 'validity' of its order and the solidity and prestige of its historic form."[10] The church, that is, begins to look upon itself as the visible incarnation of the invisible ideal church. It is simply not correct or appropriate to call opposition to such a position anti-catholic. It is not anti-catholic to believe that the one church is wherever the gospel is preached and the sacraments delivered. It is surely much more anti-catholic to claim that one institution is the one church now and forever. That is a transgression of the eschatological limit set down by the *satis est* which spells, in the end, tyranny.

What is the faithfulness to which the *satis est* calls us? If one looks at the matter in the light of the recovery of Luther's theology, perhaps we can avoid some of the endless debates of the past and needless debates of the present. What the *satis est* calls for is agreement not on a whole list of things or doctrines, but on the specific activity of teaching (preaching) the gospel and administering the sacraments according to that gospel. The debates of the past have generally gotten bogged down in arguments about doctrinal agreement—about "how much" is necessary. More lately the drive towards "visible unity" seems to incline its advocates to add some things by way of communal life and discipline. It is no accident that it was the Reformed theologian/ecumenist Lukas Vischer who coined the slogan, *satis est non satis est*. As a good Calvinist he wanted to add something about discipline and such. And even our bonny Lutheran theologians at Strasbourg seem to want to add things beyond the limits drawn by the *satis est*. They talk of the necessity of "lived unity" and such niceties—even statements to the effect that "to attempt to realize . . . the unity described in *satis est* without the relations of 'full communion' is to live in self-contradiction."[11] Whenever something gets added, the teeth of the law begin to show!

Is this not simply the same old game? Whenever the eschatological line is drawn in Lutheranism by the gospel and the sacraments, someone always wants to add something more. The gospel and the sacraments are never enough. Always, always, someone gets nervous and demands something more. The statements about adding things to the *satis est* list sound remarkably like the dreary business of the third use of the

---

10. Reinhold Niebuhr, *Faith and History* (New York: Scribner's, 1949), 239.
11. Rusch, *Ecumenism: ELCA*, 111.

law, now applied to our ecclesiology. Those who refuse to add more "things" to the list are even accused of "satis est reductionism"![12] And, given the nervousness, such changes are consequent. Whenever the line is transgressed, the old being escapes. And where old beings escape the appointed end, the church has to take steps to bring them under control. The church becomes a surrogate for eschatology, a kind of eschatological vestibule! And that always turns out to be a prison.

The *satis est* calls us, surely, to believe and confess that the gospel and the sacraments are indeed enough. No doubt the irony of it all is that that seems precisely the hardest thing for churches and theologians to agree on. But what can be done about that? If we have listened to Luther, and learned anything at all from the recovery of his theology, I expect we will just have to say, "nothing!" It is simply not a matter of attempting to repair the supposed inadequacy of the *satis est* by adding or subtracting this or that. It is not a matter of a list of "things," doctrinally or otherwise. It is rather a matter of the specific activity of preaching the gospel—learning how to do that and sticking to it. If we don't know how to do that, or don't do it even when we know how, nothing can help us. No tinkering with a list of things and no bolstering of offices is going to help because the office is to preach the gospel. If one does know what the gospel is all about, one is certainly not concerned to play the game of expansionism or reductionism. If we are in trouble on this score, we are really in trouble. Nothing can be done about it except to do what the *satis est* is all about: to return to the preaching of the gospel and the doing of the sacraments with faithfulness until those who hear and receive have finally had "enough" and can consequently confess: *satis est*, I have had enough! What more could one ask?

---

12. Michael Root, "*Satis Est:* What Do We Do When Other Churches Don't Agree?," unpublished paper read at the Convocation of Teaching Theologians of the ELCA, Techny, Illinois, 1991, 27.

Lex semper accusat? Nineteenth-Century Roots of Our Current Dilemma

Do we then overthrow the law by this faith? By no means! On the contrary, we uphold the law.
—Romans 3:31

J. Edgar Hoover liked to quote Lincoln's saying that reverence for law should be the political religion of the nation.[1] But we seem today to have arrived at a point where such words meet with something far less than enthusiastic or unanimous approval. Indeed, the very fact that they are thrown at us by the head of a major law-enforcement agency is likely only to increase antipathy in many circles. Reverence for law is just not "in."

There are, of course, many reasons for this general malaise in the attitude toward law—reasons that arise out of the complex political, social, and cultural situation in which we find ourselves today. My purpose here cannot be an attempt to untangle that mess, much as that is needed. Rather I would like to reflect a bit on the *theological* understanding of law and to ask whether theological development may have contributed, perhaps unwittingly, to the current difficulties and if so, how these might be sorted out. Such a restricted theological approach cannot pretend, to be sure, to provide a comprehensive answer to the problem of law today, but it might at least help Christians to find their bearings in a confusing time.

To do this I think we must look back a bit to the century immediately preceding our own, for it is here that we will find the roots of many of our current difficulties. Perhaps also before we begin it should be made clear that in considering the theological understanding of law we are

---

1. See his article on that subject in *Event*, January 1969, 3–6.

dealing with the problem of law in a more-or-less general sense, not with particular laws or legal systems as such. There may be particular laws or even legal systems that one would not want, as a Christian, to support. But our question here is the more general one of the theological understanding of the function of law as such. The question is: What ought the Christian attitude to law and the rule of law to be?

THE REFORMATION VIEW

When the question is put in this way, it becomes immediately apparent that Christians have had a difficult time giving a positive answer. The reason, of course, is that law has always suffered from its unfavorable contrast with the gospel. The law makes irksome and even impossible demands that "the flesh" in its weakness cannot fulfill. The gospel, on the other hand, grants forgiveness and comfort. In this scheme of things the law was granted a primarily *negative* function. The law exposes man's weakness and shortcoming *so that* he will turn to the gospel for help. As Melanchthon put it, *lex semper accusat*, the law always accuses. In contrast to the gospel the law is looked upon as a tyrant from which one hopes to be delivered by the gospel.

Now the question is, if this is the case, how is one to come to an understanding of the positive function of law? It would be interesting to speculate, no doubt, about the part this primarily negative view of law might have played in the development of the modern antipathy to law. But such speculation would lead us, I think, too far afield. The reformers, it should be noted, did have devices by which they sought to establish a more positive attitude to law. This came in their distinction between the *uses* of the law. The accusing function of law related to its *theological* use, i.e., its use for man's relationship to God. Here the law always accuses. That is to say that man can never use the law to earn his way to God, to establish his own righteousness in the final judgment. The situation was quite different in relation to human society, however. Here one encounters the law in its civil use. Here the law is understood as a force, backed by the power of the state as God's representative in civil matters to restrain evil and to preserve human society. In this it could be argued that there was at least the beginnings of a more positive evaluation of the place of law. Christians must have respect for law as the means through which God intends to preserve and extend human society.[2]

---

2. Some of the reformers, of course, liked to speak also of a third use of the law, the law used as a guide to conduct for the redeemed Christian. Since, however, this is a rather specialized use, pertaining to the Christian life alone and not to the attitude toward the laws of society in

THE NINETEENTH-CENTURY PROBLEM

By the time of the nineteenth century, however, the Reformation view of law had been largely forgotten or discredited. The major reason for this, no doubt, was that man, full of the confidence inspired by the Enlightenment, came to resent the idea that he needed a gospel backed by ecclesiastical authority to help him.

What the Enlightenment and, with some reservation also, the nineteenth century rebelled against was what they called the "positivity" of the Christian religion, the fact that it was supposed to be revealed in positive historical facts unrelated to reason. A truth revealed in historical facts and imposed by ecclesiastical authority could only appear arbitrary, a heteronomy, a law imposed from without. And it was, of course, the gospel that suffered from this attack. The law, on the other hand, was quite reasonable, being the presupposition of the universal natural religion of mankind. It was, you might say, a new kind of gospel discovered now really for the first time in man's "coming of age," his "enlightenment," his newfound independence from feudal and ecclesiastical heteronomies.

With revelation and the gospel thus discredited, the religion of reason, i.e., morality and law, gradually took over the theological scene. Thus it was that Immanuel Kant came to write his treatise on *Religion Within the Limits of Reason Alone*, a work that was epoch-making in the theological understanding of law and in many ways decisive for the nineteenth-century problematic. The very title is significant. Reason, once the repressed poor relative of revelation, has now expanded its province to take in all that is essential in religion.

But this could only mean that religion would be reduced to the dimensions of law and its rewards. There were, of course, difficulties in doing this. For our purpose the most formidable one was the problem of freedom. If religion is to be reduced to the dimensions of law, how could man be said to be free? Having just escaped from the heteronomy of ecclesiastical law was man now to be bound by a new and perhaps even more exacting taskmaster, the moral law of reason?

To solve this problem (as well as other related ones that we leave unmentioned here) Kant fell back on the idea of the moral law *within*.

---

general, it can perhaps be left out of account here. I say *perhaps* because some would no doubt dispute this. But to enter here into the complex debate about the third use of the law would be impossible. For further guidance the reader is directed to W. Elert, *Law and Gospel*, Facet Books, Social Ethics Series 16 (Philadelphia: Fortress, 1971), and P. Althaus, *The Divine Command*, Facet Books, Social Ethics Series 9 (Philadelphia: Fortress, 1963).

Man hears *within* himself the voice of the moral law demanding that he do the good for the sake of the good. And since the moral law comes from within, it is at the same time the guarantee of freedom. That is to say, man is not subject to any legislation from without because he is a law unto himself; he is autonomous. This freedom is finally impervious to any threat that might be posed from without, be it that of ecclesiastical or political heteronomy, or scientific or psychological determinism. Man hears within the call, "*du kannst denn du sollst*" (you *can* because you ought). Nothing short of degeneration into bestiality can silence that call, and man's highest religious duty is to recognize it as the call of God. "Religion is (subjectively considered) the recognition of all our duties as divine commands."[3]

This surely is the high-water mark, in modern times, of the positive appreciation of law. The moral law is the guarantee of the most precious gift: freedom—the ultimate deliverance from all heteronomies. Action in accordance with that law can alone be called truly good. The inner law evoked, for Kant, virtually a religious veneration. Two things, he said, filled his mind with ever new and increasing awe: the starry heavens above and the moral law within him. The pinnacle upon which law has been placed presages in an interesting fashion the words that Hoover borrowed from Lincoln: "The highest goal of moral perfection of finite creatures—a goal which man can never completely attain—is love of the law."[4]

The similarity between Kant's statement and Lincoln's is not, I think, just coincidental, for an understanding of law like Kant's is basic to modern liberal democracy.[5] Man is liberated from feudal heteronomies and external legal persuasion to the extent that he becomes a responsible citizen, a law unto himself. Respect for law is the foundation of social existence.[6] But is this the positive view of law we are looking for? What-

---

3. Immanuel Kant, *Religion within the Limits of Reason Alone,* trans. T. M. Green and H. H. Hudson (New York: Harper, 1960), 142.

4. Kant, *Religion within the Limits of Reason Alone,* 136.

5. The term *liberal democracy* is used here and throughout the paper not in a partisan sense, either theological or political (i.e., not as a contrast to conservatism), but simply to designate modern Western democracy *per se.*

6. There is, of course, something of a tension here between the law within and external statutory law. When Kant extols love of law as the highest moral perfection, he means the law within. But love of the law within does not take place at the expense of respect for statutory or external law. It means rather that one enters a higher state of moral existence in which external law is no longer needed. To oversimplify a somewhat complex picture, Kant sees man's moral progress in three basic stages. The first stage is one of "lawless external (brutish) freedom and independence from coercive laws." This is a state of savagery, "a state of injustice and of war, each against each." Man must leave this for the second stage, that of a political commonwealth where the war of each against each is restrained by coercive laws. But on this stage there is still

ever its advantages, the fact is that most nineteenth-century theologians recoiled in horror from this stringent moralism. Indeed, one could say that from one point of view, the very problem posed for the nineteenth century was that of escaping from the rigors of Kant's view of the law. And this certainly indicates an important point about the search for a positive understanding of law. When law is made so absolute that it dominates everything in this fashion, it becomes intolerable. Men turn away from it in horror. From a theological point of view I suppose I can say that the trouble is that there is no end or limit to law. There is nothing outside it or beyond it, no "promised land" beyond its reach. And that is to say that there is no gospel, no eschaton to alleviate the unbroken reign of law. Kant did not escape the *lex semper accusat*, he succeeded only in making it more absolute.

THE NEGATION OF LAW

There were many attempts by nineteenth-century theologians to escape the moralism of Kant. If one can generalize without too much oversimplification, I think one can say that these attempts were of three sorts. More traditionally minded theologians did not attack the view of law frontally, but sought to use it as proof of man's need for grace and supernatural help. This attempt, in some ways laudable, could not really succeed however, since the idea of revelation had been so seriously eroded. Its only recourse was to fall back on an idea of scriptural inerrancy that meant a return to the heteronomy men were trying to escape. Thus its attempt to mitigate Kantian moralism was frustrated by the tendency to make the gospel itself into a new law.

Others, like Schleiermacher, sought escape by falling back upon an immediacy prior to law and conceptualization, in the dimension of feeling. Kant, it was held, *had* done violence to the moral life by picturing it as a constant and never-ending struggle between the principles of virtue and natural inclinations. What they sought was a harmony between inclination and will in which the problem of law could be more

---

conflict between the true inner law, the principles of virtue and the inner immorality provoked by coercive law—the immorality of doing good only in order to receive personal advantage. Thus the truly moral person must bestir himself to join an ethical commonwealth (Kant's idea of the church) where one lives freely according to the inner law and does good for the sake of the good alone. But looking down from this height, the virtuous man respects statutory law, the laws of the political commonwealth. Love of the law within and the freedom it grants is the source of one's respect for statutory law See Kant, *Religion within the Limits of Reason Alone*, 88.

or less bypassed. What is needed, they thought, was the cultivation of the proper feelings that would restore the lost harmony.

Such feelings and sentiments could be aroused, for Schleiermacher, through the Christian gospel, through the communication of the perfection reached in Jesus. We need not dwell here on the intricacies of this theology. Suffice it to say that here law is virtually eclipsed. Like all conceptualization, law is always at one remove from the immediacy of feeling. The question of law for Schleiermacher can arise for the Christian only as "an accident of memory."

To be sure, he admits, "something like legislation will always exist in Christian life in . . . certain spheres," but this is only "to guide the actions of those who lack insight." And this is where civil law and such things enter the picture. But law itself can be conceded no value whatsoever in the sphere of sanctification for, says Schleiermacher, "love always is, and does, more than law can be or do." Thus Schleiermacher counsels the dropping of the imperative mood altogether in Christian ethics, preferring instead simply a description of how men live in the kingdom of God.[7] This type of thought gave birth to a long line of purely descriptive ethics in the nineteenth century that sought more or less simply to bypass the problem of law—at least for the Christian.

Undoubtedly there are many things that could be said in favor of attempts like Schleiermacher's. For certainly everyone—and not just Christians—would find quite desirable a state of harmony in which law is no longer necessary. That, surely, must be what the kingdom of God is about. The question is, however, if such a state is attainable in Schleiermacher's fashion, i.e., by returning to a state of immediacy prior to law. Does such an attempted return really take the concrete realities of the human situation under law seriously enough?

However one may answer that question today, G. W. F. Hegel in the nineteenth century answered it in the negative. This brings us to the third and for modern times, I think, the most important reaction to Kant. Though he shared with Schleiermacher the desire for a harmony beyond the reach of Kant's grim moral struggle, Hegel did not think one could find it by a retreat into feeling prior to law and conceptualization. To sink back into undifferentiated and indefinite feeling was to sink, he said, into that "night where all cows are black." "The spirit," as he put it, "appears so poor that, like a wanderer in the desert who languishes for a simple drink of water, it seems to crave for its refreshment merely the

---

7. F. Schleiermacher, *The Christian Faith*, ed. H. R. Macintosh and J. S. Stewart (Edinburgh: T&T Clark, 1956), 522–24.

bare *feeling* of the divine in general."⁸ One cannot escape the Kantian law by retreat; one can overcome it only by going *through* it to something *beyond* it. And this, in Hegel's mind, demands the hard labor of thought and not merely the cultivation of appropriate feelings. One must conquer the problem of law through understanding, not emotion.

But how is this to be done? The beginnings of Hegel's attempt to move beyond Kant can be seen especially in one of his early writings, "The Spirit of Christianity and Its Fate." His complaint is that Kant did not really reach the goal he set for himself, that of freeing man from the "positivity" (heteronomy) of religion. For simply to move the moral law from without to within is not really to set man free. It merely means that whereas once God was seen as being external to man demanding obedience without question, now God is within. Whereas once there was opposition between Jehovah and his creatures, in Kant there is opposition between the moral law within and man's natural inclinations, which are coerced rather than freely persuaded to acquiesce. For even if the voice of law comes from within, man is still a slave, if only to himself.⁹

In this early writing, Hegel asserts that one can get beyond law only when something higher than law takes the place of law and thus annuls or negates law in its legal form. This "something higher" is the love that Jesus taught and exemplified. Love is a concrete thing, an "is," which is the fulfillment and thus the negation of law in which law loses its form as law. Love is therefore the unification of inclination and moral will missing in Kant.¹⁰

The important thing to notice, it seems to me, is the way in which even in this early essay, Hegel tries to get beyond the problem of law by employing the idea of negation (*Aufhebung*). The form of law, its character as an abstract universal command, is negated or *aufgehoben* when the concrete love that it demands is realized. In comparison to Schleiermacher this means that one does not sink back into an indefinite state of feeling prior to law but that one moves through the negation of law to a higher state. Kant's mistake, then, was not his discovery and formulation of the moral imperative, but his inability to get beyond it.

One must have law, and one must conceptualize if one is to escape the "night where all cows are black." But such conceptualization must in turn be negated by a higher concrete realization. Such negation does not mean, of course, direct obliteration or cancellation. It means rather

---

8. G. W. F. Hegel, *Preface to the Phenomenology of Mind*, in *Hegel: Texts and Commentary*, ed. Walter Kaufmann (Garden City, NY: Doubleday, 1965), 16.

9. G. W. F. Hegel, *On Christianity*, trans. T. M. Knox (New York: Harper, 1961), 211.

10. Hegel, *On Christianity*, 209–16.

a suspending in which what is essential is taken up on the higher state. Thus Hegel speaks of the *form* of law (its universality, its character as abstract demand) being annulled while its *content* is realized in the concrete instance of its fulfillment.

But what is this higher concrete realization, this higher state reached through the negation of law, and how does such negation actually take place? Quite obviously, if man is to be released from the coercive domination of law both from without and within, he will have to be taken up in a higher community in which he does his duty freely and spontaneously, in which he freely relinquishes his individual inclinations for the sake of the whole. The higher community will then supersede the Kantian inner law. In *The Spirit of Christianity and Its Fate*, this higher community is the community of love inaugurated in Jesus which is the fulfillment and thus the negation of law. Attractive as this idea may be, Hegel is not at this early stage very clear about how this community comes to be or just what the negation involves. He toys rather vaguely with the idea that the Spirit that was in Jesus is to become the common spirit of the group. But this, I shall argue later, is precisely where a fruitful beginning comes to naught. The idea of negation is a fruitful one, but Hegel does not, I think, know how to exploit its full theological potential.

Hegel's own assessment of the failures of the community of love is decisive for the road he was to take in developing his mature system. The trouble was that the original community of love founded by Jesus was not and could not be universal enough. It was a small and restricted group existing in opposition to the world. But the true religion must be universal; the true God is the God of the whole. If Christians were set in opposition to the world, they were, in effect, without God. Thus, they were without a proper object for their worship. And to make up for this lack they made the earthly Jesus, now understood to be risen from the dead, the object of their worship. Instead of *becoming* love themselves, they worshiped the *symbol* of love. This was the sad fate of Christianity. Thwarted from true universality because of its separation from the world (and thus from God) it became a positivistic and heteronomous sect in opposition to the world.

This devastating critique of Christianity already indicates the direction in which Hegel will have to move in order to find his higher community in which law can be negated and there will be a more universal and concrete unification between inclination and moral will. It must be a community more universal than the church, involving all the people and all of life. But since it was at the same time to be concrete, it could not be just "the world" or "humanity in general," for that, too, was an abstraction—the favorite abstraction of enlightenment. The only answer then was that it must be the nation, the concrete state. It is in the state and its ethos that man is caught up in something higher than himself to which he freely gives his allegiance. In Hegel's view, the restraints that one's country lays upon one will not be experienced as imposed from without, they will not have the alien character of Kant's moral law.[11] On submitting to the state one is not submitting to external control, but only to what is really an extension of oneself.

This is an idea which, of course, sounds excessively dangerous to modern ears. It is usually cited as the reason why Hegel's thought could lead to political absolutism of the most arbitrary sort. Whatever the justification for such charges—and we cannot argue them here—one must not overlook the fact that Hegel felt himself protected from them because his understanding of the state was the culmination of his philosophy of history, the long struggle of human freedom, the process by which the spirit comes to realize its true self in perfect freedom. And it is in this process, finally, that we see what has happened to the idea of negation.

The spirit progresses toward realization of itself, toward freedom, through the process of negation. This is, of course, a difficult thing to grasp. If we can oversimplify it and put it in terms of law, perhaps we can say it looks something like this. As society progresses its needs are conceptualized in the form of law. But law as a universal and abstract concept is alien to life itself; it is itself a negation of life. However, the alien form of law is itself negated when what the law demands is concretely realized. There is a higher synthesis through the negation of the alien form of law, through a continual process of conceptualization and negation something like this: the Spirit reaches in man the ultimate harmony between what ought to be and what is, and this ultimate harmony is absolute freedom. The state is therefore the current expression of this progress toward freedom. The law as a form alien to concrete life is negated in the perfect harmony between national ethos and individual inclination. In other words, one might say, Hegel had dissolved the problem of law and gospel into a philosophy of history, culminating in the bourgeois state.

---

11. "The state is the actuality of the ethical idea. It is ethical mind qua the substantial will manifest and revealed to itself, knowing and thinking itself, accomplishing what it knows and insofar as it knows it. The state exists immediately in custom, mediately in individual self-consciousness, knowledge, and activity, while self-consciousness in virtue of its sentiment toward the state finds in the state, as its essence and the end and product of its activity, its substantive freedom." G. W. F. Hegel, *The Philosophy of Right*, in *The Ethics of Hegel*, ed. W. H. Walsh (London: Macmillan, 1954), 45.

LAW AND REVOLUTION

Whatever one might say for the intellectual brilliance of Hegel's attempt, the suggestion that history culminates in the bourgeois political state, that here man finds his true home, virtually cries out for critical protest. This is true especially in those instances where it becomes evident that the liberalism of the bourgeois political state is hard pressed to solve its problems. Hegel's own followers were, as is well known, of two minds. Those who were quite satisfied with things as they were (the right-wing Hegelians) used Hegel to justify the status quo. At best they were in favor of extending the system and instituting liberalizing reforms to patch up the cracks. On the other hand, those who felt victimized by the bourgeois state, or who were sensitive to the manner in which it did victimize people (the young, or left-wing Hegelians) drove the system on toward one more ultimate negation: critical attack and revolution against the bourgeois state itself. This kind of negation reached its fruition in Karl Marx.

We need not argue here which of these groups were true followers of Hegel or whether the revolutionary program of Marx is a materialist inversion of Hegel's dialectic. The important thing for us to see is the way in which the revolutionary impetus has grown quite directly out of the attempt to solve the problem of law, the attempt to escape the *lex semper accusat*.

It is the result of the search for "the promised land" beyond law, the haven of true human freedom beyond heteronomy. Hegel sought to get beyond the endless moralism of Kant by means of a higher synthesis in the bourgeois state. For someone like Marx, however, the bourgeois state does not liberate man, it only enslaves and alienates the major part of its citizenry. The so-called "rights of man," the laws of the state, are not universal human rights, they are merely bourgeois privileges, laws that protect and perpetuate the greed of the moneyed classes over against the less fortunate. What is needed, therefore, is one further act of negation, a revolution that will eventually abolish the state itself and lead to the land of true and universal human freedom. The significance of this progression, in the light of current problems, can hardly be exaggerated. The animus against law culminates in revolution.

But what is the promised land beyond the bourgeois state, beyond the "long arm of the law"? What does it look like and is it in fact attainable? These are questions, of course, that do not admit of easy answers. For Marx it was the classless society, the communist society. It is instructive to note, however, that not all of his fellows among the young Hegelians agreed with him on this.[12] Max Stirner, for instance, declared that Marx, too, had not gotten rid of the last vestige of heteronomy because he had simply subjected the individual to the demand of the whole of society in general.

Stirner believed in a society of absolute egoists in which each individual, free from all universal concepts and demands, makes of his life what he can. Marx rightly retorts that this was nothing other than the apotheosis of the bourgeois Protestant individual, a return to the primeval battle of "each against each" from which man sprang. Bruno Bauer, on the other hand, seemed to look not for the end of the state, but for its strengthening, a new kind of absolutely secularized state in which bourgeois freedom and egoism would be surrendered. He longed for a ruler strong enough to take over and create this "paradise." Others, like Donoso Cortes, opted in favor of a Christian dictatorship. And there were other suggestions as well.

This argument among the young Hegelians is significant, I think, because it anticipates in such an interesting way the confusion of today's revolutionary. The violent reaction to the bourgeois liberal concept of law may have its justification, especially where such law has become oppressive. But where does one go beyond law? Hegel dreamed of a "higher synthesis" in the state. Marx found this oppressive and sought a higher freedom in the classless, eventually stateless, society. It is a sobering fact that this allowed his disciples to pay lip service to the ideal of freedom while actually implementing totalitarianism.

THE RETURN TO LIBERALISM

The latter half of the nineteenth century found itself unwilling or perhaps even incapable of dealing further with these problems. Perhaps it was because the times were such that they were not yet forced to face them, perhaps it was due to sheer exhaustion of spirit. At any rate, the theology of the time as well as the philosophy and the politics quite generally forgot the questions of the young Hegelians and returned to the liberalism of Kant.

Theology busied itself mainly with historico-critical questions and "degenerated," to use Karl Löwith's somewhat harsh words, "into history of dogma and church history, comparative religion and psychology of

---

12. See the informative book by David McLellan, *The Young Hegelians and Karl Marx* (London: Macmillan, 1969).

religion."[13] It is hardly surprising, therefore, that the most influential theology of the late nineteenth and early twentieth century was a Ritschlianism built largely on the foundations of Kantian liberalism and remembered mostly for its historical research.

This means, I think it fair to say, that in the mainstreams of thought there were no really new attempts to grapple with the problem of law.[14] To be sure, the harshness of the Kantian moralism was ameliorated somewhat by assimilating the moral imperative to the commandment to love—a love inspired by being taken into the historical community made possible by Jesus' redemptive act. But Christianity is viewed, nevertheless, in Kantian fashion as the perfect moral and spiritual religion in which one is raised above the restrictions and inhibitions of natural inclination and natural causality. Freedom is achieved when one acts spontaneously out of love, independent of natural necessity or reward. As with all Kantian-based liberalisms, such a view would seek to solve the ills of society by persuading men to leave nature behind and to join the kingdom of moral and spiritual freedom, the kingdom of love, the kingdom of God. It will advocate reform rather than revolution, reform that will seek to extend the benefits of individual freedom to the largest possible group.

Such a view makes it rather easy, of course, to associate the cause of the gospel with advancing social reform. The words of Adolf von Harnack are perhaps typical. The gospel aims at founding a community among men as wide as human life itself and as deep as human need. As has been truly said, its object is to transform the socialism which rests on the basis of conflicting interests into the socialism of a spiritual unity.[15] One cannot fault the nobility of such aims. The question, however, is whether the comfortable association of the gospel with the liberal faith can remain viable. Is it really possible to transform a socialism of conflicting needs into a socialism of spiritual unity? Our own time hardly encourages optimism of that sort.

---

13. Karl Löwith, *From Hegel to Nietzsche,* trans. D. Green (Garden City, NY: Doubleday, 1967), 118.

14. This is not to say, however, that there were no important developments in lesser-known circles that were to bear fruit later. For an account of such developments see R. Schultz, *Gesetz and Evangelium in der Lutherischen Theologie des 19. Jahrhunderts,* vol. 4, Arbeiten zur Geschichte and Theologie des Luthertums (Berlin: Lutherisches Verlagshaus, 1958), and my book, *The Law-Gospel Debate* (Minneapolis: Augsburg, 1969).

15. Adolf von Harnack, *What Is Christianity?* (New York: Harper, 1957), 100.

THE END OF LIBERALISM?

It begins to appear now as though the return to liberalism, with its existentialist aftermath between the wars, might have been only an interlude. At any rate it is apparent that liberal democracy is finding it increasingly difficult if not impossible to cope with the problems of contemporary society. The attack upon law from all sides, the erosion of public morality, can only mean that the liberal faith is dying or is already dead. And liberalism is nothing without its faith, without the belief that the telos toward which man strives is the true "ethical commonwealth" where there is a perfect wedding between natural inclination and law, where man spontaneously and freely does the good for the sake of the good. Without that faith the liberal state degenerates into a system of competing needs, where law is the enemy of natural inclination, and the battle of each against each is always a threat if not a reality.

In such instances the liberal state is forced against its will to become totalitarian. The majority enforces its will by sheer weight of numbers. In the wake of such developments, the sinister character of some "law and order" campaigns is evident. But if liberalism is dead, this spells the end of its noble attempt to foster a positive attitude toward law as well. Though it was in many ways theologically naïve, its passing is hardly a cause for rejoicing. The fascism of the reactionary right and the nihilism, the grim self-righteous confusion of the revolutionary left, are certainly vastly inferior, to say the least.

TOWARD A POSITIVE VIEW OF LAW

We must attempt, nevertheless, to pick up the pieces. The rebellion against the liberal view of law that has been incubating for so long has in recent days burst upon us with a fury that has shocked and surprised. If we had been more attentive to the history of the nineteenth century, perhaps what is happening would not seem so strange. The rejection of liberalism means that we are once again confronted with all the questions raised by the young Hegelians and the confusion resulting therefrom. In attempting to develop a positive view of law in a postliberal age, perhaps we need to go back to that time and try to discover, from a theological point of view at least, what went wrong.

The difficulty lies, it seems to me, in the development of the idea of negation. Hegel quite rightly saw that it would take a negation of law, at least in its form as law, to get beyond the moralism of Kant. But Hegel is not exactly clear, I think, about how such negation is possible or who actually accomplishes it. He seems to think that man does the negating, or at the very most the Absolute Spirit immanent in human society working through the human spirit. Once one rejects Hegel's doctrine of spirit, however, as did the young Hegelians, the result is unambiguous: man is the negator of law. Thus the idea of negation, shorn of whatever Christian trappings it may have had in Hegel, produces the revolutionary, the man who takes upon himself the right to negate the law and bring in the golden age of freedom.

From a Christian point of view this is impossible. For the Christian view is surely that only God can negate the law and that such negation can only be eschatological; it can come in its completeness only with the passing of "this age." That does not mean, however, that one must wait in submission to law until the end of the world. For it is in *the gospel* that such negation has occurred in our time in Jesus Christ. But such negation is not mere negation of law in a purely objective historical sense; it is rather more the negation of the man who lives under the law and for whom law is necessary. It is, in theological terms, the death of the "old Adam" and the raising of the new. In other words, this age and its law remains until the new man appears who no longer needs it.

But this new man appears not as a matter of course, not as the result of the legal process, not as the fruit of the dialectical progress of Spirit, and not as the product of a revolutionary program, but as the result of the death and resurrection of Jesus Christ who works that ultimate negation and new life in men. From the Christian point of view, the end of the law, the freedom from heteronomy, for which all men seek—the search to which the nineteenth century bears such eloquent and tortured witness—is available. It is the gift of the gospel.

This theological understanding of the idea of negation provides a vantage point from which one must raise questions about the Hegelian idea and its revolutionary offspring. If man is the negator of the law, he can easily usurp for himself the place of God. Perhaps that is why some revolutionaries find it so easy to preside over questions of life and death. Perhaps, too, that is the reason for the grim, humorless, self-righteous piety of most revolutionaries. It is a tough and serious business to play at being God! And perhaps as well that is the reason for the confusion of the revolutionary.

Having supposedly negated the law, he doesn't really know what to do with the world. Either he will have to end by imposing much more stringent and totalitarian laws than ever before in order to realize his revolutionary goals or, recognizing the incongruity of that, settle for permanent negation, permanent revolution. This is not to say that there may not be legitimate forms of revolution, revolutions in which a Christian ought to participate. Nor is it an argument for the status quo in society. It is merely to point out that there is at the root of the modern idea of revolution something incompatible with the Christian gospel. This, I think, is something that needs to be said today. For if one sees that it is God and not man who holds the ultimate power of negation and that he has done this in such a way in Jesus Christ as to negate not merely law but the old Adam, things begin to look quite different.

From this vantage point, too, perhaps we can begin to develop a more positive attitude toward the use of the law. The nineteenth century, as we have seen, spent a good deal of its energy trying to escape the idea of endless law. It was quite rightly recognized that it was the very endlessness of law that made it impossible to bear. They were wrong, however, in thinking that law could be ended by theological or philosophical artifice or even by revolution. Here, I suppose one could say, the *lex semper accusat* still holds. There is no escape from law in that way. But there is an end to law far more real than that, the end that comes with the breaking in of the new in Christ, the end of the old Adam and the creation of the new. It is when man realizes that there is really and truly an end, a goal, a telos, that he can begin for the first time to listen to the law, to let it speak to him and hear what it has to say. When one sees that the end, the goal of it all, has happened and is on its way through God's initiative one can begin to see law in a positive light. For then one sees that law is not forever; it is for this age, for this world.

The point is that faith opens up an entirely new sphere of possibility and action, *this* world bounded by the end. Here the law can be viewed in a positive way. That is why, I think, the reformers could speak about a "civil use" of the law according to which actions here and now could be judged as good. If the law is eternal, if there is no distinction between this age and the next, there is no way to speak of the goodness of our actions in and for this age; everything is judged by the moral absolute.

There is little chance, too, then, of really arriving at a positive attitude to law. For it is the supernatural pretension of law, its unbreakable absoluteness that makes it unbearable and drives man in his endless quest to be rid of it. When it has an end, however, a real end, one can see its positive use. In view of the end in Christ we can see that the law is intended for *this* world and that a new kind of goodness is possible, a goodness in and for this world, a "civil righteousness." Faith in the end of the law establishes the law in its proper use.

To say this is not, it must be insisted, to defend the status quo or to fall into the old trap of unqualified obedience to the state. That kind of thinking arises only when one has not grasped what faith in the end of the law means—both on the part of its proponents and its critics. For faith in the end of the law leads to the view that its purpose is to take care of this world, not to prepare for the next. That means that we do not possess absolute, unchangeable laws. If the law no longer takes care of this world, it can and must be changed. As even Luther put it, we must write our own decalogue to fit the times. Furthermore, whenever anyone, be he reactionary or revolutionary, sets up law or a system by which he thinks to bring in the messianic age, that is precisely the misuse of law against which Christians must protest. That is why, I would think, not even revolution is entirely out of the question for the Christian if that appears the only way to bring about necessary changes. But it must be a revolution for the proper use of the law, for taking care of this world, in the name of purely natural and civil righteousness and not in the name of supernatural pretension. That is to say, it must be a positive revolution and not a revolution of negation.

It is too much (or perhaps too little?) to say, I think, that respect for law must be the political religion of the nation. That seems to imply that law is an absolute before which we must all unquestionably bow. It would be better to say that care for the proper use of the law must be our constant and never-ending concern in this world. For we are not called merely to be law-abiding, but to take care of this world, and law must be tailored to assist in that task.

PART VI
Theological Method

Systematic Theology Is for Proclamation

Systematic theology is for proclamation. When properly done, it fosters, advocates, and drives to proclamation. This presupposes at the outset a basic distinction between systematic theology and proclamation. Indeed, a major difficulty in usual discussions of the matter is that systematic theology and proclamation tend so easily to be confused. When that happens it is invariably proclamation that is obscured. Proclamation gets displaced by explanation, teaching, lecturing, persuasion, ethical exhortation, or public display of emotion about Jesus. So at the outset we need to distinguish between systematic theology and proclamation and to relate them in at least a preliminary fashion.

Proclamation, as we shall use the term in this study, is explicit declaration of the good news, the gospel, the kerygma. It is at once more specific and more comprehensive than preaching, even though, as will also be the case here, we often use the two terms interchangeably. Proclamation is more specific than preaching because not all that we ordinarily call preaching—teaching, edifying, ethical exhortation, persuasion, apologies for Christian living—is necessarily proclamation. At the same time, proclamation is more comprehensive because it occurs apart from formal preaching, most notably in the sacraments and the liturgy, but also in the everyday mutual conversation of Christians.

How is such proclamation to be distinguished from systematic theology? It is helpful at the outset to make a distinction between primary and secondary discourse. Proclamation belongs to the primary discourse of the church. Systematic theology belongs to its secondary discourse. Primary discourse is the direct declaration of the Word of God, that is, the Word *from* God, and the believing response in confession, prayer, and praise. Secondary discourse, words *about* God, is reflection on the primary discourse. As primary discourse, proclamation ideally is present-tense, first-to-second-person unconditional promise authorized by what occurs in Jesus Christ according to the scriptures. The most apt paradigm for such speaking is the absolution: "I declare unto you the gracious forgiveness of all your sins in the name of the Father, the Son, and the Holy Spirit." Proclamation is not "about" something other than itself. It does not point away from itself. It does not signify some other thing. It is the saying and doing of the deed itself, for example, "*I* baptize *you.*" The deed is done, unconditionally. It is not an account of what happened in the past, such as, "God so loved the world that he gave his only begotten Son," true as that is and, indeed, as much as it authorizes the primary discourse. Such accounts are past tense. Proclamation is present tense: I here and now give the gift to you, Christ himself, the body and blood of the Savior. I do it in both Word and sacrament. This is God's present move, the current "mighty act" of the living God.

The only appropriate response to such primary discourse is likewise primary: confession, praise, prayer, and worship. Proclamation as primary discourse demands an answer in like discourse be it positive or negative: "I repent, I believe" or "I don't, I won't, I can't." In other words, when the proclamation announces, "I declare unto you the forgiveness of all your sins," the appropriate response is not, "Well, that's your opinion!" Perhaps the only thing the absolver could say to such irrelevancy would be, "No, that's not my opinion. If I were to give my opinion about you it would likely be something else! We are not dealing with human opinion here, but with the Word of God!" The only appropriate response has to be primary: "I believe" or "I don't believe it." The primary language of proclamation evokes and expects the primary response of confession and worship or its refusal. Systematic theology, however, belongs to the sphere of secondary discourse. It is not the Word of God, it is words about God, reflection on what has been heard. Above all we must be clear that systematic theology is not what is to be proclaimed. To use an analogy, proclamation is like saying, "I love you." Systematic theology is like a book on the nature of love or the art of loving. It is secondary discourse. It attempts to put things in order, to focus, to lend coherence, and to measure the church's discourse on the basis of its established norms, scripture, the creeds, and confessional documents.

It is essential that these two kinds of discourse not be confused or that one gets substituted for the other. Perhaps this can be clarified by pressing the love analogy further. Imagine the lover and the beloved at a critical moment in which the primary language is to be spoken. "Do you love me?" asks the lover. And the beloved answers, "Well, that is an interesting question. What is love after all?" And so launches into a discussion about the essence of love. After patient waiting, the lover finally gets another chance. "Yes, that's all interesting, but do you love me?" Then the beloved takes another diversionary tack and says, "Well, yes, of course. You see, I love everybody!" (A universalist!) The lover protests, "That's not what I mean! You haven't answered the question! Do *you* love *me*?" So it goes. In spite of all the helpful things it does, secondary discourse makes the would-be lover look ridiculous when substituted for primary discourse.

There is only one type of discourse that will do the job in the case of the lovers: primary discourse, the proclamation, the self-disclosure in present tense, first-to-second-person address, the "I love you," and the subsequent confession, "I love you too!" What happens in the church's proclamation is often similar: secondary discourse gets substituted for primary and so proclamation never occurs. Proclamation as primary discourse must be carefully distinguished from and not confused with systematic theology as secondary discourse. In spite of much apparent antipathy to systematic theology today, that is what is heard mostly from our pulpits—albeit systematics of a second-rate or rather unsystematic sort!

If proclamation and systematic theology are to be distinguished, then how are they to be related? They are necessarily correlated: one is impossible without the other. Without systematic reflection there will be no conscious proclamation. Proclamation may perhaps happen instinctively. But this is more accidental than purposed. Systematic reflection is necessary to make the move to proclamation conscious and explicit. This is entailed in the contention that systematic theology is for proclamation. It ought to be the kind of reflection that fosters and drives back to the proclamation. Indeed, to make distinctions as I have done here is to begin such systematic reflection. Without such reflection one would probably not come to a clear understanding of what proclamation is and so would not do it. One might do a lot of things—exegete, lecture, explain, persuade, teach, orate effectively or poorly, edify—all of which may be fine in their place, but one will not proclaim.

I take systematic theology, therefore, to be the kind of reflection that takes place between yesterday's and today's proclamation. One who hears the proclamation reflects on it so as to say it again in a different time and context. It is a reflection that takes place between the ear and the mouth. If nothing happens there, one is not needed and would best just get out of the way. The hearers would be better advised to read the Bible or yesterday's sermons. But then there will likely be no proclamation for today. Systematic theology is indispensable for such proclamation.

But with such assertions, the correlation is not yet complete. For without the proclamation and an understanding of its place, systematic theology will either not be done at all or is likely to go wrong. Everyone knows and generally agrees that systematic theology exercises a critical function over against the proclamation of the church. But if there is a genuine correlation the proclamation needs to reflect back on and raise critical questions about systematic theology. If today's proclamation does not turn out right, or is not really done at all, something went wrong with the reflection. All too often what happens is that the systematic theology short-circuits the process and usurps the place of the proclamation. The secondary discourse about love displaces the "I love you." One ends then by delivering some species of lecture about God and things rather than speaking the Word from God. When this occurs it matters little whether the lecture in question is conservative, liberal, evangelical, or fundamentalist. That only means the lecture is to one degree or another theologically correct. But that is of no great moment if it does not issue in proclamation.

The secondary discourse is relatively pointless if it does not drive to proclamation, to actual primary discourse. A central concern of this study is to show that proclamation is not just practical or pastoral application of arguments already completed and wrapped in neat packages in the systematic, but that *the move to proclamation is itself the necessary and indispensable final move in the argument*. If and when systematic theology looks on itself as the conclusion of the argument—the means by which ultimate persuasion is to take place so that there is no room or place for proclamation—it has overstepped its bounds and falsified itself. That is, the systematic reflection should not only leave room for the proclamation but must make the move inescapable. The argument must leave one in a position where proclamation is the only move left. If systematic theology does not leave such room and make such a move inescapable, it falsifies itself by denying its purpose. It then usurps the place of proclamation and retreats behind the ivied walls of academia, never to be heard from again except, perhaps, at professional societies where one has long since forgotten its purpose.

Thus proclamation and systematic theology must be intimately correlated: Without systematic theology there will be no proclamation; but without proper understanding of proclamation, systematic theology will overstep its bounds and falsify itself. I intend to show that both proclamation and systematic theology will be understood and done differently where such correlation is observed and maintained. Proclamation is neither second-rate or popularized systematic theology nor the practical application of systematic arguments. Systematic theology, likewise, will operate under certain critical limits. It will insist on and leave room for the proclamation. In following out its reflective task it will make certain characteristic moves and refuse to make others, realizing that it cannot usurp the place of the proclamation. Proclamation has to be the final step and thus set a critical limit to the systematic. The purpose of this study in this regard is to point out how this happens and thus to establish the critical function of proclamation vis-à-vis systematic theology.

When one looks at the history of the church from the perspective of the relation between proclamation and systematic theology, it becomes apparent that a perpetual problem has been the eclipse of primary discourse, especially in the form of proclamation, so that it tends to get truncated or to survive only marginally. Almost from the start the gospel proclamation tended to lose its present tense. It was thought that the eternal Logos made a one-time appearance, came down, acquired a body, was crucified and raised, and then absconded with his body, never to be heard from again. The heavens were silent, the great acts of God were over and done with, and there were no more prophets. Jesus became, in today's parlance, "history," past tense. The good news became old news. The only place where the present tense survived in some fashion was in the sacraments. That is why they became so important. But even in sacraments specially authorized successors of the dead-and-gone Jesus were necessary to perform the miracle of making him present tense again. Meanwhile, the discourse of the church, its proclamation, became more and more just secondary, past-tense discourse about God and his Christ. However, as long as such secondary discourse was an ecclesiastical affair, done by the bishops and catechists and doctors of the church, and ancillary to the church's liturgy, it did stay tied to the church's mission. When it later became oriented mainly to the schools the relation began more and more to unravel. The direct proclamation survived at best only as a part of the Sacrament of Penance where it was carefully hedged by conditions and kept in the closet of the confessional.

The Reformation was at best a temporary interruption in this tendency to concentrate on the secondary discourse of the church. It was an attempt to get the primary discourse out of the closet of the confessional into the common discourse of Christians and into the public pulpit. It survived by fits and starts in the churches, but increasing separation between university and church could only mean that theology would become more and more an academic rather than an ecclesiastical discipline. Secondary discourse again crowded out primary discourse.

Through it all, in varying degrees in both Protestantism and Roman

Catholic camps, the secondary discourse—the words about God, the history, the infallible facts of the Bible, the old news—properly attested ecclesiastically tends willy-nilly to become the object of faith in place of the promise, the proclamation. The great crisis for the church is that the modern world since the Enlightenment sets serious question marks over this past-tense, secondary discourse. Not only does its historical veracity come under critical scrutiny, but even more seriously, its heteronomous character becomes odious. In other words, as a teaching about a past event it partakes of the uncertainty of all such past events. But even if true, it appears heteronomous (that is, an arbitrary or alien law imposed from without).

The Enlightenment sought to liberate the world from such heteronomy. It saw clearly that old news was bad news. Those who think that an inerrant or infallible historical record solves the problem mistake the gravity of the crisis. An inerrant record only makes matters worse. Old news remains bad news even if it is inerrant. Gotthold Lessing put the question that hangs over the modern era like a marsh gas: How can accidental truths of history be proofs of eternal truths of reason?[1] The Enlightenment rejected such heteronomous "positive" historical religion for "natural" religion, a religion fitted to the autonomy of enlightened and rational beings—as Immanuel Kant was to put it, a "Religion Within the Limits of Reason Alone."[2]

For theology that was a fateful moment. It put an end to ecclesiastical hegemony and demoted theology to one among many academic disciplines. It signified in turn a hermeneutical divide: from that moment on, Scripture would have to be interpreted according to the canons of practical reason. As a result, academic theology tries to manufacture a gospel by turning accidental truths of history into eternal truths of reason, even if only "practical reason." This is the triumph of secondary discourse. Whatever has to do with proclamation is banished to the realm of "practical theology."

Ever since, the church has been on the defensive. On the "left," the strategy of theology has been that of accommodation, apologetics, and theological cosmetics. It has been engaged in a valiant effort to rescue the secondary discourse itself from complete demise by attempting to make it acceptable, credible, palatable, and amenable to human autonomy, to hone down and blunt the sharp edges of the message. The nagging ques-

---

1. Gotthold Ephraim Lessing, "On the Proof of the Spirit and of Power," in *Lessing's Theological Writings*, trans. Henry Chadwick (London: Adam and Charles Black, 1956).

2. Immanuel Kant, *Religion within the Limits of Reason Alone*, trans. T. M. Greene and H. H. Hudson (San Francisco: Harper and Bros., 1960).

tion of what this accomplishes still remains. Does the defensive strategy actually defend anything? Or does it gradually erode the faith?

But how is the problem to be met? On the "right," conservatives and reactionaries insist that we are safe only if everything is, so to speak, set in stone. We are protected from the erosions of time only by an inerrant scripture, infallible secondary discourse. But this is likewise an undermining of the present-tense proclamation. Old news remains bad news even if it is supposedly inerrant or infallible.

The ecumenical question in many ways only highlights and aggravates the problems. As long as one operates on the assumption that the secondary discourse is the object of faith and hence a species of "absolute truth," one can only choose up sides and compare such secondary discourse and hope to reach some "convergence." Failing that, one can only surrender to pluralism—all too often just a plea for the right to hold a private opinion without subjecting it to rigorous public scrutiny. Theology then becomes a matter of taste. There can, of course, be no argument about taste! *De gustibus non disputandum est* ("taste cannot be disputed") becomes the final authoritative utterance in theology.

Recapturing the distinction and proper correlation between primary and secondary discourse and, with it, the idea of a systematic theology that is for proclamation promises help not only in ecumenical conversation but also in the church's conversation with the contemporary world. The defensive strategy of theology in the modern world has resulted not in saving but rather in eroding the faith. The conservative and reactionary right has correctly seen that. But its attempt to avert erosion by insistence on setting the secondary discourse in stone is only postponement of eventual disaster. It is time to take a different tack. What the church has to offer the modern world is not ancient history but the present-tense unconditional proclamation. The strategy of accommodation and defense has resulted in the sentimentalization and bowdlerization of almost everything. It is time to risk going over to the offense, to recapture the present tense of the gospel, to speak the unconditional promise and see what happens. To do that it will be necessary to construct a theology that is for proclamation, for going over to the offense, not for defense.

This book, an attempt in that direction, is something between an essay and what used to be called an outline of systematic theology. It is like an essay because it represents an initial testing of a thesis. I have not attempted to argue the case by meticulous comparison with other systematic works since that would disproportionately increase the length of the work. At the same time it is something of an outline (what German systematicians call a *Grundriss*) because it traverses traditional dogmatic topics and tries to show how a systematic theology that is for proclamation might look. It does not pretend to be rigorously systematic in the sense often employed among academics, but a serious systematic proposal is being made. The term *systematic theology* is used more to indicate the arena and type of reflection required than to claim that a seamless web is being woven. Nor does the work by any means claim to be a complete systematic theology. Since it concentrates on proclamation and the related problematic, it has a somewhat limited scope.

This book is, furthermore, a preliminary sketch. This is not to imply that some dogmas or doctrines are of more importance for proclamation than others. It is simply that the matter must be presented within certain limits of time and space. There is, for instance, no complete or explicit discussion of the doctrine of the Trinity, but the substance is radically trinitarian throughout. The very understanding of proclamation it proposes is radically trinitarian: that God speaks to me in the address of a fellow human today is possible only if God is triune, only if that person can speak to me in the Spirit the Word of the God who does himself speak to us in Jesus. The logic of the argument would not, I suspect, allow for the easy collapse of the immanent into the economic trinity inspired by Karl Barth and Karl Rahner and prevalent in much current systematic reflection. But this awaits further work. In some instances where a more complete investigation of my own views is possible the reader is directed to other writings and articles. Such expositions do not yet exist, however, in every case. Omissions will have to await a more complete treatment in subsequent work.

The Preached God

And how are they to believe in him of whom they have never heard? And how are they to hear without a preacher?
—Rom 10:14

Systematic theology is reflection between yesterday's and today's proclamation. Having heard and been claimed by the Word of God, we reflect on how to say it again. We begin such reflection with the God we have heard. That is proper since "God" is the word we use for the beginning, as well as the ending, of all things. "In the beginning, God . . ." (Genesis 1), and in the end God shall be all in all (1 Cor 15:28). Having heard the word of God we are, in turn, impelled to speak it, to proclaim it. But how shall we reflect on God so as to foster proclamation? That is the fundamental question for systematic theology.

GOD NOT PREACHED

It is customary in systematic theology to begin with a discussion about how we can know and speak of God. We investigate possible sources for the knowledge of God: nature, experience, reason, and finally special revelation in the scriptures of the church and its traditions. We review the norms for our speaking of God: the canons of the church, its scriptures, its creeds, and its liturgies. Such surveying and reviewing have their rightful place in the theological enterprise. When systematic theology is understood as the kind of thinking that takes place between yesterday's and today's proclamation, however, reflection about God takes a shape different from the usual. Being captivated by the proclamation, our thinking about God is radically altered. We encounter not just talk about God, but God speaking to us.

GETTING GOD OFF OUR BACKS

The hearing of the proclamation makes us aware of a fundamental distinction, as Luther once put it, between God preached and God not preached. In the proclamation we hear something we have not heard before and cannot hear elsewhere: "What no eye has seen, nor ear heard, nor the heart of man conceived, . . . God has prepared for those who love him" (1 Cor 2:9). The distinction between God not preached and God preached helps us to reflect and speak honestly about God.

To begin with, assuming we have heard God in the proclamation, we can be honest about the fact that outside the proclamation God is something of an onerous burden. We see that apart from God preached, we are estranged from God. Rather than being the one we are allegedly always seeking, God not preached appears more as the one we can never quite get off our backs. As such, "God" is the name for whomever or whatever is "out there," "up there," "in the depths," "transcendent to us," and messing with us. "God" is the place where the buck stops. "God" is responsible for it all. God is an enigma for us. Is there anyone, anything, "out there," "up there"? We are not quite sure, and our attempts to either prove it or to disprove it fall short. Outside the proclamation both theistic and atheistic theologians are strangely one. Both are trying to get God off our backs. The theist most often does it by trying to make God "nice," to bring God "to heel," so to speak, and the atheist does it by trying to make God disappear. Both attempts have a similar outcome from the point of view of the proclamation: they only subvert it.

Nevertheless, for better or for worse, neither theistic nor atheistic appeals seem to work for long. We may find an argument temporarily convincing, but then something else overtakes us—some tragedy, some joy, some fortune or misfortune, some deed or happening that inflates or deflates our ego—and we are back where we started. No matter how persuasive the argument, the next generation, even the next thinker, acts as though it had never been made, or it could not be done, or it did not really work because there were some "holes" in it. The arguments are done, redone, and redone again. We never seem to get God off our backs. God just persists. And that is our problem. That is, in part, what it means to say that we live under the wrath of God and cannot escape.

Thus God apart from proclamation is a rather intractable problem for us. We neither get along very well with God, nor without God. We are at best ambivalent about God. On the one hand, we like the idea of an eternal "anchor" to things, or an eternal goal that is also the source and guarantor of all the things we seek: eternal truth, goodness, beauty, and so on. On the other hand, God is a threat to us: the ruler, the judge, the almighty One who has the final say. We are caught between seeking and fleeing God's presence. The psalmist sings, "As a hart longs for flowing streams, so longs my soul for thee, O God" (Ps 42:1). But then, "Whither shall I go from thy Spirit? Or whither shall I flee from thy presence?" (Ps 139:7). Our thinking does not exactly help us, at least not in a direct positive sense. The problem is that when we think "God" we come up against an awesome string of sheer abstractions, what Luther meant, perhaps, by the "naked God in his majesty" (*deus nudus in sua maiestate*), the "bare idea" of God. God is absolute, immortal, immutable, infinite, timeless, passionless (*apathos*), omnipotent, omnipresent, and omniscient; God is the eternal ruler, judge, and disposer of all things, by whose power and will all things come to be and not to be. God is, by definition, God.

It is the very god-ness of God that causes all the difficulty in our thinking. For if those fearsome abstractions convey truth, "God" is the end of us. That is, should God be all those things, we are left with nothing—no significance, no freedom, no place to stand. God as sheer abstraction, as "the naked God," is an inescapable terror for us. God "not preached" is a God of wrath. This concept may be unpopular but it is true. Otherwise, people would not feel the need nervously and desperately to hide it, to cover up or paper over the naked God with pages torn from theology texts. Outside the proclamation God is unavoidably wrathful.

GOD THE ABSCONDER

God not preached is therefore a confusing, nefarious brew of presence and absence, of sheer timeless abstractions. Yet the abstractions do not reveal so much as hide God from us. They tell us more about what God is not than what God is. God is infinite (that is, not finite), immutable (that is, not changeable), not mortal, not suffering, not limited by time or space, not relative to anything. As such, God amounts to a deified minus sign.

So even though inescapably present, God is terrifyingly absent in this presence. God is, as the tradition (especially Martin Luther) put it, "hidden" (*absconditus*). The Latin has a more active flavor to it than the English, as when someone absconds with the "goods" and leaves behind only an absence, an emptiness, a nothingness. Moses experienced this active absence when he asked to see the divine glory: "And the Lord said, 'Behold, there is a place by me where you shall stand upon the rock; and while my glory passes by I will put you in a cleft of the rock, and I will cover you with my hand until I have passed by; then I will take away my hand, and you shall see my back; but my face shall not be seen'" (Exod 33:21–23). Not preached, God is the absconder, the one who will not be seen and leaves behind only an emptiness, a blank space. In that sense, God is not merely "hidden" (that is, more or less passively unseeable or unknowable), but the one who actively hides from us, always "gives us the slip."

There is, of course, both a positive and negative aspect to this absconding. On the one hand, that the naked God hides from us and saves us from destruction: "No one can see God and live." The constant temptation of the theologian of glory in us is to try to penetrate the "hidden majesty" of God. Were we able to do that this side of the Parousia, nothing but destruction would result. Enough mischief is accomplished by our unsuccessful attempts to do so. There is a "hidden grace" in the hiddenness of God. On the other hand, the negative aspect is that apart from the proclamation we live under the wrath of the divine hiddenness—the terror of the naked abstractions, the divine absence, the nothingness. As the ever-present absent One or the terrifying abstractions, the One who is the end of us, God not preached merges into and becomes confused with Satan, the accuser and destroyer. This is suggested in the idea of the "masks" (Latin, *larva*) of God. The Latin word also means "ghost" or "demon." The masked God—the God not preached—is hardly distinguishable from Satan.

We can, of course, become fascinated with the emptiness, the nothingness, thinking perhaps that it in itself provides some avenue of escape from the burden of God. Those so fascinated can become enticed by a living negation, a mystical way of self-denial by which one becomes something of an abstraction oneself. Piety becomes almost a holy suicide. Thus even in this there is no escape from the wrath of God. God not preached remains an intractable problem for us.

SHUFFLING THE MASKS

God not preached is the absconder, one who hides behind the naked abstractions, and there is nothing theology as such can do about that because theology is a collection of abstractions. It is only in the concrete proclamation, the present-tense Word from God, spoken "to you" the listener, that the abstraction is broken through for the moment and God no longer absconds but is revealed. This is what theologians with too few exceptions through the ages have either failed or refused to see. When the distinctive correlation between systematic theology and proclamation is overlooked, the theological impulse will of necessity be to attempt the impossible: to go to work on the abstractions, to attempt to remove or see through them, to tear the mask from the face of the "hiding" God. When the proclamation is not heard, there is no other recourse. One attempts, against Luther's frequent caveat, to "peer into the hidden majesty of God."

Systematic theology has lately subjected itself to futility because of its preoccupation with such attempts. The attempt is futile because it only shuffles masks. Just when one thinks that he or she has removed one terrifying mask, another mask emerges and turns out to be even more threatening, though the perfidy may not be immediately apparent. Such theologizing only substitutes another seductive abstraction for the proclamation. For example, nineteenth-century liberalism proposed Jesus' proclamation of "the Fatherhood of God" as a surrogate for the gospel. Yet "Fatherhood," severed from its trinitarian moorings, has turned out to be just another frightening mask to many in our day. We should learn from this that similar masks such as "the Motherhood of God" will turn on us as well. They turn on us because the abstraction replaces the proclamation. Instead of the "I love you," of the almighty one, we hear a lecture on a God who is in general "love." The "solution" only creates an even greater problem. Instead of a word from God we hear theological opinions about God. We go out of the frying pan and into the fire! Recall our lover who at the crucial moment claims, "Of course, I love everybody!" or even perhaps "I am love," instead of saying, "I love you!" What is the beloved to say or do about that? If the message is merely that God is love in general, then everything is turned back on us. "If God is love, what is the matter with me? Why am I such an unloving clod?" The generality, the abstraction, whatever its place, only turns on us because it can never do the job of the concrete, self-revealing proclamation. Theology simply cannot unmask God.

This move to tear away the masks, to penetrate, modify, or erase the abstractions, has reached epidemic proportions in the last century. This is no doubt a consequence of the demise of proclamation among us. We seem to have become very sensitive about a timeless, immutable, impassible, and omnipotent God, and have attempted to replace these "masks" with those of suffering and self-limitation. Ronald Goetz sets the issue clearly: "The age-old dogma that God is impassible and immutable, incapable of suffering, is for many no longer tenable. The ancient theopaschite heresy that God suffers has, in fact, become the new orthodoxy."[1]

Goetz's list of theologians attacking the impassibility and immutability reads virtually like a "who's who" of contemporary systematic theology: Karl Barth, Nicolas Berdyaev, Dietrich Bonhoeffer, Emil Brunner, John Cobb, James Cone and liberation theologians generally, Hans Küng, Jürgen Moltmann, Reinhold Niebuhr, Wolfhart Pannenberg, Rosemary Ruether and feminist theologians generally, William Temple, Pierre Teilhard de Chardin, and Miguel de Unamuno.[2] Others could be added.

Indeed, Goetz finds this move to a suffering God to be the one point of consensus today in an otherwise discordant and chaotic pluralism. It is, he avers, a "doctrinal revolution" the implications of which are "enormous," affecting every classical Christian doctrine.[3] Particularly remarkable, Goetz finds, is that this "theopaschite mind-set" has developed as a kind of "open secret."

The doctrine of the suffering God is so fundamental to the very soul of modern Christianity that it has emerged with very few theological shots ever needing to be fired. Indeed, this doctrinal revolution occurred without a widespread awareness that it was happening.[4]

Goetz lists a number of factors which he thinks have contributed to the rise of contemporary theopaschitism: the decline of Christendom; the rise of democratic aspirations; the problem of suffering and evil; and scholarly critical work on the Bible in the light of the foregoing.[5] While Goetz does not claim his list to be exhaustive, it seems apparent from the point of view of this study that something more internal to theology itself is a major cause: the failure to see that proclamation is the only vehicle for reconciliation with God. Systematic theology, consequently, has thought itself obliged to repair God's damaged reputation.

The problem is at least twofold. On the one hand, a God stripped of the masks and abstractions is no longer worthy of the name. On the other, such a God ultimately turns out to be more reprehensible and frightful than before. The logic of the masks plays itself out. In Goetz's words:

> The doctrine that God is limited in power solves the problem [of evil] by sacrificing God's omnipotence. However, to my mind, any concept of a limited deity finally entails a denial of the capacity of God to redeem the

---

1. Ronald Goetz, "The Suffering God: The Rise of a New Orthodoxy," *The Christian Century* 103, no. 13 (April 16, 1986), 385.
2. Goetz, "Suffering God," 385.
3. Goetz, "Suffering God," 385.
4. Goetz, "Suffering God," 385.
5. Goetz, "Suffering God," 386.

world and thus, ironically, raises the question of whether God is in the last analysis love, at least love in the Christian sense of the term.[6]

There is no doubt a sense in which theology will want to speak of God's suffering. This needs to be done more carefully, however, in terms of the trinitarian relations and the difference between God not preached and God preached. Why, for instance, do the systematic attempts to displace the impassible God always fail? Why do they have to be done and redone and redone again? What impels us forever to keep trying unless it is that, no matter what, the impassible God "sticks in our craw"? Do we sense that the mask remains in spite of all our efforts? Has systematic theology not demonstrated its futility in the matter? The point is that frontal attacks on the naked abstractions do no good. The assertion that God suffers accomplishes nothing apart from a systematic theology that fosters a reconciling proclamation. The assertion that God suffers tends to degenerate into sentimental drivel about how God somehow identifies with us in and is supposedly enriched by our suffering. The result is little more than a kind of "misery loves company" theology that is much worse than belief in an impassible God. Again in Goetz's words, "God the fellow sufferer is inexcusable if all that he can do is suffer."[7] The frightful logic of the masks works itself out. God the sufferer is in the end more offensive than the impassible God.

The fact that God, though sympathetic with the suffering of humanity, is nonetheless enriched by it, would seem little more impassive than the pathos of the sentimental butcher who weeps after every slaughter. If the purpose of our life and death is finally that we contribute to "the self-creation of God," how, an outraged critic of God might demand, does God's love differ from the love of a famished diner for his meat course?[8]

The impassible God is indeed frightening enough, but at least that God did not eat us for lunch! Theology—biblical, systematic, or otherwise—cannot tear the masks from the face of the absconding God. If it does not see itself as driving to proclamation it succeeds only in shuffling masks and making matters worse.

The problem here is deeper than the reasons suggested by Goetz. It is not just that certain peculiarly modern misfortunes have happened to theology more or less from without, but that there has been a fundamental miscalculation about the very purpose and limitations of the systematic enterprise itself. Theology undertakes to reconcile us to God by seeking to penetrate the masks, to get behind the abstractions. The

---

6. Goetz, "Suffering God," 388.
7. Goetz, "Suffering God," 389.
8. Goetz, "Suffering God," 388.

result, however, is only to disenfranchise God and water God down. But God is not mocked. We do not by such artifice escape the divine wrath. We are delivered willy-nilly into the hands of "the judge" or perhaps of Satan, the accuser, the "attorney for the prosecution." For apart from the proclamation God and Satan are virtually indistinguishable.

WHO KILLED COCK ROBIN?

Who is responsible for the demise of God in the modern era? The intellectual historian James Turner tracks down the culprits for the modern American scene in *Without God, Without Creed*.[9] Traversing American intellectual history and particularly the work of nineteenth-century theologians and preachers, Turner concludes that the theologians and preachers themselves were the real cause of unbelief. Adapting belief to modernity, they succeeded only in reducing God to human dimensions, and in doing so,

> [they] made unbelief a more attractive possibility. Put briefly, unbelief was not something that "happened to" religion. . . . On the contrary, religion caused unbelief. In trying to adapt their religious beliefs to socioeconomic change, to new moral challenges, to novel problems of knowledge, to the tightening standards of science, the defenders of God slowly strangled Him. If anyone is to be arraigned for deicide, it is not Charles Darwin but his adversary Bishop Samuel Wilberforce, not the godless Robert Ingersoll but the godly Beecher family.[10]

What the theologians and preachers muted or jettisoned altogether tended to be those aspects most closely associated with the terrifying masks and the naked abstractions—the transcendence, incomprehensibility, and hiddenness of God. This occurred in three dimensions. First, God the Ruler of nature was abstracted into naturalistic scientific explanations. Second, God the moral Governor was identified with purely human activities and aspirations. Third, and most importantly for our purposes here, God—the mysterious Lord of Heaven Who struck human beings with awe and humility—was much diminished, as believers shifted the main focus of their concern from God's transcendence of earthly things to His compatibility with humanity, its wants, its aspirations, its ways of understanding. What remained of awe before divine

---

9. James Turner, *Without God, Without Creed: The Origins of Unbelief in America* (Baltimore: The John Hopkins University Press, 1985).
10. Turner, *Without God, Without Creed*, xiii.

mystery was transformed into reverence for such surrogates as nature, art, and humanity itself.[11]

The "fatal slip" of many religious leaders, in Turner's view, was that they forgot "that their God was—as any God had to be to command belief over the long term—radically other than man."[12] It is to be expected that Turner's analysis would fit in cultures other than the United States'. It is, after all, a very old game. As St. Augustine remarked long ago of Cicero's attempt to enhance human freedom by rejecting divine providence, "Seeking to make men free he succeeded only in making them sacrilegious."[13] Or as Luther put it when Erasmus attempted the same thing, "The gouty foot laughs at your doctoring!"[14] The "God-pain" is like the gout. The more theological doctoring is attempted, the worse it gets.

THE CLASSIC DISTINCTION

The only solution to the problem of the abstract, naked, absconding God is the proclamation: God preached. The failure in systematic theology to attend to the fundamental distinction between God not preached and God preached has been disastrous. This distinction comes from Luther, though perhaps not even he exploited its full significance. Luther's distinctions in the doctrine of God are well known. God clothed in the flesh is set against the naked God (*deus indutus* versus *deus nudus*) and the revealed God against the hidden God (*deus revelatus* versus *deus absconditus*). The distinctions were made with such gusto and confidence because he knew that no one—no earthly theologian certainly—was going to dislodge, spy out, or unmask the naked, hidden God. The naked, hidden God needs no theological proof, apology, or defense. The problem, Luther saw clearly, was neither how to find God nor even to prove God's existence, but how to get God off our backs. Yet only God could do that. The distinctions are not theoretical but descriptive. They are accurate descriptions of the way things are. Only God can deal with God.

Thus there is a battle. It is God against God. The abstract God cannot be removed but must be dethroned, overcome, "for you" in concrete actuality. The clothed God must conquer the naked God for us. We can never escape on our own. The revealed God must conquer the hidden God *for you* in the living present. Faith is precisely the ever-renewed

---

11. Turner, *Without God, Without Creed*, 265.
12. Turner, *Without God, Without Creed*, 267.
13. St. Augustine, *City of God*, trans. Marcus Dods (New York: Random House, 1950), 153.
14. Martin Luther, *The Bondage of the Will*, LW 33:53.

flight from God to God: from God naked and hidden to God clothed and revealed. Thus Luther insisted that we must cling to the God at his mother's breasts, the God who hung on the cross and was raised from the tomb in the face of the desperate attack launched from the side of the hidden God/Satan. There just is no other way. The question at stake is whether one will believe God in face of God.[15]

All of that is common knowledge. Less well known, however, is that there was a third pair of concepts in Luther's "dialectic of God" which set the preached God over against God not preached. This third pair is at once the most neglected by systematic theology and the most critical, for it determines the way one does theology. Systematic theology can cope with distinctions between the naked and clothed God or between God hidden and revealed. These distinctions can be reduced, supposedly, to reasonably approximate "abstractions," permitting systematics to straddle the dialectic in some fashion, even though it complains a bit and puzzles about what is hidden and what is revealed in our "knowledge" of God. Indeed, howls of dismay are often heard when a theology is questioned for removing the "masks" that are its particular targets. So the protest often runs, "How can Luther know so much about the hidden God?" The question betrays a common theological myopia resulting from failure to see that the naked God, the hidden God, can and is to be left alone only when one has heard and knows the place of the proclamation. From the point of view of the proclamation alone one can "let God be God." Not only is it impossible to dislodge this God, but also, the proclamation itself gains warrant and authority only if we let God be God.

But if the hidden/revealed dialectic is puzzling, what is systematic theology to make of God not preached versus God preached? Where does systematic theology place itself? It would be unseemly for it to place itself on the side of God not preached, for then it would open itself to the suspicion of being an abstraction with little to say. Yet if it were to place itself on the side of God preached it would seem to reduce itself to homiletics. The distinction is difficult for systematics because it calls for a different understanding of the function of theological discourse. Indeed, it calls for two different types of discourse—that which preaches God versus that which does not and neither pretends nor aspires to do so but sees its purpose as serving and fostering the preaching. Systematic theology does not seem to like such distinctions—perhaps because it is unwittingly accustomed to putting itself in the place of preaching.

---

15. The reader will notice that we are perilously close to preaching here. But that is perhaps just an illustration of my point. Systematic theology drives to proclamation, leaving one in the position in which that has to be the next move because every other road is cut off!

THE SOURCE OF THE OFFENSE

A principal reason why the distinction has been ignored and neglected, however, is the perplexing and even offensive context in which it finds its classic statement: Luther's disagreement with Erasmus over the bondage of the will. The discussion in which it appears turns on some biblical passages that Erasmus believed allowed him to infer freedom of choice. The specific passage in question is Ezek 18:23: "I desire not the death of the sinner, but rather that he should be converted and live."[16] Erasmus argued that if God does not desire the death of the sinner, such death can only be due to the wrong exercise of free will. In other words, since God does not desire it, human free will must be the reason for it. If, Luther was right in saying that all things happen by divine necessity, Erasmus reasoned, then God would be the ultimate cause of the sinner's death, and the claim of the passage that God "desired not the death of the sinner" would be absurd.

Luther, however, claimed that Erasmus's inference of free choice made a horrible confusion of law and gospel.[17] It turns a sweet proclamation of the gospel promise into a terrible statement of law: "If you want to escape death, you had better exercise your free will, stop sinning, and convert!" One may as well exhort the alleged free will to stop our dying! The inference of free choice always has the effect of turning gospel into law, turning the proclamation into a project to be accomplished rather than a promise freely given. Moreover, if the inference is true at all, it proves too much even for Erasmus. It proves only that Pelagius was right: the will is free enough even to avoid sin and death and thus to dispense with the Spirit and grace altogether. As one would suspect, the consequences of such a move for systematic theology are serious as well. If the Word "I desire not the death of the sinner" is taken as a statement about God in the abstract, a general or universal truth about God not preached, both the need for proclamation and the very god-ness of God are undercut. If it is generally and universally true that God does not desire the death of sinners, then proclamation is not needed, for surely the desire of God will be realized. The difficulty, however, is that reality undercuts confidence in such generalities, for in fact, sinners are dying like flies! Either they are dying without God's knowledge, or God is unable to do anything about it. In either case, the very god-ness of God is sacrificed. We

---

16. LW 33:136. Erasmus quoted Ezek 18:23, 24, 27. Luther summed it up with Ezek 33:11, as then translated: "I desire not the death of the sinner."
17. LW 33:137.

are left with a God who "desires not the death of the sinner" but either is ignorant of or cannot—or will not—do anything about it.

The point of Luther's argument is that proclamation cannot be confused with or turned into abstract, general statements about God. Luther insists that the "I desire not the death of the sinner . . ." is the sweet voice of the gospel, that it is true of the preached God, but is not to be construed as a general truth any more than, for instance, "I forgive you all your sins." Luther saw that the Ezekiel passage was in fact not a general statement about God in the abstract but part of God's instruction to the prophet on what he should preach to the house of Israel. One should no more make a general statement out of that than out of a prophecy of doom and destruction. Theology needs to recognize the difference between God not preached and God preached, between our general, abstract statements about God and the proclaimed Word of God to us. Theology that attempts to make God "nice" ends only with a polite, societal deity whose "goodness" is at once ineffectual, patronizing, oppressive, and ultimately terrifying.

A viable doctrine of God requires the distinction between God not preached and God preached. The classic statement of the position comes at that point in the argument between Erasmus and Luther where the question arises as to why, if there is no freedom of choice, some believe and others do not. The proclamation of the gospel comes effectively to those who have been brought to despair over sin through the law. Why then are some touched by the law and others not? Here, Luther insists, our theologizing has reached its limit. The ultimate answer to the "why" lies in that hidden and awful will of God whereby he ordains by his own counsel which and what sort of persons he wills to be recipients and partakers of his preached and offered mercy. This will is not to be inquired into but reverently adored, as by far the most awe-inspiring secret of the Divine Majesty, reserved for himself and alone and forbidden to us.[18]

This is a crucial moment for systematic theology because a limit has been reached. Theologies can be characterized by whether they observe this limit or not. The limit means that discourse about God breaks into two different sorts. The distinction between God preached and not preached is added to the dialectic of God and explicitly heads the list.

We have to argue in one way about God or the will of God as preached, revealed, offered, and worshiped, and in another way about God as he is not preached, not revealed, not offered, not worshiped. To the extent, therefore, that God hides himself and wills to be unknown

---

18. LW 33:139.

to us, it is no business of ours. For here the saying truly applies, "Things above us are no business of ours."[19]

We can, indeed we must, talk about God in two different ways. In the one we have to do with God preached, revealed, offered to us, and worshiped by us, while in the other we have to do with God not preached, not revealed, not offered, not worshiped. Care must be taken that we speak properly in these two different ways. But just here we come to the critical point. For it is precisely Luther's talk about the preached and not-preached God and especially the way the two kinds of talk are related that have provoked vehement protest. Here just about everybody, including most Lutherans,[20] abandon ship. Let us look carefully at the source of the offense in the passages immediately following the quote above. And lest anyone should think this a distinction of my own, I am following Paul, who writes to the Thessalonians concerning the Antichrist that he will exalt himself above every God that is preached and worshiped (2 Thess 2:4). This plainly shows that someone can be exalted above God as he is preached and worshiped, that is, above the word and rite through which God is known to us and has dealings with us; but above God as he is not worshiped and not preached, but as he is in his own nature and majesty, nothing can be exalted, but all things are under his mighty hand.

The God who is to be preached is the God who comes in lowliness and humility. It is possible for human and satanic perfidy to vaunt itself above the preached God, as exemplified by the antichrist. God not preached, revealed, offered, or worshiped, however—"God as He is in His own nature and majesty"—poses a particular kind of limit for us and consequently for proper theological discourse. If one is to speak properly about this not-preached God, one must recognize that such a God simply is the limit. In other words, we do not have to do with a limit that theology may or may not choose to impose on itself, but one about which it can, finally, do nothing. "Above God as he is not worshiped and not preached . . . nothing can be exalted." Luther means that we simply can do nothing about the not-preached God. Such a God just remains God "in his own nature and majesty." God not preached is the God we can never get off our backs, the God who always comes back to haunt us when we think we have at last managed to escape by theological artifice, the God we invoke in curses even when we do not believe, the God about whose existence or nonexistence we argue in vain, the God whom we absolve from evil in our theodicies but in whose face we must shake

---

19. LW 33:170.
20. See the study by Klaus Schwarzwäller, "*Sibboleth*," in *Theologische Existenz Heute* 153, ed. K. G. Steck and G. Eichholz (München: Kaiser Verlag, 1969).

our fist anyway, even the God to whom Jesus cried, "Why have you forsaken me?" and received no answer.

But how then are we to regard the not-preached God? How then is God not preached to be related to God preached? This is the most critical point in the discussion.

> God must therefore be left to himself in his own majesty, for in this regard we have nothing to do with him, nor has he willed that we should have anything to do with him. But we have something to do with him insofar as he is clothed and set forth in his Word, through which he offers himself to us and which is the beauty and glory with which the psalmist celebrates him as being clothed. In this regard we say, the good God does not deplore the death of his people which he works in them, but he deplores the death which he finds in his people and desires to remove from them. For it is this that God as he is preached is concerned with, namely that sin and death should be taken away and we should be saved. For "he sent his word and healed them" [Ps 107:20]. But God hidden in his majesty neither deplores nor takes away death, but works life, death and all in all. For there he has not bound himself by his word, but has kept himself free over all things.[21]

What are we to do about God not preached? Nothing. We are to leave the not-preached God alone and pay attention to the God clothed and displayed in the Word. But how can we do that? Only, of course, to the degree that we are grasped by the preached God. In Luther's terms we cannot—will not—do it by ourselves, not apart from the proclamation. To put it bluntly, everyone theologizes here as they must. A veritable battle is being fought over us between God not preached and God preached. God not preached devours sinners without regret, but the preached God battles to snatch us away from sin and death.

All that, though difficult to swallow theologically, is understandable and perhaps acceptable. What puts everyone off, however, is the last sentence: the assertion that God hidden in majesty "has not bound himself by his word, but kept himself free over all things." The usual objection is this: if God not preached (God hidden in majesty) is not bound by God preached (by the Word of promise) but is free over all things, then there is no basis for certainty or confidence that the promise of the preached God will stand. The fearsome specter of a God hidden in majesty who can arbitrarily wipe out the promise has haunted theology ever since.

The driving impulse of this haunted theology has been the persistent attempt to banish the specter of this terrifying absolute God (*deus ipse*) from sight, to try to bind this God not preached to theology's understanding of the revealed Word. But the only result of this attempt has

---

21. LW 33:140.

been to forsake proclamation for an explanation. Ironically, such theology abandons the real weapon it has against the unpreached God. For the point is that not theology, but God preached is the only defense against God not preached.

What prompted Luther to leave the specter of a God who has not "bound himself by his word, but has kept himself free over all things" to haunt us? There are at least three major reasons that should now be obvious. First and foremost, Luther recognized the primacy of the oral, spoken word, that particular type of discourse called proclamation, the living voice of the gospel. The burden of the passage quoted above is his insistence that we must take explicit theological note of this primacy and observe careful distinctions in our speaking between God not preached and God preached. Luther let the absolute God be, precisely to make room for the proclamation. So we have the remarkable circumstance that the argument Luther used to save the proclamation is the very one most systematic theologians since have thought would endanger it. The antithesis could hardly be more clear.

This is the classic illustration of how a theology that understands the place of proclamation will make certain moves and refuse to make others. Luther knew that only the proclamation—only the preached God, the living Word here and now—could save us from the God not preached, the absolute God. A theology that intends to save us by attempting to remove or render the God not preached harmless in the system makes just the wrong move. It fails to recognize the nature of the battle for the human soul. It maintains that it can bind God not preached to the Word and so "save" us. It makes the fatal assumption that it can accomplish more than the living Word. Theology must recognize its limits. It must understand that only the concrete address, the "I absolve you," the "I baptize you," will save us from the threat of the absolute God. Absolution is the only solution to the problem of the absolute!

The second major reason why Luther did not banish the absolute God from his theology is already implied in the first. Such banishment cannot be accomplished by any kind of theological artifice. Luther left the absolute God there in his theology because he knew he could do nothing about it. Nothing can be exalted above the absolute God. It simply is not true that God in general is bound even to an abstraction called the revealed Word. As Luther put it, "God does many things that he does not disclose to us in his word; he also wills many things which he does not disclose himself as willing in his word."[22] What would happen if we were to claim that the absolute God is bound and limited by the Word?

---

22. LW 22:140.

We would revert to the situation in which the preached Word—"I desire not the death of the sinner"—becomes a general statement by which God is bound and limited. But that is not true, nor does it accord God any particular honor. For sin and death continue, and nothing—certainly not theology—alters the reign of the absolute God except ("when and where it pleases God!") when the concrete proclamation interrupts and creates faith. Not even God can do anything about wrath in the abstract. Not even God can somehow unmask God in the abstract. The proclamation of the concrete, incarnate word set against the absolute God so as to create faith is the only way out. Faith means precisely to be grasped by the proclamation in the face of the terror of the absolute God, in the face of tribulation (*Anfechtung*), as Luther put it. Theology, no matter how sweetly done, does not cure tribulation. Theological opinion may provide momentary relief, but rarely does it survive the heat and evil of the day.

The third reason that prompted Luther to leave the specter of the absolute God alone is his knowledge that we as sinners live under the wrath of God. Our efforts—even the best of them—afford no escape. Theology, no matter how cleverly devised, cannot deliver us from the wrath of God. It may twist and turn to remodel God, try by every artifice to fashion less-frightening masks, but in the end such masks only turn on us. We are sinners confronted by masks we cannot see through. We cannot see God. Luther was not merely stating opinions at this point. He was describing as honestly as possible the actual state of things. No doubt only faith can risk such honesty.

Faith itself is endangered when the attempt is made theologically to bind the hidden God to the Word as abstraction. The nature of faith is transformed. Faith strives to become sight, to render the hidden God visible. Faith's object is not the proclaimed God, not the sacramental deed of God "for you" in the living present, but certain alleged truths about God in the past tense. Indeed, the very freedom of faith is consequently lost. Theology becomes a tour de force, an attempt to induce or perhaps even subtly force belief in the God one has conjured up. But faith is a matter of being set free from the God of the past tense. It is not a matter of deferring to the authority of this or that theologian, but a matter of being set free by the proclamation itself, by an actual word from God. Faith comes by hearing and being grasped by the proclamation. God speaks to you. Faith is the Spirit-fired free flight from the hidden to the revealed God.

The fact is that the terror of the absolute God reigns until the proclamation that creates faith announces its end and liberates the believer from it. Theology must learn to speak the truth about this. Theology must know its own limitations and speak honestly about the way things are. It must not tell sweet lies about God. It must assess the true nature of the battle so that it can be joined in proper fashion. Ironically, a theology that sets out to protect the proclamation by tying the absolute God to the revelation only undercuts the proclamation itself and bowdlerizes God. Small wonder that we find ourselves today with only tenuous belief in a platitudinous God and little consciousness of what God wills to say to us. So we talk mostly about ourselves. Where the distinction between God not preached and God preached is not observed, we are gradually reduced to complete silence.

Where systematic theology is informed by the distinction between God not preached and God preached, however, the way is open for a profound and exciting view of the nature and place of the act of proclamation. The deed of proclamation in the living present is the deed of the living God! It is what God has in mind for us. The mighty acts of God are not over, not relegated to the past or to some philosophy or theology of history. The proclamation itself is the mighty act of God in the living present. Everything that God has done in Jesus Christ has been poured into this moment. The incarnation, death, and resurrection of the Son of God in Jesus is the authorization for the proclamation of the will of God in the living present. The preacher needs the "nerve"—the Spirit—to act on that. Systematic theology needs to understand itself so as to drive the preacher to that point. It must be constructed so as to leave its practitioners at a point where they can do no other than proclaim. Where systematic theology overlooks or blurs the distinction between God not preached and God preached, thereby usurping the place of proclamation itself and leaving us with a lecture instead of the promise, all will be lost.

THE ELECTING GOD

If we are to proclaim and not merely explain God, what are we to say? In speaking of God it is important to start with the very first principle: What is to be proclaimed is what God has decided, in fact, to do. The word for what God has decided to do is election. The God of the Scriptures is an electing God. The God of the Scriptures is "the God of Abraham, Isaac, and Jacob," the God who chooses Israel and disposes over its entire history, the God who comes in Jesus to break down the wall of separation between Jew and Gentile so that the election shall know no bounds, the God who sends apostles so that this "mystery hidden for ages in God" may now be revealed to all, even the "principalities and powers in the heavenly places," through the ministry of the church and its proclamation (Eph 3:7ff). The God of the Scriptures is an electing God and, therefore, a God who speaks and enjoins those who hear, believe, and follow to speak the Word of God, to go and do the electing.

This sending forth of preachers to do the electing is the aim of the God of the Scriptures (the proclaimed God) as distinguished from all the gods of idealisms (the explained God). The explained God is the God not preached who does everything in general, and so in the end does nothing in particular, no matter how much one may talk about the "mighty acts of God in history." These "mighty acts" are all turned into the past tense, and thus treated as mere occasions for further explanation. The history finally becomes material from which one distills one more explanation, as the philosophers of old did from the myths. Whether the material comes from biblical history or from the myths makes little difference if all that comes of it is one more explanation. That is why arguments between revelation in history and in nature soon become sterile. The explained God always turns out to be one of the gods of idealism, the alleged goal and rewarder of the idealist project, as Regin Prenter points out.[23] The explained God is not the God who seeks the lost, but the God whom the lost (even if with the aid of grace) must seek and attempt to appease, the just rewarder of pious effort, the God of law who always turns against us.

PREDESTINATION, A TEST CASE

The electing God of the Scriptures is the God of predestination. Such an assertion, however, puts systematic theology once again at a crossroad, facing the question of the next move. Election or predestination is a crucial test case because it is such a persistent, intractable, and offensive problem for us. The usual move is predictable: attempt to remove the threat or domesticate the offense by systematic adjustment, to pretty up the mask, so to speak, with theological cosmetics. The most direct and honest move is to obscure predestination altogether. The scriptural evidence is ignored, explained away, or treated perhaps as a species of ancient mythology to be demythologized in some fashion. The most subtle move is to fabricate some kind of synthesis between divine election and the idealist project. God obligingly elects those who in one way or another fulfill the necessary conditions. One then only needs to negotiate minimal or maximal conditions.

---

23. Regin Prenter, *Spiritus Creator*, trans. John M. Jensen (Philadelphia: Muhlenberg, 1953), 19ff.

Such moves are, of course, quite natural. Election—predestination—as a general or abstract idea is threatening to us. Even if it is a "revealed" truth, it remains an idea and as such carries no comfort. Once again we encounter at the outset one more frightening mask of God. We know the "that" of it, but we do not know the "why" or the "who." Added to the list of magnificent abstractions, it becomes the last straw. The idea that the almighty, timeless, immutable, impassible, infinite, immortal, omni-everything God also elects can only be taken to mean that such a God has decided things in eternity once and for all, and there is absolutely nothing further to be said or done about it.

Such a God is the end of us, the absolute end of all our idealistic hopes and aspirations. Kant, the father of modern idealism, saw the matter with chilling clarity in his attempt to construct a *Religion Within The Limits of Reason Alone*. Speaking of the possibility of faith in a God who is no longer within the limits of reason alone, but who actually invades time and history to create faith, Kant says,

> Yet were this faith to be portrayed as having so peculiar a power and so mystical (or magical) an influence that although merely historical, so far as we can see, it is yet competent to better the whole man from the ground up (to make a new man of him) if he yields himself to it and to the feelings bound up with it, such a faith would have to be regarded as imparted and inspired directly by heaven (together with, and in, the historical faith), and everything connected even with the moral constitution of man would resolve itself into an unconditional decree of God: "He hath mercy on whom he will, and whom he will be hardeneth," . . . which, taken according to the letter, is the *salto mortale* [death leap] of human reason.[24]

Kant saw with utmost clarity that the actual intrusion of God into time to create faith meant election and that to admit to it is the "death leap" of human reason, the end of the "old being." Kant, of course, resolutely turned his back on the prospect. In so doing he made the only move humanly possible. For there is nothing we can do but deny, disown, or dismantle such a God. It is a matter of self-defense. This fact describes what is called the bondage or servitude of the will. It is the essence of sin: We are unreconciled to and will not trust such a God. As such it is the presupposition disclosing the need for proclamation. Were there no

---

24. Kant, *Religion within the Limits of Reason Alone*, 111. This is, of course, not all that could be said about Kant's volume; I believe that this passage is a watershed in the history of modern hermeneutics and systematics: from that point in time, all scriptural assertions that smacked of election had to be trimmed to fit the dimensions of "practical reason" and the religion of the autonomous self. Not even biblical fundamentalists or so-called evangelicals seem to have escaped. Theology so construed turns the whole into a matter of our decision rather than God's.

such bondage there would be no need for proclamation. An explanation would do.

A systematic theology that understands the place of proclamation will make a quite different move. It will understand that there is no "abstract" theological cure for the problem of the electing God. It will realize that attempts to remove the electing God are futile. It knows that no amount of persuasion can prevent the idea from returning to haunt us—"What if . . . ?" It knows that anyone who reads the Bible with faithful discernment will soon lose confidence in theological cosmetics.

What is to be done about an electing God? Our only recourse is to make the move to proclamation. We are not, of course, to proclaim that God is an electing God; everybody knows that already and is scared to death by it. Rather, we must do the electing ourselves. One must have the nerve—or better, the Spirit—to do the unheard-of thing and say to those listening "You are the elect!" or "You are the one." "Just as surely as I am here and you are there, this is the moment the almighty, eternal, electing God has planned on, the 'mystery hidden for ages' and now revealed 'through the church,' the actual revelation of the will of the hidden God!" We have to do with that shepherd (Matt 18:12–14; Luke 15:3–7) who left the ninety-nine and went after the one that was lost! The point is that since God is an electing God, the only real solution to the problem of being unreconciled to the God not preached is to do the deed of the preached God: "Once you were lost but now you are found."

TWO FALSE SOLUTIONS

The two most prevalent attempts of idealism to reach a solution must be rejected. The first is universalism: the idea that we can defuse the dynamite of election and predestination by saying that God "elects" everyone. Quite apart from the fact that the Scriptures give us no particular warrant for asserting this, the idea does no real good at all. It substitutes an abstract idea about God for a concrete self-disclosure of the divine will, leaving the hearers under wrath. The error is not in the hope it expresses. It is certainly more legitimate and gracious than a so-called evangelical theology that insists hell must be populated to complete the divine plan. The error of universalism is that it simply cuts off the move to proclamation. As a result, the God who supposedly loves and elects everyone never gets around to saying it to anyone. The opinion of the "universalist" is no better than that of the double predestinationist who likewise subverts the proclamation by the abstract notion that the election of some to heaven and others to hell has been determined before all time.

Ideas of universalism do not save anyone. Even the slightest hint in the Scriptures of the possibility of a different outcome is enough to shatter one's confidence in such ideas.

> The argument about universalism is usually wrongly stated and takes different shape when one thinks in terms of proclamation. The scriptures do indeed contain statements which appear universalist. But like the "I desire not the death of the sinner" discussed above they are misused if taken as abstract general statements or ideas about God. If one interprets scripture in that fashion, one will then have to find some way to cope with other statements as well that seem to indicate different ideas about God—the possibility, for instance, of being cast into the "outer darkness" where there is "weeping and gnashing of teeth." The point is that ideas afford no real comfort when one's ultimate destiny is at stake. Searching for a "general consensus" in scripture or counting passages for or against an idea is no protection for the "conscience." One is not saved by a scriptural consensus. The smallest hint or just one passage is enough to shatter confidence and to raise the specter of being lost.[25]

Once again, the move must be made to the proclamation. The element of truth in the universalist position is that the gospel demands to be proclaimed universally, that it knows no bounds, imposes no conditions. The preached God comes to do battle against sin and death precisely through such limitless proclamation. The preacher is authorized to say it—to do the election—to everyone within earshot.

The second attempt to defuse the dynamite is to fall back on some version of human responsibility or "free will" as an explanation for the gospel's success or lack thereof among us. Election is discounted since we are the ones who make the ultimate decisions. The reason why some are "saved" and others not rests in our hands. At first this seems to remove the threatening mask from the face of God, but in the end it only makes matters worse. "See to it yourselves then!" would be the divine message to us. The result, once again, is the loss of the proclamation. Instead of the Word that does the deed here and now, the hearer gets explanations about how "nice" this God is who does not elect anyone. A "systematic theology" that thinks itself able to persuade supposedly free beings gets substituted for the proclamation. Exhortations abound—all prettied up in high-sounding phrases like having Jesus as "your personal Savior," or "letting Jesus into your heart"—to choose this abstraction.

A systematic theology that understands the nature and place of proclamation consequently will not waste its time trying to avoid or explain the election away. Instead it will endeavor to get preachers to go and do

---

25. LW 33:161.

it. It will recognize precisely that systematic theology has to make room for the proclamation, foster it, drive to it, leave its practitioners with no other recourse but to do it.

THE PLACE OF THE PREACHER

A systematic theology so constructed will understand that to be of any use the proclamation must be able authoritatively to answer the crucial question about what God has decided to do here and now, that is, about election or predestination. The crucial question is not the whether or why of it, but the who. The preacher must claim the audacious and unheard-of authority to say who is intended, to actually speak for God. The answer, to anticipate, is always you: "You, now that you are here within earshot." This is the place of the preacher. There is only one question about predestination we can answer with any authority, and it is the only one that matters: Who?

The preacher acts on the presupposition that only the present-tense, here-and-now deed of God, the proclamation itself, can be the solution to the problem of God. The proclamation is the end result, the culmination, of the great acts of God in history. The preacher ought to have the consciousness of standing in that place knowing that the Word and sacrament are themselves the end (*telos*), the purpose of it all. The concrete moment of the proclamation is the doing of the mighty act of God in the living present. It is not a recital of past acts, but the doing of the act itself now. Only when there is an authoritative Word from God in the present tense do we escape the threat of the hidden God. Only then can a faith be created to stand in the face of that threat. As Paul wrote, "Faith comes from what is heard, and what is heard comes by the preaching of Christ" (Rom 10:17), "for . . . it pleased God through the folly of what we preach to save those who believe" (1 Cor 1:21).

LET GOD BE GOD

Now we can see what is to be gained by leaving the absolute God alone, by not attempting systematically to tear the mask from the face of the hidden God. Precisely because one allows God to be God, by whose will and appointment all things happen, one is able to declare that the concrete moment of the proclamation (the absolution, the sermon, the baptism, the supper; all given *for you*) is the divine act of God in the living present. Of course, that "for you" cannot be spoken except in the proclamation. We are left in the position where we can only move to the proclamation because it is a matter of the present tense, here and now. The moment of proclamation is the revealed will of God "for you." When you are there, when you are within earshot, you are the target. The almighty, immutable, God breaks through the hiddenness to speak the concrete word of election to you.

Faith comes by hearing! One must be still and listen (cf. Ps 46:10). Faith alone hears and trusts that the unchangeable God of election stands behind the proclamation. That is the mystery hidden in God, now revealed in the church. Where the electing God, the hidden God, the absolute God has already been dismantled, we are not dealing with the Word "of" God, but only our words and opinions "about" God. There everything collapses into uncertainty. Perhaps it was just by social custom or parental whim that we were hauled before the congregation and doused with water, or only an accident that we happened to hear the gospel word. We cannot be certain we were intended to hear it. Where one allows God to be God—whatever that may cost or entail in subsequent theological consequences—the moment of proclamation is the doing of what God has in mind for us. God makes no mistakes. Were this not the case, all would be lost in the arbitrariness of opinion and the black hole of the self.

A systematic theology operating under such auspices will take a different shape from what usually trades under that name, though it needs to cover much the same ground. Since the question is not whether but who God elects, a different set of questions becomes central. Who has the authority to say so? Where does such authority come from and how is it granted? Who are the hearers of the proclamation? How can one announce with such confidence, "You are the elect"? What does one presuppose about such hearers and what shape must the proclamation consequently take? What is the expected and hoped-for outcome of the proclamation? Such questions abound. Systematic theology has to deal more intentionally with questions about the presuppositions for and the authority of the present-tense proclamation.

Heidelberg Disputation, Theses 19–21

THESIS 19. That person does not deserve to be called a theologian who looks upon the invisible things of God as though they were clearly perceptible in those things that have actually happened (or have been made, created).[1]

How is the great divide to be described? Luther begins by asserting that there is a fundamental presumption about "sight" involved—so fundamental indeed that those who so presume do not really deserve to be called theologians. We might call them philosophers or moralists or metaphysicians or even ethicists, perhaps, but hardly theologians. Actually, of course, Luther does concede the title (thesis 21) but qualifies it by calling them "theologians of glory" in contrast to "theologians of the cross." This is the shorthand way of designating the great divide.

How do theologians of glory operate differently from theologians of the cross? That is the issue for this section of the Disputation. Theologians of glory operate on the assumption that creation and history are transparent to the human intellect, that one can *see through* what is made and what happens so as to peer into the "invisible things of God." There is a kind of oxymoron in the thesis in speaking of "seeing the invisible," but it is intended, no doubt, to indicate the presumption involved. How do we see the invisible? Obviously we can't, directly. However, theologians of glory work, as one would say today, by analogy. The assumption is that the visible creation yields clues, if not directly at least

---

1. There is an ongoing debate about the translation of the final clause of this thesis, *ea, quae facta sunt*, literally, "those things that have been made." Does "have been made" here refer to creation? If so, then the knowledge of God that Luther intended would be that gained by analogy from creation. But elsewhere in the Disputation the argument centers more on the attempt to mount up to God via human works, as in thesis 22. The translation of LW is ambiguous, no doubt intentionally, so I have added a parenthetical clause. I have tried in my comments to encompass both possibilities by suggesting that the "knowledge" the theologian of glory arrives at can be understood as both divine perfections and therefore also goals for human "works."

by analogy, to what is invisible in God, to the nature and logic of God. We can, that is, figure out something of what God is like by looking at the world he has made and how it works. The "invisible things of God" we can supposedly "see" by this mode of operation are, in Luther's mind, such things as "virtue, godliness, wisdom, justice, goodness, and so forth."[2] They seem to be a collection of those things humans are to strive for and that find their perfection in God, essences and qualities, both divine perfections and therefore also human goals. The claim to be able to "see" in that sense would lead to the assumption that we could set up a way to God. There would be, so to speak, a glory road, which should eventually lead to God.

But why should one who operates in that fashion not deserve to be called a theologian? Is this not the business of theology, to figure out the logic of God and his action in the world? This is precisely where the great divide becomes apparent. One who proposes to "see through" creation and divine action actually ends by dissolving the power of the cross in a sea of abstract universals and consequently undercutting the present actuality of the word of the cross. Our "theologians," that is, undermine the very proclamation they are supposed to foster and so forfeit their right to the title. Perhaps an example will help to make this audacious claim more clear. Theologians from time immemorial down to the present have worried about divine attributes like timelessness and immutability, attributes of divine majesty. They seem to cancel out the freedom and responsibility of the creature, especially when questions about election and predestination are raised. If God immutably elects "before all time," how can there be freedom? So what do theologians do? They go to work with philosophical presuppositions to solve, remove, or in some way explain away the problem of objectionable attributes.[3] They think, that is, that they are able to see into the invisible things of God through the things that are made.

But what is accomplished thereby? First, it can be observed that it never seems to work. The attributes of divine majesty keep coming back like a song. The attempt to do something about them has to be redone, it

---

2. LW 31:52.

3. This has been attempted in ways too numerous to mention here. It has long been the favorite parlor game of philosophers and theologians. Generally speaking, among theologians who wish to preserve at least the facade of Christianity, it appears to happen in one of two ways: either Jesus and his cross are taken into the divine, that is, they assume the character of "timeless truth" of a philosophical sort available to our choices; or, more recently, the divine is collapsed into time in the event of Jesus and the cross. "Timelessness" and "immutability'" and such "masks" of God (as Luther would have called them) are supposedly removed. Of course, the question remains to haunt us: Do they really go away at the fancy of the philosopher/theologian? Can theology actually pull the mask from the face of the hidden God?

seems, by every new generation. We never seem quite convinced by the theology. Theologians, you might say, are like Sisyphus, condemned in Hades to rolling a huge stone up the hill, only to have it constantly roll back down. Incidentally, it is interesting to note that Sisyphus was condemned in that manner because he had discovered some of the secrets of Zeus! Second, even if such attempts were to succeed, theology would only make God ludicrous. For what is God without the attributes of divine majesty? No doubt that is why we sense something is amiss, and the stone keeps rolling back down to crush us.

Third, and most importantly all that such theology accomplishes in the end is to pull the rug out from under the proclamation. This is the ultimate reason why those who operate in this manner do not deserve the title "theologian." What they do is, of course, easily enough done. But the radical nature of works like the Heidelberg Disputation is to expose the fact that it is not a neutral or harmless enterprise. Those who indulge in it never seem to understand that there is no abstract theological solution to the problem of the divine majesty. The only solution is the cross itself and the subsequent proclamation of the word of the cross as a divine deed, the work of the Spirit, in the living present. That is to say, as fallen creatures and not creators we will *always* be threatened by God, who is hidden by the masks of divine majesty. Like conscience they will never go away and stay away. They are always there, always ready to attack. They don't submit to manipulation. The only refuge is the word of the cross in the here and now. Through the *preaching* of the cross in the living present, not through theological explanations, we are defended from the terror of the divine majesty. Precisely against the threat of supposed divine timelessness and immutability we are claimed in the concrete word of the cross in the living present; through baptism and Supper we are washed and fed. We feel and taste the truth in the here and now. To believe means precisely to be claimed by the cross and its word, to cling to that and find one's assurance there. The "solution" to the problem of God, that is, is not in the classroom but in church. When theologians do not grasp that, or when they forget it, they no longer deserve the title. In spite of grand and high-sounding theologies, they will likely just undercut the church's task. There is a great divide here. To be grasped by that fact is to be on the way to becoming a theologian of the cross.

On the other side of the divide, however, is the temptation always to operate on the assumption that we can see through the divine masks to the divine majesty. That is, of course, the presupposition necessary to the claim that we can prepare for grace by doing our best with our natural powers. For the most part we will, no doubt, be modest enough to admit that we cannot go the whole way on the glory road without the help of grace. But then Christ gets called into the scheme to make it work. Christ and the cross are taken up into abstract doctrines. The result is that the cross too is looked upon as though it were transparent. Theologians of glory will claim not only to be able to see through creation but also to *see through* the cross to figure out the final "Why." Why did Jesus have to die? Apparently to pay for our failures and mistakes in the pursuit of "virtue, godliness, wisdom, justice, goodness, and so forth." Thus, the cross is not really just what is visible. It becomes a launching pad for speculative flights into intellectual space, into the invisible things of God. It is not simply that a man sent from God is suffering, forsaken, and dying at our hands—as if that were not enough!—but he is a payment to God (whose justice one has supposedly peered into and figured out) in some celestial court transaction.

Theologians of glory are thus always driven to seek transcendent meaning, to try to see into the invisible things of God, to get a line on the logic of God. They look at the cross and ask, "What is it all about?" They wonder what is "behind" it all. There is a reason for this, of course. If we can *see through* the cross to what is supposed to be behind it, we don't have to *look at* it! It is, finally, a matter of self-defense. He was "as one from whom men hide their faces" (Isa 53:3). If the cross can be neatly folded into the scheme of the self's glory road, it will do no harm.

Luther apparently does not think it necessary at this point to spend much time refuting this position. The proof he offers for this thesis is among the shortest of the Disputation. Perhaps he assumes that by now the presumption inherent in the position ought to be obvious. At any rate, he contents himself simply with pointing to Rom 1:22, where St. Paul speaks of those who claim to be wise but are nevertheless fools. The context of the Romans passage should perhaps be filled out a bit. The fools are they who knew God but "did not honor him *as God* or give thanks to him but became futile *in their thinking* and their senseless minds were darkened. Claiming to be wise they became fools" (Rom 1:21–22, emphasis added).

How shall fools be made wise? The problem is that at the deepest level we have here not just a set of teachings, theological opinion, or that which we might take or leave at will and which might be corrected by better information, but *temptation*. As we have already indicated, it is a matter finally of self-defense. Thus the proof concludes with just a brief parting shot about the uselessness of this method of operation in making one either worthy or wise. Peering into the "invisible things of God" only "puffs up, blinds, and hardens" (cf. thesis 22). Luther's indication of what such invisible things might be has already been given: virtue, godliness, wisdom, justice, goodness, and so forth. Knowledge of divine essences and qualities, Luther asserts, does not make wise men out of fools. Indeed, it is more likely to make fools out of the wise! Essences and qualities are abstractions; they are what is left when all the action, particularly the suffering and the dying, has been stripped away. There is a fundamental misdirection in seeing. Our theologians must be taught where to look and what to see. That leads to thesis 20.

> **THESIS 20.** That person deserves to be called a theologian, however, who comprehends the visible and manifest things of God through suffering and the cross.

Theologians of the cross see things differently. They can't get around the cross. They can't see through the cross to what is "behind" it. They can't escape the realization that virtue, godliness, wisdom, justice, goodness, and so forth are exactly what put Jesus on the cross. The cross is not transparent but more like a mirror. Our line of sight is bent back upon itself, upon ourselves and our world. We "see," so to speak, in the reflected light of the cross. Instead of trying to see through the world and the cross to the invisible things of God, we are turned back to what is "visible and manifest" of God here among us, and we "comprehend" it through suffering and the cross.[4] Suffering and the cross become the key to the comprehension of one who deserves the title of theologian.

What is meant here by the 'visible and manifest things of God"? The Latin original furnishes a hint as to what Luther had in mind. The word here translated as "manifest" is *posteriora*. It means "back" or "hinder parts." This indicates that the discussion is intended to call to mind the event in Exod 33:18-23 in which Moses asks to see God's glory—even Moses has the aspirations of a theologian of glory! God tells Moses that no one can see God's face and live. Consequently, Moses is to hide in a cleft in the rock when God approaches. God covers Moses' eyes and allows him to see only his back, the *posteriora*, as he passes by. God, that is, actually prevents Moses from seeing his glory. To be sure, that is on the one hand a gracious act since no one can look on God's face and live. But for a theologian of glory it is on the other hand a supreme put-

---

4. The Latin original of theses 19 and 20 has a chiasm that neatly expresses the difference in what our theologians look at and what they see. The chiasm is difficult to translate into English. The "seeing" of thesis 19 is *intellecta conspicit,* whereas that of thesis 20 is *conspecta intelligit.* Perhaps one could say that the theologian of glory of thesis 19 contemplates the invisible intellectually, whereas the theologian of the cross of thesis 20 comprehends the visible contemplatively (through suffering and the cross).

down. God won't let even Moses see, what every theologian of glory so desperately wants to see. God allows Moses to see only his back when he has passed by. In Luther's mind here it is the suffering, despised, and crucified Jesus that takes the place of God's backside. No doubt Luther uses this somewhat offensive image precisely to shock the theologian of glory in us. This comes out in his proof for this thesis:

> The manifest and visible things of God are placed in opposition to the invisible, namely, his human nature, weakness, foolishness. The Apostle in 1 Cor 1[:25] calls them the weakness and folly of God. Because men misused the knowledge of God through works, God wished again to be recognized in suffering, and to condemn wisdom concerning invisible things by means of the wisdom concerning visible things, so that those who did not honor God as manifested in his works should honor him as he is hidden in his suffering.[5]

God refuses to be seen in any other way, both for our protection and to put down the theologian of glory in us. Theologians of the cross are therefore those whose eyes have been turned away from the quest for glory by the cross, who have eyes only for what is visible, what is actually there to be seen of God, the suffering and despised crucified Jesus. It was the pagan Pilate who said it: *Ecce Homo!* Behold the man! Faulty eyesight is to be corrected by the cross.

Correcting the sight of the theologian of glory is a drastic business. In his proof Luther uses language taken from St. Paul (quoting Isaiah) in 1 Cor 1:19, "I will destroy the wisdom of the wise." The cross therefore is actually intended to destroy the sight of the theologian of glory. In the cross God actively hides himself. God simply refuses to be known in any other way.

> As the Apostle says in 1 Cor 1[:21], "For since, in the wisdom of God, the world did not know God through wisdom, it pleased God through the folly of what we preach to save those who believe." Now it is not sufficient for anyone, and it does him no good to recognize God in his glory and majesty, unless he recognizes him in the humility and shame of the cross. Thus God destroys the wisdom of the wise, as Isa [45:15] says, "Truly thou are a God who hidest thyself."[6]

The cross cannot be considered therefore as one option among several in our attempts to see God. The cross shuts down alternatives. It destroys the wisdom of the wise. It blinds the sight of the theologian of glory.

5. LW 31:52.
6. LW 31:52–53.

What is revealed is precisely that we don't know God. Our problem is not that we lay claim to such little knowledge of God but that we think we know so much. So God hides from us. As with Moses, he puts his hand over our eyes. God refuses to be known according to the schemes of a theology of glory. What is vital here is absolute concentration on the rejected, crucified Jesus.

> So also in John 14[:8], where Philip spoke according to the theology of glory: "Show us the Father." Christ forthwith set aside his flighty thought about seeing God elsewhere and let to himself, saying, "Philip, he who has seen me has seen the Father" [John 14:9]. *For this reason true theology and recognition of God are in the crucified Christ, as it is also stated in John 10 [John 14:6]: "No one comes to the Father, but by me." "I am the door" [John 10:9], and so forth.*[7]

Theologians of the cross are those from whom all support other than the cross has simply been torn away. The situation is not that we might sit back and upon reflection calmly choose to be this or that sort of theologian. If we look at it instead of through it or behind it, the cross tears away all other possibilities. So as theologians of the cross we operate on the premise that faith in the crucified and risen one is all we have going for us. All the supports of the theology of glory are destroyed by the cross. The cross is the end result of the theology of glory. So it is finished. There are no escape hatches. By faith we become a human being, a person of this world, a truly historical being, because there is nothing to do now but wait, hope, pray, and trust in the promise of him who nevertheless conquers, the crucified and risen Jesus. By faith we are simply in Christ, waiting to see what will happen to and in us. As Luther could put it in his most famous saying in the commentary on the first twenty-two Psalms from about this time, "The cross alone is our theology" (*CRUX sola est nostra Theologia*).[8] More must be said about this, but for now we turn to our next thesis.

> **THESIS 21.** A theology of glory calls evil good and good evil. A theology of the cross calls the thing what it actually is.

This is the way the thesis reads in the earlier printings of the American edition of *Luther's Works*. I use the translation purposely here as a kind of object lesson. The Latin original speaks not of a *theology* of glory or of the cross, but, as we have been insisting all along, of a *theologian*.

---

7. LW 31:53.
8. WA 5:176.32.

Later printings have, fortunately, made this correction. But the mistake illustrates a persistent tendency. Our temptation is always to change the subject. In this case the blame is switched from us to theology. The assumption is that we can more or less easily escape the error described by just disavowing the theology. "Call evil good and good evil? Who? Me? No way! I don't hold with the theology of glory!" So the matter is settled—supposedly. Yet we have seen all along in the preceding theses and their proofs how we actually do get drawn into calling evil good and good evil. The theologian is the culprit here, not the theology as such. The theologian is always the acting subject, indeed, the ultimate reason why the theology comes out as it does. The point here is that the theologian of glory is *impelled* to act in a certain way. We can even say that over against the cross all theologize as they *must*. This is the outcome of the great divide. Faulty seeing leads inexorably to false speaking. The cross, as Luther could put it, finds us out (*Crux probat omnia*).[9]

The theologian of glory calls evil good and good evil. A theologian of the cross calls a thing what it is. The great divide in seeing leads to a completely different way of speaking. It leads to plain and honest talk about what we do and what happens to us. The theologian of glory has all the value signs exactly reversed. How can we grasp this? Previously we have seen how the value signs are reversed with reference to works that we do. Here, however, a deeper dimension opens before us, one of the most profound and difficult dimensions of what being a theologian of the cross involves: how we speak of and cope with suffering. Before we hurry to comment, we must listen to Luther's words in his proof for this thesis:

> This is clear: He who does not know Christ does not know God hidden in suffering. Therefore he prefers works to suffering, glory to the cross, strength to weakness, wisdom to folly, and, in general, good to evil. These are the people whom the Apostle calls "enemies of the cross of Christ" [Phil. 3:18], for they hate the cross and suffering and love works and the glory of works. Thus they call the good of the cross evil and the evil of a deed good. God can be found only in suffering and the cross, as has already been said. Therefore the friends of the cross say that the cross is good and works are evil, for through the cross works are dethroned and the Old Adam, who is especially edified by works, is crucified. It is impossible for a person not to be puffed by his good works unless he has first been deflated and destroyed by suffering and evil until he knows that he is worthless and that his works are not his but God's.[10]

---

9. WA 5:179.31. Martin Luther, *Luther's Commentary on the First Twenty-two Psalms*, vol. 1, trans. John Nicholas Lenker (Sunbury, PA: Lutherans in All Lands, 1903), 294–95.
10. LW 31:53.

Direct, plain, clear, entirely unsentimental, but for that reason difficult and offensive words. What we have to say about suffering is usually a prime example of the faulty speech of the theologian of glory. Suffering is called evil and works good. The word of the cross, however, *inflicts* the very suffering they talked about. The words are difficult just for the reason Luther says they are. We are inveterate theologians of glory. We are tempted and bound to be so. We invest all our capital in works. There is then a necessary relation between works and the way we regard suffering. We work to *avoid* suffering—mostly for here but sometimes also for the hereafter. Or, if we don't work to avoid suffering, we run from it. We might even work to stave off the fear of death, not to say the suffering of hell. We depend upon and glory in our works, and we call these self-serving deeds good. Suffering, we insist, is bad. If it comes upon us, we immediately begin to wonder if we have failed somehow in our works. Since theologians of glory shy away from the depth of the cross and its forgiveness, there can be no honesty about reality and the way things are. The self that invests in its own works has no recourse but to defend itself to the end.

As a result we look on suffering from the outside. It is painful and generally to be avoided. From this position of Olympian transcendence we may on occasion feel guilty enough to descend into the world of suffering to express our solidarity with the oppressed, the poor, and the afflicted. We will call it "Incarnational Theology" or something of the sort. (Notice how easily one can slip over into calling it a theology! Then one can espouse it without doing much. One can take occasional trips to impoverished or ravaged areas and come home to talk about it.) Jesus is set up as our model. "Misery loves company" is the prime Christological motif. Christ humbled himself and descended into the world of suffering so we ought to too. If, on occasion, this causes a bit of pain or discomfort, we can tally it up on our ledger of good works.

Thus theologians of glory are not above turning even "The Theology of the Cross" to their own advantage. So it can even happen as we see today that "The Theology of the Cross" comes into a certain vogue. It provides additional levers for therapists and ethicists.[11] As a "theology," the theology of the cross turns very easily into a negative theology of glory. Our occasional pain becomes our good work. If we can't make it by escaping suffering, perhaps we can by entering into it. So we hear a good bit of sentimental talk these days about entering into solidarity

---

11. See, for instance, the article by Larry Rasmussen, "Returning to Our Senses: The Theology of the Cross as a Theology for Eco-justice," in *After Nature's Revolt: Eco-justice and Theology*, ed. Dieter T. Hessel (Minneapolis: Fortress, 1992).

with those who suffer, as though it were something we might do on weekends.

Contemporary theologians talk much about the problem of evil. Some think it is the most difficult problem for theology today and one of the most persistent causes of unbelief. One wonders, however, just how much this is itself the result of the faulty speech of the theology of glory. Since suffering is itself classified as evil, it is of course simply lumped together with disaster, crime, misfortune of every sort, abuse, holocaust, and all manner of notorious wrong as one and the same problem. So it is almost universally the case that theologians and philosophers *include* suffering without further qualification among those things they call evil. Of course there are different sides to the question. Evil does cause suffering—but not always. Indeed, the usual complaint is that the evil don't seem to suffer. However, the causes of suffering may not always be evil—perhaps not even most of the time. Love can cause suffering. Beauty can be the occasion for suffering. Children with their demands and impetuous cries can cause suffering. Just the toil and trouble of daily life can cause suffering, and so on. Yet these are surely not to be termed evil. The problem of suffering should not just be rolled up with the problem of evil. Only false speaking lures us into doing that.

Identification of suffering with evil has the further result that God must be absolved from all blame.[12] Thus, the theologian of glory adds to the perfidy of false speech by trying to assure us that God, of course, has nothing to do with suffering and evil. God is "good," the rewarder of all our "good" works, the pot of gold at the end of the rainbow of merit. But is this prettified God the God of the Bible? Is it not quite probable that just these attempts to whitewash God are the cause of unbelief?[13] Meanwhile, suffering goes on unabated. If God has nothing to do with

---

12. It is remarkable that there were so few attempts to construct theodicies prior to the 18th century. Certainly there was no shortage of suffering and disaster. Life was "nasty, brutish, and short." In Luther's own day the black death had decimated the population of Europe and still threatened. Villages and towns lived in constant dread of fire and natural disasters, and so forth. Yet attempts to absolve God were deemed foolish. Is it not curious that only when life seems to be easier do thinkers set out to "justify" God? Is it perhaps that when we think ourselves to have done so well we question God for being so inept? Perhaps it is as Hannah Arendt remarks, "When men could no longer *praise,* they turned their greatest conceptual efforts to *justifying* God and His Creation in theodicies" (Hannah Arendt, *The Life of the Mind,* vol. 2, *Willing* [New York: Harcourt Brace Jovanovich, 1977], 97).

13. James Turner believes that to be the case. See his penetrating work, *Without God, Without Creed: The Origins of Unbelief in America* (Baltimore: Johns Hopkins University Press, 1985). Turner indicates that it was precisely the attempt on the part of theologians and preachers to accommodate God to current modes of thought that led to unbelief, not the fear that God was truly God in majestic awesomeness. God was turned into a patsy not worthy of commanding belief.

suffering, what is he involved with? Whoever does not know God hidden in suffering, Luther asserts in his proof, does not know God at all.

The result of false speech is that attitudes toward suffering today are fraught with ambiguity. On the one hand, suffering is virtually identified with the problem of evil. Some, perhaps mainly feminist theologians today, launch a polemic against the cross claiming that in it Christianity glorifies suffering. A Father-God who demands the suffering of his Son is guilty of "divine child abuse"! Suffering, it is claimed, is never redemptive.[14] On the other hand, from much the same point of view, a negative theology of glory decrees that we ought to enter into solidarity with suffering. If we can't escape it, we can still use it to our advantage. There is even much talk about the suffering of God in this vein: God makes himself "vulnerable" in Jesus, so we ought to too. Misery loves company.

In the face of all this, the claim here is that it is only *through suffering and the cross* that sinners can see and come to know God. So theologians of the cross must be able to speak honestly and forthrightly, to "say what a thing is." This suffering is from God and it is good. That is the deepest reason why we call the Friday of the crucifixion *good*. But now we must be careful. What is meant by suffering here? It seems obvious that Luther does not mean just physical pain. He himself experienced much excruciating pain during his life, but never to my knowledge does he identify that pain with the suffering worked by the cross or use it to make claims for himself as a sufferer. For Luther the sufferings of the spirit, the pangs of conscience, the terrors of temptation (*Anfechtungen*), were always more agonizing and serious than the physical pain he also knew well. Even physical death, though heartrending enough for loved ones, was a far lesser matter than the kind of death experienced when the wrath of God assaults the sinner.

So the suffering Luther has in mind first and foremost is the result of God's operation on the sinner. One can find reference to that throughout his writings.[15] The suffering Luther has in mind is something God

---

14. See Joanne Carlson Brown and Rebecca Parker, "For God so Loved the World?," in *Christianity, Patriarchy and Abuse: A Feminist Critique*, ed. Joanne Carlson Brown and Carole R. Sohn (New York: Pilgrim, 1989), 1–29. The claim that suffering is *never* redemptive is surely somewhat shortsighted. To live, to love, to care, to be concerned about others will mean, certainly, to suffer in one way or another. Even to write controversial articles and have to bear the criticism and even scorn that follow will mean, no doubt, to suffer! And one hopes, I expect, that it will be in some small measure redemptive.

15. The exposition of Psalms 1–22 from roughly this same time (*Operationes in Psalmos, 1519–1521*, WA 5) contains countless instances in which suffering is the result of the divine action in reducing works and merits to naught. The following are some good examples:

"Other virtues may be perfected by doing; *but faith, hope, and love, only by suffering*, by suffering I say, that is, *by being passive under the divine operation*" (WA 5:176.1); "The soul is taken

inflicts on us just by virtue of the fact that he moves against the presumption of our works. He is out to do it all. We suffer this unilateral action of God. We suffer because we don't like it. We don't like to be put out of control. It means that we are rendered totally passive by the divine operation through the cross and resurrection of Jesus. "Passive" has, of course, become something of a bad word in contemporary speech. It is taken to mean lack of assertiveness, lack of motivation, lack of care, extreme lassitude. But we should recall that it comes from the same root as "passion" and means literally the same thing as suffering—as in "the passion of our Lord." Luther used it constantly to describe the proper disposition of the sinner to the grace of God. Precisely because the sinner has taken up an active position (the "active potency" of thesis 14!) in relation to God's activity on the basis of works, God's action over against the sinner can only result in suffering. The sinner is therefore rendered absolutely passive, put totally out of commission, we might say today. The sinner can only suffer the divine action. The comment on Ps 2:9, "Thou shalt break them with a rod of iron," gives a good picture of the kind of suffering Luther has in mind:

> For since the Word of Christ is the Word not in the flesh but in the spirit, it must suppress and cast out the salvation, peace, life, and grace of the flesh. When it does this, it appears to the flesh harder and more cruel than iron itself. For whenever a carnal man is touched in a wholesome way by the Word of God, one thing is felt, but another actually happens. Thus it is written [1 Sam 2:6-7]: "The Lord kills and brings to life; He brings down to hell and raises up; He brings low, He also exalts." Isaiah also beautifully portrays this allegorical working of God when he says [28:21], "He does His work—strange is His deed; and He works His work—alien is His work!" It is as if he were saying: "Although He is the God of life and salvation and this is His proper work, yet, in order to accomplish this, He kills and destroys." These works are alien to Him, but through them He accomplishes His proper work. For He kills our will that His may be established in us.

---

hold of [by the pure Word of God] and does not take hold of anything itself; that is, it is stripped of its own garments, of its shoes, of all its possessions, and of all its imaginations, and is taken away by the Word . . . into the wilderness . . . to invisible things, into the vineyard, and into the marriage chamber. But this leading, this taking away, and this stripping, miserably tortures [the soul]. For it is a hard path to walk in, and a straight and narrow way, to leave all visible things, to be stripped of all natural senses and ideas, and to be led out of all those things to which we have been accustomed; this, indeed, is to die, and to descend into hell" (WA 5:176.16–24). Luther knows of course, that such passages have the ring of mysticism about them. So he goes on a bit later to criticize mysticism for understanding the matter as "elicited acts," that is, as something we do: "They do not believe them to be the sufferings and feeling sensations of the cross, death, and hell. The CROSS alone is our theology" (WA 5:176.32). It is significant that the last sentence so often quoted is directed precisely against a theology tempted to turn the suffering involved into something to do rather than something done to us.

He subdues the flesh and its lusts that the spirit and its desires may come to life."[16]

The very indignation and resentment we harbor and/or express when we come up against the absolutely sovereign action of God in these matters indicates the truth of what is being said. The anger and indignation is the beginning of the suffering! Like Job we protest against God. Why? Because in actual suffering all theorizing is over. One enters into contention with God. Precisely in his rash protest over his suffering Job unwittingly speaks the truth about God.[17] In his suffering he cries out to God as the ultimate answer to it all. As with Job, it is only through suffering that sinners come to know and speak such truth. As inveterate theologians of glory, we are bound to shy away from such truth and, like Job's friends, try to make excuses for God. We adjust our doctrine of God to fit our glory projects. If God doesn't "play fair," how can our works count? Thus do we render God innocuous by our flattery. Instead of being brought to the praise of God, we bend our efforts to justify him.[18]

True knowledge of God, therefore, does not come on a theological platter. We are predisposed to distort things, to see wrongly, and to speak falsely. We construct a doctrine of God amenable to our projects. So the only way to know God is through suffering, the suffering of the one who saves us. God, so to speak, has to get our attention so that we will see at last. Knowledge of God does not comprise sets of doctrinal truths that may be taken or left at our discretion, not even if those truths call themselves "A Theology of the Cross," which we subsequently take

---

16. LW 14:335.
17. I am indebted in this section to the fine essay by Klaus Schwarzwäller, "'Nun hat mein Auge dich gesehen': Leiden als Grundproblem der Theologie," in *Einfach von Gott reden: Festschrift für Friedrich Mildenberger zum 65 Geburtstag*, ed. Jürgen Roloff and Hans G. Ulrich (Stuttgart: Verlag W. Kohlhammer, 1994), 190–225. What was it that Job "saw" when God spoke to him out of the whirlwind that he had previously only "heard by hearing of the ear," so that he despised himself and repented in dust and ashes (Job 42:5–6)? Job had persistently held God to account in his protests over against his "comforters," who tried to exonerate God by their "theodicies." Job's friends thought his speech laying the responsibility on God was outrageous and blasphemous, but Job insisted on crying out against God since God is, according to "the hearing of the ear" (perhaps we might say "the doctrine of God!"), the one who is supposed to be in charge. Now God, in declaring his awesome and universal majesty out of the whirlwind, actually approves what Job had said over against all the explanations of the "theologians." So God declares (42:7–9) that Job had spoken the truth, terrifying as it was and is. Job now *sees* that in the voice of his suffering he had unwittingly spoken the truth, and he is terrified by it: "I have uttered what I did not understand, things too wonderful for me which I did not know" (42:3). Job *sees* that through suffering the truth had literally been wrung out of him. He sees where previously he had heard and complained. He thus "despises himself and repents in dust and ashes."
18. See above, 238n4.

steps to put into practice. Whether *we* take it or whether *we* leave it makes no difference. As long as we think the matter is at *our* discretion, we remain the acting subjects. God is ultimately an insignificant cipher. There is no way through here. God can be known and had only through suffering the divine deed of the cross. The cross does not merely inform us of something, something that may be "above," or "behind" it. It attacks and afflicts us. Knowledge of God comes when God happens to us, when God does himself to us. We are crucified with Christ (Gal 2:19). The sinner, the old being, neither knows nor speaks the truth about God and consequently can only be put to death by the action of God. Such is the way one becomes a theologian of the cross, who can begin to speak and proclaim the truth of God, to "say what a thing is."[19]

19. The assertion that the truth about God is spoken out of suffering is common in Luther, sometimes in very radical form. In general it appears in the well-known insistence that God reveals himself "under the form of opposites" in weakness and suffering, or that God does his "alien work" of killing, afflicting, and bringing down to hell before he does his "proper work" of making alive, comforting, and raising to new life. Perhaps most radical are those instances where he speaks of God first becoming a devil for us before becoming God, and vice versa.

> Outwardly . . . grace seems to be nothing but wrath, so deeply is it buried under two thick hides or pelts. Our opponents and the world condemn and avoid it like the plague or God's wrath, and our own feeling about it is no different. Peter says truthfully [2 Per. 1:19] that the Word is like a lamp shining in a dark place. Most certainly it is a dark place! God's faithfulness and truth always must first become a great lie before it becomes truth. The world calls this truth heresy. And we too are constantly tempted to believe that God would abandon us and not keep his Word; and in our hearts He begins to become a liar. In short, God cannot be God unless He first becomes a devil. All that God speaks and does the devil has to speak and do first. And our flesh agrees. Therefore it is actually the Spirit who enlightens and teaches us in the Word to believe differently. By the same token the lies of this world cannot become lies without first having become truth. The godless do not go to hell without first having gone to heaven. They do not become the devil's children until they have first been the children of God. (LW 14:31)

These strange words begin to yield some sense when one thinks as a theologian of the cross and "tells it like it is." Unconditional grace must first be an absolute threat to us as theologians of glory. There is no "cure" for the theology of glory. No mere "change" of mind or opinion is possible. Grace therefore can only appear as nothing but wrath. The executor of the wrath of God, however, is the devil. God therefore first becomes a devil. All that God says and does, the devil must say and do first. One must first go to hell before one can be raised. There is no other way here. God must be accorded the absolute right to do this.

The sinner must suffer this if there is to be life. More radical perhaps is a comment from the 1519-21 *Operationes in Psalmos* occasioned by Isa 42:3, "A bruised reed he will not break and a dimly burning wick he will not quench."

> And I will say one thing more in my free and bold way. There are none nearer to God in this life than these haters and blasphemers of him, nor any sons more pleasing to him and beloved by him! And you can in this state make more satisfaction for sin in one moment than ever you could by repenting for many years together under a diet of bread and water. Hence it is true that in death (where this temptation prevails most), a Christian may in one moment get rid of all his sins, if he but act wisely under temptation. Here it is that those "groanings that cannot be uttered" are at work and prevail [Rom. 8:26]. (WA 5.170.25-5.171.3)

Remarkable passage! It makes no sense at all to a theologian of glory, but if we think of Job (above n. 16), for instance, it begins to make more sense. Like Job, the "blasphemer" at least does God the honor of acknowledging God as God. In extremity the sufferer is finally provoked enough, perhaps ultimately in death, to send complaint to the right address. Perhaps we can imagine God saying, "Ah, at last! I got you to talk to me! You spoke the truth about me in spite of yourself!" The promise is that he will not break the bruised reed nor quench the dimly burning wick. As with Job the situation is such that the suffering leads to truthful speech. No doubt Luther has Jesus' "blasphemy" in mind, the cry of dereliction from the cross. The theologian of glory always has great difficulty with that cry. In pious restraint the theologian of glory will refrain from such "blasphemy" and flatter God by absolving Him from all blame. But such pious speech simply robs God of the right to be God. So Luther could say that there are none closer to God in this life than "blasphemers," who at least do God the honor of letting Him be God!

PART VII

The Ministry

Speaking the Gospel Today

PREACHING THE GOSPEL TODAY: THE KILLING LETTER AND THE LIFE-GIVING SPIRIT

The Futility of Antinomianism

In the first section I proposed that if we look at what has happened to the preaching of the gospel from within rather than from without we will begin to realize that everything has gone soft and mushy. Our real problems are within. A decadent pietism has set in. There is no "bite" anymore to the Word. The hammer does not break the rock in pieces. The salt has lost its savor. An insipid gospel of sympathy has to do double duty for the law. Church documents aver that they are going to settle the social and ethical controversies confronting us "according to the principles of the gospel." Whatever happened to the law? (One synod actually voted down a motion to the effect that they should be guided by both law and gospel. So a synod of the ELCA is actually on record espousing Antinomianism!) Sympathy and intimacy—good things become substitutes for pastoral ministry. All this can be laid, I proposed, at the door of the basic antinomian presupposition and method of modern theology and practice, the assumption that theology can, so to speak, overpower eternity, that it can make a gospel that will be attractive to the world by accommodation, by erasing or ameliorating the offense. So what one hears from the pulpit all too often is gospel *Schwärmerei*, just "sweet Jesus" schlock of one sort or another, or perhaps lately the kind of thing leaking out of the Jesus Seminar, "Jesus as Sage," and so forth. As someone has quipped, we shall have to rename our churches "Our Sage's Lutheran Church"! But the trouble with that seems to be that we cannot be sure that he said any of the things attributed to him after all. Perhaps we shall have to rename the churches "Our Silent Sage's Lutheran Church"!

Now the difficulty with antinomianism is that it just does not work. On the objective level the law or the offense does not go away, it just changes its "mask" and becomes more subtle. On the subjective level as well it does not finally help people. It is supposed to emancipate from childhood tutelage (Kant: enlightenment) and build self-esteem. But when it becomes apparent that it is only superficial word-playing, self-esteem can soon turn to self-loathing. Luther was certainly already aware of this in his own battles. Writing against the antinomians he says,

> The devil knows very well that it is impossible to remove the law from the heart. . . . But the devil devotes himself to making men secure, teaching them to heed neither law nor sin so that if [it actually happens] sometime that they are suddenly overtaken by death or by a bad conscience, they have grown so accustomed to nothing but sweet security that they sink helplessly into hell. For they have learned to perceive nothing in Christ but sweet security. Therefore [when such real terror comes] it is taken as a sure sign that Christ (whom they understand as sheer sweetness) has rejected and forsaken them. That is what the devil strives for, and that is what he would like to see.[1]

When it begins to appear that the Little Engine That Could actually cannot, we have double trouble. On the one hand, the gospel itself is discredited and useless. It becomes just "sweet security," to use Luther's term (that is, false security). It cannot stand when the going gets rough, when death, tragedy, or bad conscience really hit. Optimism is no cure. We are constantly being exhorted and/or exhort ourselves. We tell ourselves, "you can quit, just do it." That optimism is supposed to build our self-esteem and so forth. But when we cannot quit we must find some way to escape the voice of the law, some way to hide what we are up to. And the supposed optimism only leads to deeper self-loathing and despair. Only an "intervention," "bottoming out," can save us. Current television culture gives an interesting picture of this. The advertisements are full of sweetness and light, promising simple and easy roads to success, the right deodorant, the right coffee, the flashy car, the fast life, and so on. But the dramas have all the signs reversed: drugs, addiction, abuse, crime, battered wives, battered children, tragic disruptions of one sort or another. The dramas take place in emergency rooms, police stations, back alleys, among the poor, the homeless, the helpless, the lost. This is socio-drama substituted for tragedy. It is an appeal for sympathy.

1. LW 47:111.

But even such drama seems more and more to be disappearing from the screen. I suppose we no longer want to see it on TV. We see it every day in the newspapers if not in actuality. So the sitcoms take the stage to cover it all over with canned laughter. We become anesthetized with the trivial.

THE WORD LOST ITS BITE?

Here is my question: If the Word has lost its bite how shall that be remedied? If the salt has lost its savor, wherewith shall it be salted? In the old days there used to be an answer for that. It had to do with the proper preaching and distinction between law and gospel. The gospel, it was insisted, must never be preached unless the law is preached first. First must come the conviction of sin before there could be the promise and assurance of grace. Pastors were supposed to master the use of that method in both preaching and the cure of souls. But it is not too big a stretch to see that it is just that method that has been a target of the attack of the antinomianism we have been outlining. Both law and gospel were an attack on the citadel of the self. The law exposed the sin and the gospel granted divine forgiveness—neither of which was particularly welcome to the autonomous self. Of course as time went on the method could lead to many abuses, the chief being that it could easily be turned into a kind of theological scare tactic, as if one could frighten people into heaven by literally scaring hell out of them. But such abuse did not circumvent but finally only reinforced the autonomous self. It appealed to the self to save itself by making the proper choices.

The outcome of the antinomian movement of modern theology has been to call the old law/gospel method into question. The outcome of this questioning is, however, still difficult to assess with complete accuracy. There seem to be two contradictory judgments. On the one hand is the persistent claim that people today no longer suffer under the burden of a guilty conscience as they did in Luther's day. We can no longer assume that people live in a world under the sacred canopy of a shared moral law. In Allan Bloom's words, there is no floor beneath our feet. We have fallen into the dark basement of the self. How can we preach forgiveness to people who do not and will not recognize guilt? We have this marvelous cure (called grace and forgiveness) but no one has the disease. So, it is thought we have to find other topologies to make what we say relevant: meaninglessness, shame, identity, self-worth or esteem, and so on. But on the other hand there is the fact that psychiatrists' offices are crowded with people plagued by guilt. So there are many who will tell us that people who come to church are already hurting and crushed, so much so that they do not need to hear more law. They have had enough of it already. All they need to hear is gospel.

So we have seemingly opposing judgments when we try to gauge the viability of the law/gospel method today. One says it will not work because no one feels guilty. The other says that people are already crushed and hurting. The reason, I suspect, is due exactly to the confusion that antinomianism breeds in theology. The aim of antinomianism is to get rid of law. But law cannot be gotten rid of. What gets eliminated then is invariably the offense of the gospel. So the attempt to erase the law only makes matters worse. The addict who cannot quit only doubles despair. And if the preacher only spouts sweet security there is probably no other place to go than to the psychiatrist's couch. Either that or the pastor, in order to have something to do, becomes a therapist.

In any case, what seems to have happened is that the preaching of the law in an effective manner has more or less dropped out. There is, of course, plenty of law. Attempts to preach gospel often end as covert law, but the *effective* preaching of law has thereby evaporated. Given the development we have been tracing, the effective preaching of law today is one of the most difficult things a pastor has to do. If we are to get the bite back in the preaching of the Word it seems to me that we need to do some serious thinking about this. The whole trend of modern theology has been to take the bite out, to pull the teeth and thus to make it just a kind of *Schwärmerei*. Antinomianism has taken its toll. What is to be done?

DOING THE WORD: GETTING THE BITE
BACK IN THE WORD

How shall we think about getting the bite back in the preaching of the Word? I would like to propose a number of considerations that I have found useful in approaching the matter of preaching today. Each of them could be the subject of a lecture or a book or two in themselves, so what we do here is just a sketch. I have attempted to sum up the outcome of all these points in what I have called "Doing the Word to the hearers," or "Doing the Text to the hearers." That is to say, preaching can be viewed not merely as exegeting the text, or explaining it, or even just expounding it, or updating it; all such exercises are necessary and useful but are preliminary. The final task of preaching is *doing* it, attempting to do again in the living present what it once did to its ancient hearers.

The aim: that the text is a living word that will make its own way, that it packs its own punch. Doing the text involves several considerations.

First Consideration: The Hermeneutics of Letter and Spirit

The first consideration is that if we are to get the bite back in the Word today it will be quite necessary to broaden and deepen what the tradition meant by rightly dividing and preaching law and gospel. To do this it is necessary to go back to what lies behind the law/gospel method, the hermeneutics (as we would say today) of letter and spirit, particularly as one can find it in studies on the early exegetical work and theology of Luther. When we do that we will see that the concept of law is rooted in the understanding of letter, and gospel in the functioning of spirit. Law, that is to say, is not only laws, but letter, the literal deposit, the whole of Scripture, the very text itself in its first instance as it strikes us bound sinners. Indeed, Luther could expand the letter even beyond the text of Scripture and speak of creation itself and all that happens therein as the *opera literalia dei*, the literal works of God. He apparently had great fondness for that passage in Leviticus about how the sound of a driven leaf shall terrify a whole army and set them to rout, so that they flee for their lives when no one pursues. There is nothing more lowly and despised, he liked to say, than a dead dry leaf. Worms crawl around on it and it is quite innocent and useless. But when its "moment" comes, it terrifies horse, rider, soldier, entire army. Are we not fine people, he remarks, driven in panic by a little leaf, when we otherwise so proudly pooh-pooh the wrath of God whenever we get the chance? Law is broadened to letter, to the way the text—the entire history of God with his people—works, even the way the creation itself impinges on the lost sinner. And what the law/letter does in the first instance is clearly specified in the passage that was always taken as the key, 2 Corinthians 3:6, "the letter kills." It is only in the second instance that we come to the function of what was called "gospel": the Spirit gives life. We will say more of this later.

But the question through the centuries has been just how, in what sense, does the letter kill and the spirit give life? Most, if not all, of the tradition, following the philosophers, held that the letter killed because it was dead, belonging to the world of appearances, change, decay, and death. So if you remain stuck just with the literal history you will perish. What is necessary is to find what the letter signifies above and beyond this world and death; one must get beyond dead letter to life-giving spirit, where spirit means a transcendent realm of truth, that which endures beyond all change, decay, and death—the transparent world. But this would mean that the text would have to be translated into what is basically a different story, the story, say, of the exit of the many from the one and its return—allegory. The letter would be a secret code, so to speak, an allegory whose true "meaning" containing the ultimate solution to decay and death (every hermeneutic is a covert soteriology!), lay elsewhere. Our first question, as it almost invariably is because we are inveterate metaphysicians—I expect this is part of our fallenness—would always be about meaning, the secret meaning and final promise of the text. We would use it as a mine from whose rough ore we could refine our doctrine and ethics. The text is always just a point of departure for some "spiritual" enterprise or other. So the text becomes just a clue, the occasion, for constructing "another world" which is supposed to be the real one. (It would be worthwhile to follow out the problem of what the letter signifies into the modern and postmodern periods. In the ancient world it signified a transcendent metaphysical realm of truth. In the modern world that realm collapsed into the interior world of the self and the psyche. In the postmodern world that too has collapsed, and the letter, it seems, "signifies nothing." But if it is not a matter merely of what the word signifies, but what it does immediately in and of itself—if it is a text that "makes its own way," so to speak, if it kills the old and calls the new into being—what then?)

But Luther, as was his wont, simply took the passage about the letter killing and the spirit giving life literally. That has as a consequence that the letter is not simply dead, but deadly. That is to say that the history of God and his people leads finally to the cross. It spells but one thing for old beings. It spells death. Only then can there be life, new life in the spirit. This is what lies behind the old method of rightly dividing and preaching law and gospel. It is not merely a matter of a guilty conscience set in the context of a fixed moral universe; it is more broadly a matter of the old self under attack by the letter, the text, the very story itself. Luther saw quite clearly what had strangely been overlooked, that the text of 2 Corinthians was actually not about interpretation as such, but about ministry—that we claim nothing for ourselves, for our sufficiency is from God who has qualified us to be ministers of a new covenant, not according to the letter but the Spirit, for the letter kills, but the spirit gives life.

When the law-gospel method of preaching is seen against the background of the letter/spirit dichotomy there is a possibility of recovering something of the bite of the Word. The Word is not intended to open up possibilities for old beings to exercise their spiritual muscles. The

Word comes not to coddle but to kill old beings, to put them out of their misery, to make way for the life-giving spirit.

A Functional Understanding of the Word

The second consideration flows quite naturally from the first. The Word, and that means Word as law and gospel, should be understood and used much more consistently in its *functional sense*. Where it is understood that letter kills and spirit gives life then it will be seen that, at least for the purposes of preaching, law and gospel do not designate sets of differing or even opposed propositions but *functions*. That which offends, accuses, attacks, and ultimately kills does the "law function." That which comforts, forgives, and ultimately gives life exercises the "gospel function."

Even though this functional understanding can seem at first glance to introduce some confusion—after all, how are we to control how our words function?—it does help us to deal with some of the questions we have raised about our preaching today. In the first place it can help us to identify more accurately the target that the antinomianism we have spoken of was aiming at but could never quite hit. It can help us define the nature of the *nomos* that virtually the entire modern world has been *anti*. It was never so entirely clear just what they were against, whether law or gospel. But if we proceed functionally it is clear that it was not really the law that they were against since that was generally rehabilitated in one way or another, but it was the gospel in its function as killing letter, the gospel as a "heteronomy," a *heteros nomos*, the very idea that God has entered into history, taken time (literally) to deal with us, to carry out his election. It was and still is, I expect, the unconditional mercy of God that is finally most offensive to the oldness of being. I can quit! The oldness in us is incensed because it senses that its kingdom is under radical attack and might lose control. One does not have to look to Enlightenment rebels to see that. It is readily apparent even in the church itself. The attitude toward the sacraments, particularly baptism, even and sometimes especially of the most pious, is a good indication. One of the most controversial issues in the church is always baptism. People are always so desperately afraid that we will "take baptism for granted" and so forth. There seems to be tremendous fear that God is going to go and spoil everything by giving it all away. Of course such procedure is dangerous. It does actually lead to death one way or another. It is quite possible for the Old Adam or Eve to twist baptism into an excuse for faithlessness and license. If so, it leads to a different kind of death, one from which there is no resurrection. But shall God, as Luther could put it, call off his goodness for the sake of the ungodly?

In the second place, more importantly, the functional understanding can help us to answer the difficult question of preaching law effectively today. If it is the case that people no longer suffer from a guilty conscience under the moral law, or if it is the case that some are already hurting and crushed, then we would do well to see that it is the very goodness of the gospel itself, the unconditional givenness that must carry out the "law function." The word of the gospel itself is in the first instance the killing letter. It is the cutting edge of the gospel that is the final crescendo of the law. The gospel in this sense is a sword that cuts both ways. It is not just a cure looking for a disease. It is not merely comfort to the hurting. As Ernst Käsemann liked to say, the gospel of the justification of the ungodly is a polemical doctrine. To be sure, the gospel exalts them of low degree. But what we seem most consistently to have forgotten is that it puts down the mighty from their seats. It is the final attack on the old self in its *securitas*. And it is the completeness, the fullness of the gift that puts the old being out of its misery. This is to pick up on what has remained an apparently unresolved question in Reformation theology. What brings about true repentance, the preaching of the law or the preaching of the gospel? This old debate can be resolved more usefully when we understand the matter in a functional sense. It is the very unconditionality of the gospel that functions as law to put old beings finally to death, whether high and mighty or of low degree. To be put to death in this sense is to be put in the position where there is nothing to do, to be rendered entirely "passive" as Luther liked to say. It is to be made a creature of grace, or better, to be regenerated, made new, to be remade a creature by the grace of God. Baptism, we teach, drowns the old Adam and Eve. A new being is pulled out of the water. We are killed, so to speak, with goodness, the very givenness, the unqualified goodness of the deed. It is the very offensiveness of this, the very thing about which we complain the most that is of the essence. Now since it is this offensive that has been the target of modern theology then I think we must sail right into the storm. Preachers must realize that precisely what upsets us the most is where the question of law and gospel is to be settled, rightly divided, and preached today. Preaching must not, in the first instance, seek to apologize the offense away but must rather use it to kill and make alive; it must seek to do the deed.

Third Consideration: Bondage of the Will

The third consideration is the question of the hearer. What shall we presuppose about those to whom we are to speak the gospel? If what we have been saying is true, if the word comes to kill and make alive then we do not come to make an appeal to the religious sensibilities, or even the guilt feelings, the good will, the supposed freedom, of old beings. We do not have to do with the Little Engine That Could or could not. Rather the presupposition for preaching, as Luther insisted, is the bondage of the will. That is to say that our problems as prospective hearers of the Word of God are rather more serious than we might have thought from the various analyses of the contemporary scene. Our fundamental difficulty is not merely that something more or less accidental has happened in our time to frustrate our desire to believe. If that were the case then a little apologetics could probably fix things. No, the problem is one that is exposed only from the inside. It begins to show up precisely when we come up against the very unconditionality of grace itself, when we come up against the sheer givenness of the sacraments, the nature of the word as killing letter and life-giving spirit. What begins to appear is that here God alone is at work. And we cannot have that.

Our fundamental problem is that we cannot get on with God. And we cannot because we will not. Our wills are bound. Now to clarify such an assertion would take considerably more time and space than we have here. Basically I think we can take it to mean not that our power to choose is somehow interfered with but rather that we do more or less what we please. And that is just the problem. We do what we are bound to do. When we come to God and the things of God we are bound to say no. "Man by nature," Luther could say, "is unable to want God to be God. Indeed, he himself wants to be God, and does not want God to be."[2] This bondage becomes most apparent when we come up against the god-ness of God. It comes to expression in those impenetrable masks usually called the divine attributes, or especially when we hear tell of such matters as divine election and predestination. When all is said and done we cannot give in to such a God. We cannot trust our eternal destiny to one who decides the matter alone. We must bargain for some leverage in the matter, even if it is just a little bit. In actuality we have no choice in the matter, not because we are coerced by outside force, jerked around like puppets, but because we just cannot.

This consideration of the bondage of the will as presupposition for preaching sets us clean contrary to what I have called the antinomian

2. LW 31:10.

method of modern theology. The basic anthropological presupposition of that method is the freedom of the will. The method proceeds on the assumption that it is the business of theology to make the message attractive enough for old beings to choose. Thus talk of an electing, predestinating God must either be removed or quietly rendered functionally inoperative. So God becomes at best the one who waits upon our choices. Inevitably that means that God becomes the God of Law and Wrath. Even if we say, as we are wont, that God is Love, Love, Love, it turns on us. God, apparently, is obligated to love everyone and so would violate his very being if he actually got around to saying "I love you" to anyone in particular. Furthermore, a God who only *is* love and never *does* anything about it always turns on us. If God is love, then what is the matter with you unloving slobs? One of the most fatal miscalculations of theology, I expect, has been to think that the message could ever be made acceptable to old beings. All that has been accomplished thereby has been to render the message trivial and dead. Here, it seems to me, lies hidden the real reason for talk about the death of God. Theologians have killed him. He is kept "alive" now, if at all, only by the artificial respiration of linguistic manipulation. As in the movie *El Cid*, the dead hero is propped up in the saddle and sent charging out of the fortress in hope that just the memory of what he once was might frighten the enemy into flight.

If preaching is to regain some vitality today, it must have a clearer vision of the predicament of the hearers to whom it is addressed. The problem, plain and simple, is that we just cannot get on with God. In biblical language, it is just that we are not reconciled to God because we cannot or will not manage it. When it comes to the Living God, we are bound to say no. And it is the triune God alone who has undertaken to do something about this. God was in Christ reconciling the world unto himself and nowhere else. We are not informed that God was in the mind of the philosopher or the theologian reconciling himself, but in Christ. This is the second move of the triune God. The third move, that of Spirit, is in the fact that he has entrusted us with this ministry of reconciliation. Much more needs to be said about this, of course, but that last bit—that God has entrusted us with the ministry of reconciliation—bids us to move on to our fourth and final consideration.

A Sense for the Present

That God was in Christ reconciling the world unto himself and that he has, *mirabile dictu*, entrusted us with this ministry of reconciliation is God's "solution" to the problem that God is for us. It is quite simple really. If God is the living, electing God, then what God has done is to find a way to go ahead and do it. There is no theoretical solution to the problem of the electing God. It is killing letter. When students clamor for solutions I usually tell them there are none, not in the abstract, at least. If you try to come up with one, you just go out of the frying pan into the fire. If you want a solution to your problems with God, you have come to the wrong place. You have to go to church and pray that the preacher knows what he or she is supposed to be doing. The solution, that is, is precisely in the move of God the Spirit into the present. If the electing God is the problem, then the solution is not to explain that God away, but to do what that God authorizes us to do—to go ahead and do the electing deed. What preaching needs is a sense for the present. Too often preaching never recovers from the classroom. Preaching goes on as though the mighty acts of God have long since ceased. God *was* in Christ reconciling. What is he up to now? God so loved the world that he *gave* . . . All those things are true, of course, but they are past, or at least we treat them as such. Preaching, however, is to move into the present, to speak "in the Spirit" of the living God. It is to assume that what I have to do now in the living present is the present edition of the mighty acts of God. There ought, it seems to me, be much more speaking in the present tense, the declaration here and now, the attempt to make it plain that this is the moment now in which the text comes true, doing what the text talks about. After all, this is what happens in the sacraments. We are authorized and instructed *to do* what is usually only *talked about*. For some reason or another the move to the present seems one of the most difficult to make. Often, it seems to me, sermons can be excellently done and one sits waiting for the final move to the present, but it never comes. Actually, of course, that just means that free choice remains the controlling presupposition. So the hearers are left to make the last move somehow for themselves. Or muttering, perhaps, "Well, that is all very nice, Reverend, but when will it happen to me?" One of the dirtiest tricks in the "evangelical" bag is to be endlessly talking about grace and justification as a free gift, and then never actually giving it. Preachers need to be much more sensitive about the move to the present.

CONCLUSION: DOING THE TEXT

When I try to put all this together I come up with the idea that we might look on preaching as doing the text to the hearers, doing the text as a word that ends the old and calls the new into being. The letter kills. The bite of the gospel is restored in that the law function is done. The Word does not present possibilities upon which free choice may exercise itself. It brings all that to an end so that the spirit can give life.[3] ...

We need simply to acknowledge that the word we preach as God's word is powerful, as law and gospel. It is a word that does what it says and says what it does. It kills and makes alive. It sets free men and women who are otherwise bound to sin, to death, and to the tyranny of the law. There is no greater privilege or joy for a preacher than to share this word, one that will raise us from our decadence and bring new life to the world. May we be so empowered to preach this word with courage, faithfulness, and integrity.

---

3. Editor's Footnote: The extracted text reads "Now in order to make this a little more concrete I always like to look at some texts to illustrate how I try to put this into practice. I realize that preaching styles differ and that there are a variety of literary devices one might use to get the job done. The selection of sermons in the last section of this volume serve not as a model for the way one must preach, but rather as an indication of how I try to practice what I have been preaching in the hope that it might be helpful to others as well." Gerhard O. Forde, *The Preached God: Proclamation in Word and Sacrament* (Grand Rapids: Eerdmans, 2007), 193–94. The sermons Forde mentions can be found in *The Preached God*, 273–321.

Something to Believe: A Theological Perspective on Infant Baptism

> Our know-it-alls, the new spirits, assert that faith alone saves and that works and external things contribute nothing to this end. We answer: It is true, nothing that is in us does it but faith, as we shall hear later on. But these leaders of the blind are unwilling to see that faith must have something to believe—something to which it may cling and upon which it may stand. Thus faith clings to the water and believes it to be Baptism in which there is sheer salvation and life, not through the water, as we have sufficiently stated, but through its incorporation with God's Word and ordinance and the joining of his name to it. When I believe this, what else is it but believing in God as the one who has implanted his Word in this external ordinance and offered it to us so that we may grasp the treasure it contains?[1]

The editor of our church magazine once remarked that baptism is one of those matters about which earnest churchgoers seem to get the most perturbed. Why should this be? Why should supposedly stalwart believers in the unmerited grace of God get so upset when that unmerited grace is given freely? The "world" has no problem with baptism. So-called marginal Christians have no problem with baptism. Infants have no problem with baptism. Apparently only adult Christians, indeed often the most pious, fear that baptism may be harmful to spiritual health. Is there a kind of *charo-phobia* (fear of grace) abroad in the church? If baptism is to be withheld from infants, should the latter not also be removed from other ministrations of grace? Perhaps the old practice of dismissing the catechumens was more consistent? But even the catechumens were allowed to come under the preaching of the Word!

Such questions bear examination. Each of them hints at fathoms on the theological depth chart that we cannot begin to plumb in this short

---

1. "The Large Catechism," in BC 460; BC-T, 440.

essay. Suffice it to say for now that baptism, particularly infant baptism, remains something of a permanent offense, especially, it seems, to the more ardent of adult Christians. This fact provides a kind of backdrop as we proceed to our task: an inquiry into the theological basis for the practice of infant baptism. Here at the outset, we should like to stipulate two clarifying strictures: First, "infant" in this essay shall be taken to mean children of Christian parents, parents who have at least enough relationship to the church to request baptism for their children; and second, the intent is to attend as strictly as possible to the theological argument, leaving aside arguments of a more pragmatic, historical, sociological, or psychological sort that might also be brought to bear on the question.

SETTING THE QUESTION

First, it is important to frame the theological question properly so that we might hope to arrive at an appropriate answer. Karl Barth looms over the contemporary discussion with an eminence that cannot be ignored, so we shall begin with him. Barth insisted, in essence, that to be valid, the practice of infant baptism must be proved to be part and parcel of the doctrine of baptism itself, grounded and anchored in baptism's very nature. Baptism, that is to say, "ought to be implicitly and explicitly, inclusively if not exclusively, the doctrine of infant baptism."[2]

The case for infant baptism therefore can be made only if it can be demonstrated that we are commanded and permitted to baptize young children, *and that it is necessary to do so* because they are the children of Christian parents.[3] Furthermore, this is to take place at a time when, according to human judgment, it is impossible for these children to have any knowledge about what is to be decided: The doctrine must prove that such practice is a faithful discharge of the divine commission in conformity with the general dealings of God with humans established in Jesus Christ.[4] If we were to set the question the way Barth did, it would seem to be this: Can it be proved from the nature of baptism that the baptism of infants is necessary? If not, we must conclude, given all the debits, that infant baptism is at best a "profoundly irregular" practice.[5] To be sure, Barth was no Anabaptist. Even though infant baptism is, as he saw it, "highly doubtful and questionable," one cannot say that it is

---

2. Karl Barth, *Church Dogmatics*, IV/4, trans. G. W. Bromiley (Edinburgh: T&T Clark, 1969), 169.
   3. Barth, *Church Dogmatics*, IV/4, 175. Emphasis mine.
   4. Barth, *Church Dogmatics*, IV/4, 175.
   5. Barth, *Church Dogmatics*, IV/4, 194.

invalid.[6] Nevertheless, dogmatics cannot any longer support the practice and must call the church to account.

A comprehensive treatment of Barth's (in many ways splendid) doctrine of baptism cannot be our purpose in this essay. Of primary concern for us is the setting of the question. Surely it is too stringent to set the question as though it were a matter of proving the necessity of the practice. Acts of grace, if they are truly grace, simply do not admit of such proof or necessity. A gift loses its character as sheer gift if it comes with the force of necessity. It becomes law. To be sure, the church in the past has often said that baptism is "necessary" to salvation, that it is the only remedy for original sin, and so forth. So it was argued that infants, too, must be baptized lest they be lost.

Arguments about necessity demonstrate, however, that it is imperative to distinguish between legal necessity and what might be called evangelical necessity. If baptism is considered a legal necessity, it becomes a requirement that must be fulfilled lest damnation ensue. The gospel becomes a law. Barth's argument seems to take on this character. Indeed, one wonders whether his demand for a necessity flowing from the nature of baptism itself is simply the final outcome of his insistence that law follows and flows out of gospel. Where such necessity cannot be proved, the practice must be rejected. One wonders as well whether the argument is not a return to the stipulation that all liturgical practices not biblically provable are to be rejected.

If, however, one operates on the premise that whatever "necessity" there is behind baptism is an evangelical, that is, a purely gospel necessity, the question about infant baptism will likely be put quite differently. The necessity involved in baptism is that of a sheer gift, necessity of the sort that evokes faith, trust, hope, and love. Whatever necessity there is, is carried within itself. To use the analogy of love, one might say that baptism has about the same necessity as that of a lover's kiss. That is certainly not a legal necessity! If it is, love has already flown. But if the lover were asked, "Is this really necessary?" what could the answer possibly be? Most likely one would reply that the question was ridiculous! What sort of necessity is behind an unconditional gift?

Such questions expose the peculiar difficulty of setting questions about acts of grace, and especially about infant baptism, properly. Most of the time, the questions presuppose a legal framework and so turn out to be traps. There is no way to answer them without imperiling the close but subtle relationship between unconditional grace and faith. Is baptism necessary to salvation? Can we simply depend on the fact that we have

---

6. Barth, *Church Dogmatics*, IV/4, 189.

been baptized? Does baptism work "automatically"? So the questions go. But they are traps. If, in the attempt to protect individual choice, one hurries to say, "No," one simply negates the grace of it. The pastor saws off the limb on which he or she is to stand. If, in the zeal to protect grace, one hurries without further ado to say, "Yes," one will likely be accused of ignoring or belittling the place of faith. Then the aim of baptism will be shorted out. The questions must be put more carefully. Perhaps the best immediate response to questions about the necessity of baptism would be: "Speak for yourself. But beware, the answer will be a confession!" Questions that are traps are best turned back to expose the questioner. In other words, one has to make it clear that the answer itself is already a faith statement.

Barth's demand for proof of necessity asks for something an evangelical argument cannot really give. When Luther was asked about necessity with regard to the sacraments, he generally refused to give a legal answer. In the quote from the Large Catechism with which we began, the reasons given for baptism as an external sign are just that faith may have something on which to stand, or that we may grasp the treasure it contains. In reply to the question why it should be necessary to eat bread and wine when all the benefits could be gotten in other ways, Luther says, "God means to fill the world and give himself to us in many different ways, to help and strengthen us by his Word and works; shall we be so complacent and bored that we hinder him and tolerate nothing but the way that happens to please us? You are a black, hopeless devil!"[7] The answer is not a legal one. The necessity involved is simply that of a gift, and the gift carries its own necessity within itself. But, of course, as Luther's parting shot indicates, refusal of the gift exposes the intended recipient. The lover's kiss is not legally necessary, but spurning it carries its own kind of peril! No doubt that is why the church has always said that it is not the absence of the sacrament (that is, where it is not available) that condemns, but the despising of it. The gift is not legally but evangelically necessary. It carries its own power within itself, in its own giftedness. To refuse it means that one is exposed as impervious to such giftedness.

It is the task of systematic theology to impel us to speak and act faithfully in the light of what God has done in Jesus Christ and continues to do through the Holy Spirit. If we are to speak faithfully about baptism,

---

7. LW 37:141. The view of necessity represented in this essay—and also, I think, in Luther—parallels that of Eberhard Jüngel on the necessity of God. God is not to be understood as a necessary being but rather one who in sheer graciousness is "more than necessary." Baptism, likewise, is not necessary but "more than necessary." *God as the Mystery of the World*, trans. Darrell L. Guder (Grand Rapids: Eerdmans, 1983), 14–35.

particularly with regard to infants, we must set the question so as not to undermine the nature of the gift itself. The question, therefore, should be put more graciously. It cannot be a question about proof or necessity in a legal sense. Given the gracious activity of God in Christ, must we not rather ask whether there are any evident or overriding grounds for excluding infant children of Christian parents from baptism? The question, then, is not whether it can be proved that we must baptize such infants, but whether we may do so, whether it is a faithful and hopeful practice to do so. The question is not whether we can prove theologically that infants must be included, but whether there are unimpeachable theological grounds for excluding them, not whether we must, but whether we *may* baptize infants. To put it most directly, is excluding infants from baptism simply because they are infants a faithful practice? Does it foster proper witness to divine grace?

BAPTISMAL FAITH

Now if we have set the question, we must seek to answer it. The biblical texts do not do this. The answer must, by the nature of the case, be grounded in the theology of the matter. Barth was certainly right about this. This is not a counsel of despair. The Bible is not a rulebook for liturgical practices. That is to say, the answers must come from the nature of baptism itself. Since the crucial question for us here is that of the relation between baptism and faith, and since Luther constantly warned us that baptism and faith should never be separated, we can best get at what we need by asking about baptismal faith.

What is baptismal faith? Baptismal faith is nothing other than faith in the activity of the triune God. It is the faith that the almighty creator of heaven and earth acts in Jesus Christ through the Holy Spirit in the living present to reclaim his lost creatures. That is to say, baptismal faith is the belief that there is a God "out there" in what Luther calls, in the quotation cited above, the sphere of this "external ordinance" (*das äusserliche Ding*, as the German more pointedly has it), a God who runs the whole show. It is the trust that this "external" event, this washing with water, is the act of the electing God. It is the belief that this happening, at a specific place and time, is the will of God "for me." In Luther's words, baptismal faith is nothing other, quite simply, than believing in God, the God "who has implanted his Word in this external ordinance and offered it to us so that we may grasp the treasure it contains."

Since it is a strictly "external thing" and not my doing, faith, as Luther says, has something to believe. Such an assertion shocks us because it implies that, without a current event such as baptism, faith has nothing to believe and therefore no ground to stand on. And that is, indeed, Luther's point. Faith is precisely the trust called forth by such occurrences of grace in the "external" world as baptism in the confidence that they reveal the will of almighty God "for you" according to his Word and promise.

Whatever the difficulty involved, there is here the belief that all things happen according to the divine will or, as Luther put it, by divine necessity. We have to do, after all, with the triune God. If it were not so, faith could not have any confidence in baptism or, for that matter, any other present advent of grace, even preaching itself.[8] If it were not so, the ultimate will behind baptism would be some form of human willing: social custom, ecclesiastical pressure, parental superstition, personal decision, or just Grandma. But if God is triune, if all things happen by divine necessity, then *whatever* the contingencies that appear to us to be operative, even "just Grandma," the ultimate will behind the event is almighty God.

Baptism is therefore never just an "accident," for the works of the Trinity are undivided. Baptism is the revelation of the will of God, something that comes to us from without, an "external" thing. Without the external thing, faith has nothing to believe except, perchance, some ancient religious history. Faith then simply collapses inward upon itself. Its only recourse is somehow or other to muster the effrontery to trust its own fervor and sincerity.

Because of its irreducible externality, baptism is a preeminent sign of the priority and therefore the offense of pure grace. The difficulty in most arguments about baptism is that the very thing objected to is the point and power of baptism. "You do not mean to say that a mere external ceremony can save, do you?" So the question forever goes. But this is the entire point of baptism. The grace is in the very offense of externality. The grace is in the fact that the triune God has intervened now "for you." The intervention from without is the declaration that the God who runs the whole show is indeed *for* you. Baptismal faith is precisely to believe this. It is simply to believe in God.

The standard worry about this seems to be that such a view will lead to a species of "cheap grace," the current pop defense against all forms of free and unconditional grace. If it is somehow mysteriously infused just

---

8. Cf. LW 33:43, "Christian faith is entirely extinguished, the promises of God and the whole gospel are completely destroyed, if we teach and believe that it is not for us to know the necessary foreknowledge of God and the necessity of the things that are to come to pass. For this is the one supreme consolation of Christians in all adversities, to know that God does not lie, but does all things immutably, and that his will can neither be resisted nor changed nor hindered." Frightening as that may be, it is nevertheless the guarantee that the promises are not lies.

by "going through the motions," does that not render all activity on our part unnecessary? Once again, the way we answer will betray us. Usually, one is tempted to turn back to the self again and set up hedges and conditions of various sorts. "No, of course it will not 'work' unless you 'have enough faith,' or are properly converted, or feel it in your heart, or show it in your life," and so on, and so on. The speech implies that one has to go somewhere and get faith and then come back so baptism can "work." The self is simply set back in the driver's seat. But the point is that the very externality of the event renders the self and its activity not only unnecessary but obsolete, old, and indeed dead.

The tragic irony of most discussions about baptismal faith is that the temptation to call on human decision to protect baptism simply undercuts it. The very point of baptism is to save us from having to depend on our own decisions. The very offense of externality is itself the only real defense against cheap grace. It is the announcement that God refuses to pander to us. Grace is not cheap, or expensive; it is free. That is the real problem. The free gift alone destroys the self who wishes to stay in control. If it were not free, the old self would still be in business. Baptism signals the end of old beings incurably turned inward upon themselves, who use even their own religiosity as the last line of defense. The self has to be turned inside out.

Baptism, we have always been told, regenerates. How so? Precisely by intervening in the endless turning of the self in upon itself, thus breaking the self's incurable addiction to itself. This is why baptism as external event is the primary attack on original sin. The church has always sensed that there is a consequent relation between baptism and original sin, but has perhaps not defined the matter as aptly as it should have. To be directed outward by baptism spells the beginning of the end for original sin, the "lack of original righteousness," that is, trust in self rather than in God. To say that original sin is "removed," as though it were a quantum rather than a relational matter, would be inaccurate since the old self obviously still persists. But as Protestantism has preferred to say, original sin is now exposed for what it is; its guilt is forgiven and just so its "reign" is over. To be reborn is to be saved from the devil, the world, and the self; to be turned inside out; to be claimed by the baptizing God, the God "from without," who truly transcends us, the triune God. Hence, we are baptized into the name of this God—Father, Son, and Holy Spirit—and no other.

Such is the nature of baptismal faith. The persistent source of difficulty and cause for complaint over against baptism is the failure to get the relationship between baptism and faith right. The most pious Christians in particular seem to be offended by the claim that "baptism saves." Protests are always forthcoming in the name of "really sincere" faith or obedience or whatever. In the name of such protests, it is often asserted that one cannot "count on baptism." But then the preacher simply shoots himself or herself in the foot, leaving faith with nothing to believe. The problem arises because of the failure to see that the claim, "baptism saves," *is* already a faith claim. It is the way faith speaks. Of course it is true, as Luther continually insisted, that faith is the only way baptism can be received. Faith is the only possible "receptacle" for grace, the only possible way to receive a promise. But faith can be faith only when it has a concrete promise to believe. Accordingly, the faith in question has always to be precisely faith in the baptism (Word and sign) itself, not merely belief in ancient religious history—even if it is the history of Jesus.[9] The devils believe the history of Jesus—even that he is the Son of God. But they do not believe that this history is "for them."

Thus we have the systematic insistence on the precedence of the external over the internal. Faith must have something to believe, something that happens in the living present to which it can cling in all adversity. Baptism does not differ in this regard from any of the other concrete occurrences of divine grace. The preaching of the gospel is an "external" event perceived by the senses, as is the Lord's Supper. As Luther asserted, "Whatever God effects in us he does through such external ordinances." The gospel promise "must be external so that it can be perceived and grasped by the senses and thus brought into the heart."[10] The proper order in this sequence is that the promise and sign from without come first, and only then the internal; the faith that receives it comes second. The fire of faith within is always kindled by the flame of the external event. Indeed, the external event comprehended in the divine Word creates the faith that receives it.

BAPTISM AND TIME

If we have correctly gauged the nature of baptismal faith, then it should be apparent that the questions about "whom" to baptize and "when" are considerably relativized. Baptism is an eschatological event and so ends all old continuities and sequences. As Edmund Schlink declares:

---

9. Cf. LW 40:213–14. "If now I seek the forgiveness of sins, I do not run to the cross, for I will not find it given there. . . . But I will find in the sacrament or gospel the word which distributes, presents, offers and gives to me that forgiveness which was won on the cross."

10. BC 460; BC-T 440, from the Large Catechism in the paragraph just following that is cited at the outset of this essay.

> In baptizing children the church knows that the temporal sequence of faith and Baptism has been relativized by God's eschatological activity. For in Baptism God encloses the entire past life of the baptized as well as that which is still in the future. The temporal sequence of events in the course of life has been eschatologically nullified in Baptism: The baptized has in Christ already experienced his future death, and the life of the one risen from the dead has already been opened for him. In this eschatological bracketing the question whether the faith of the person to be baptized must necessarily precede Baptism fades away, and the temporal sequence of faith and Baptism cannot be made the norm of validity.[11]

Since the appropriate sequence is from the external to the internal, the external event always establishes its priority over its internal reception. There is no essential difference on this score between infant and adult baptism. Indeed, Jesus seemed to think that the adult should become as a child, not vice versa! In baptism the adult, too, is "born again" as a child of God through the external sign and the promise: To be baptized is to be put under the divine priority. To believe this is precisely to let God be God. Whatever one was prior to this event is not to be prolonged but "drowned" in the gracious water. As we have suggested, this is the very root of the offense and the reason why baptism is a persistent target of attack. Old beings always resist the priority of grace.

Included in this view is the understanding that baptism quite obviously can never be a "once upon a time" event. As old beings, we never give up. So baptism continues to work, putting the old being to death, by its very externality, until the end. Whoever is baptized, infant or adult, must be nurtured in this faith until the new self who believes in the God "out there" at last arises. The order is baptism-faith, not faith-baptism. This sequence must maintain itself, whatever the age or maturity of the recipient.

There is, therefore, no overriding theological reason for withholding baptism from infants. Baptismal faith is neither clarified nor promoted thereby. Such practice only invites reversal of the proper theological order with its disastrous consequences. A "faith" based on such reversal may be ever so pious, but Luther's question still remains: Does it have anything to believe but itself? To be sure, the baptism of infants in itself is no guarantee that proper baptismal faith will be forthcoming. And one can, of course, readily recount the failures of the practice.[12] But in infant baptism the sequence is maintained and the possibility of baptismal faith is permanently opened. Since baptism is, in any case, a permanent

---

11. Edmund Schlink, *The Doctrine of Baptism,* trans. Herbert J. A. Bouman (St. Louis: Concordia, 1972), 160.
12. Schlink, *Doctrine of Baptism,* 161–62.

offense to old beings, what is needed is proper nurture, not belittling, questioning, discrediting, or postponing. An evangelical pastor must not begin by sawing off the limb on which he or she stands. Our speech about baptism must be more faithful than it has been of late. The only cure for the abuses surrounding baptism is to teach and preach it properly, not to withhold it.

As with all ministrations of unconditional grace, the church here stands at a critical crossroad. In the face of all the difficulties and failures in baptismal practice, evangelical preachers must learn to either become more radical about grace or give it up. Of course we all know about the failures. Of course we all know that arousing faith to be grasped by its heritage is the only solution. But the mistake of the past has been to turn to preaching faith, exhorting, describing, cajoling, or threatening. Now we have to consider whether this was not precisely the wrong move. Preaching faith is like trying to make flowers grow by pulling on them. The very thing one wants to promote is killed. So the church is dying. Faith does not grow by preaching faith but rather by proclaiming and nurturing the hearers in the grace given in baptism.

THE GREAT DIVIDE

Now it is obvious in all this that the question of infant baptism entails not just the doctrine of baptism but the broader dogmatic system and its use in its entirety. The ultimate root of difference in our speech is that there is a great divide in the way Christians look upon baptism. It is not just a difference in practice—say, whether to baptize infants or not—but a difference in theology. Edmund Schlink, in his study of baptism, speaks of this difference as an "antithesis," which marks "the most profound difference" in the understanding of baptism. "That antithesis," he maintains, "is the understanding of baptism as God's deed or as man's deed, as the sign given by God or as the sign of human self-obligation before God."[13]

All of which is to say that the root issue is whether in baptism we have to do with divine election or in some way with the self-disposition of the human will. Obviously, where it is assumed that baptism is a sign of human self-obligation before God, infants cannot be baptized. Infants are not capable of such heroics. But the problem is even deeper than this. Wherever it is held that salvation depends in any way or to any degree on the free choice of the will, infant baptism will always seem a highly questionable practice, even in those churches where it is regularly practiced, for then the self always moves into the center as the real subject

13. Schlink, *Doctrine of Baptism*, 168–69.

of the baptismal act. The faith of the self becomes the primary focus, or perhaps even the faith and sincerity of the parents. The claim that God is actually doing something fades from view, and infant baptism becomes a pious communal custom whose theological rationale has long since been forgotten or surrendered.

This turn to the inner life of the self has, of course, been the sad fate of Christianity since at least the Enlightenment. Rejection of infant baptism as a matter of theological principle is but a surface manifestation of this fundamental alteration. Given the presupposition of free choice, traditional definitions of the sacraments themselves contribute to the problem. When it is said, for instance, that a sacrament is a "visible sign of an invisible grace," the implication is that grace is a mysterious something, perhaps in the water, which somehow empowers the weakened but nevertheless free will. All attention is then directed inward. One tries to determine whether it has "worked." If it has not, blame will eventually be unloaded on the self, which is to say that grace becomes a secret agenda. One must search the inner self to discover whether one has it or not.

Yet this leaves sacraments in a precarious position. Given the presuppositions, the house divides itself into those who believe that baptism somehow imparts such "invisible grace" and those who, for fear that the will of the self will be bypassed, reject it. The idea that the sacrament bestows an invisible grace just by being performed is rejected as "magic." The self must then find other ways (for example, conversion or immediate experience) to assure itself of divine favor. The sacraments consequently become mere signs of the supposed success of this venture. That is the end of the road. Everything turns inward upon the self. The self is never set free. The modern self is something like a black hole, endlessly gaining incredible density by sucking everything into itself.

The claim that baptism should be seen as the act of the triune God external to the self and all its continuities, an external deed that itself creates faith, presents us with an alternative to both the traditional view of an infused invisible grace and the modern turning of the self in upon itself. What the church needs today is to be grasped by the audacity of acts of unconditional grace like baptism. God simply breaks into, intervenes, in our lives because God knows what is good for us.

To baptize is to have the confidence that sinners who are bound will be set free. Freedom is not violated if one is set free. So it is that baptism is a "cure" for sin. Sin is addiction to self, no matter how pious its form. An intervention from without is necessary. The dead are not consulted, nor do they play any part in their resurrection. God takes over such matters. We can be saved by divine intervention alone. The external act is as necessary to save the pious from themselves as the impious. So it is never completed in this life and must hit us daily until at last it is done with us, and we finally whisper, "Amen!" Baptism saves us.

If we get an inkling of the audacity of the divine intervention, a consequence even more shocking to the self comes into view. The real question is not whether baptism should be withheld from infants, but whether it can legitimately be withheld from anyone at all! If all we have said here is true, so the question goes, should we not simply go out in the street and "hose 'em down in the name of the triune God"? The question is, once again, a trap, perhaps a last desperate act of self-defense. Answer with a shocked, "No," and the battle for grace is lost. The smile is lost and pessimism sets in. Answer with an unqualified, "Yes," and the grace-faith relation could be lost. In such instances the best reply is a question that might expose the questioner. One might simply ask, "Would that not be fun? Would it not be marvelous if we were in a position to do that?" Mass baptisms of that sort have been done before, even in Scripture, and in some instances are still being done.[14] Most of us, after all, would probably not be Christian today if it were not for some such wild event far back in our history.

Certainly it should be the first desire of the evangelical preacher not to restrict but to spread abroad the grace of God as widely as possible. The fact that we have to refrain from doing so does not follow from the theology of the matter but from the sobering fact that we are not in a position to follow the action with the nurture that is needed. But the fault is then neither in the theology of baptism nor in the candidates for baptism but rather in us. Restricting baptism, that is to say, should never be a matter of theological principle and certainly not a cause for rejoicing. Rather it can only be cause for regret. We have to ask whether it is not really a sign of loss of confidence in both the truth claim of the Christian message and the future of the church's mission. In one of his more audacious statements, Luther could put the matter this way:

> Since God has made a covenant with all the heathen through the gospel and ordained baptism as a sign thereof, who can exclude the children? If the old covenant and the sign of circumcision made the children of Abraham believe that they were, and were called the people of God, according to the promise, I will be the God of thy descendants [Gen. 17:7], then this new covenant and sign must be much more effectual and make those a people of God who receive it. Now he commands that all the world shall receive it.

---

14. I understand from our church officials that some five thousand Masai are to be baptized en masse this summer in Tanzania!

On the strength of that command (since none is excluded) we confidently and freely baptize everyone, excluding no one except those who oppose it and refuse to receive this covenant. If we follow his command and baptize everyone, we leave it to him to be concerned about the faith of those baptized.[15]

Think of that! A covenant with all the heathen! To be sure, we are not obligated necessarily to baptize everyone; no one can be forced, and we must do everything we can to nurture the baptized. There must be proper pre-baptismal counsel and proper baptismal addresses and sermons. But the church must look first to itself in these matters. No good is accomplished by complaining about lack of sincerity or discipline in parents. If what we have said here is true, it is likely that there is more of the vestigial remains of baptismal faith in the "superstition" and "magic" that impel some to the font than there is in all the posturing about self-obligation. What are we to say to the fact that most people are still willing, even eager, to have their infants baptized, but are reluctant to let the church have any more to do with them? Should we not wonder, at least occasionally, whether that is more a judgment on the church than on them? Could it be, perhaps, that baptism is about the only gospel left in the church, the only place left where the church is more or less forced by its own agenda to do what it ought? At any rate, the church would do well first of all to look to itself in these matters before it settles the blame for the sorry state of affairs in baptismal theology and practice on someone else. For a church that has largely neglected or failed in the nurturing task now to think to remedy people's ignorance of the sacraments by taking them away would certainly be rather cynical.

Grace is not a hidden agenda. The grace of baptism calls us to turn from the endless preoccupation with self and the pessimism that has virtually destroyed the sacrament to the glorious action of the triune God "out there" in his world. The grace is in the very externality of it. It is to be announced and spread abroad, not withheld. None of the abuses attributed to a "too liberal" practice of infant baptism will be corrected by withdrawing it. That is like withholding food from the starving until they have a proper concept of nourishment. We do not need to protect the Lord from the Lord's own generosity! In the current "post-Constantinian" age, withholding baptism does not end but only fosters a more legalistic preoccupation with the self. To be sure, there is wholesale confusion and misunderstanding about the sacraments, just as there is about Christian theology in general. But we do not plan to stop preaching just because it is poorly done or misunderstood. The only real weapon left to

---

15. LW 40:257–58.

the church is the proper teaching and preaching of baptism as the gracious and saving action of the triune God. And that, certainly, is about as it should be.

The Lord's Supper as the Testament of Jesus

THE FOUNDATION

The claim that godless sinners are justified by faith alone without the deeds of the law entails also the claim that the Lord's Supper is properly understood and used only when it is administered and received as gospel—as sheer, unmerited gift. It is a *beneficium* not a *sacrificium*. What happens in the supper, that is, is simply *the gospel*. What our Lord did at supper "on the night in which he was betrayed" must therefore be conceptualized, taught, and claimed as pure gospel if we are to approach what might be called a "Lutheran" understanding of that supper. The absolute basis for such understanding and practice is first, last, and always that it is gospel promise.

THE CONTEXT

From time immemorial theologians have argued about the context by which to extract keys to interpret the supper. Is it or is it not a Passover meal? Is it the last of the eschatologically charged meals of Jesus with his disciples? Is it a covenant meal of some sort? A Torah thank offering? All such contexts are no doubt important. But it appears that something very obvious has usually been missed. Missing is the simple fact that the texts of the supper themselves set forth the essential context within which it is to be understood. That is the fact that it took place *on the night in which he was betrayed*. Any reading of the texts demonstrates that the accounts are laced through and through with the fact of the betrayal. Argument about whether or not it occurred on the night of the Passover meal is rendered more or less irrelevant. What occurred is indelibly stamped by the fact that it took place in the context of the betrayal.

What occurred in the supper is therefore first and foremost encompassed and comprehended within its own concrete and particular story. Jesus was not symbolically or ritually previewing or acting out something that would "really" happen at some other place or time. Disregard for what the texts actually say is largely responsible for the fruitless searches for a context that will supply the supper with some "sacramental" meaning not immediately apparent. All of that is far overshadowed, if not simply canceled, by the fact that it took place in the context of his betrayal. Think on it! He, just when his very body and blood are being "handed over," "surrendered up," to the "authorities" of this age, both religious and civil, takes bread and cup and in contradiction and defiance of the betrayal says, "This is my body given *for you, this cup is the New Testament in my blood shed* for you *for the forgiveness of sins*." And along with it the eschatological promise: I shall not drink of this cup again until I drink it new with you in the kingdom. It is a new testament.

In other words, his body is handed over and his blood shed by the authorities of this age, but he remains sovereign and with the bread and the wine as his testament bequeaths his body and blood to his disciples. One calls to mind Jesus' words from the Gospel of John: "No one takes my life from me, I lay it down of my own accord." On the night in which he was betrayed Jesus gives his body and blood to his own.

THE CONCEPTUALITY

As Luther rightly perceived, the conceptuality at work here is that of testament, as in "last will and testament."[1] The conceptuality of testament clearly sets forth and insists upon the gospel character of what occurred. Jesus, in the face of his betrayal, makes his last will and testament and designates his heirs. "This cup is the New Testament in my blood shed for you and for many for the remission of sins." The point here is that what happens on the night of the betrayal is not simply to be conflated with and interpreted by what happens on the day of crucifixion. When that is done, what happened in the upper room necessarily gets subsumed under one's interpretation of Golgotha. It becomes a symbolic anticipation of what happened on the cross.

To be sure, the testament is inextricably related to what happened

---

1. Reinhard Schwarz has demonstrated how Luther saw this conceptuality as exegetically necessary from the very beginning of his career. See Reinhard Schwarz, "The Last Supper: The Testament of Jesus," trans. Gerhard O. Forde, *Lutheran Quarterly* 9 (1995): 391–403. Also Reinhard Schwarz, "Der hermeneutische Angelpunkt in Luthers Messreform," *Zeitschrift für Theologie und Kirche* 89 (1992): 340–64.

at Golgotha. Most obviously, of course, the testament does not go into effect until the death of the testator. But the conceptuality of testament should not be subsumed under one's theory about the atoning significance of the death. In the history of the tradition that has meant overwhelmingly that the supper is understood in sacrificial terms: a sacramental and ritual reenactment, representation, or remembrance of the vicarious satisfaction by Jesus of what humans owe God. The "sacrifice of the mass" in Roman Catholicism and the sacrificial character of the eucharistic prayers in Lutheran and Protestant rites are the liturgical offspring of this (mis-)understanding. Reinhard Schwarz puts the matter quite clearly.

> The underlying test for every conception of the Supper is that of the manner in which it can align itself with the situation of Jesus "in the night in which he was betrayed" . . . In the late medieval doctrine of the Supper, the act of consecration, the central part of the sacrifice of the mass, was expressly connected with the last meal of Jesus with his disciples. In that meal celebration, therefore, Jesus had ostensibly acted out a sacramental rite of sacrifice, in a sense a previewing of his own sacrificial death. He was thereby supposed to have transferred to his disciples themselves the priestly duty of redoing retrospectively a sacramental representation of his sacrificial death. In a sense, the sacrificial rite at the Last Supper of Jesus with his disciples therefore relates to the church's sacrifice of the mass in mirror-image-like fashion. The symmetrical axis lies, so viewed, in the sacrificial death of Christ whose sacramental representation once previewed by Jesus is now again retrospectively celebrated. The sacramental activity of Jesus among his disciples therefore finds its meaning in the supposition that Jesus intended to institute the churchly celebration of the sacrifice of the mass.[2]

But this draws the supper into an entirely different hermeneutical scheme.[3] It becomes a symbolic event, a ritual repetition of something that happened long ago, or a liturgical "re-presentation" or "memorial" of the "sacrifice" on Golgotha. The result is that direction is reversed. The body and blood are offered first and foremost to God and returned to the people only in the form of "sacramental grace"—with all its attendant problems. One is no longer justified by faith alone in the promise and testament, but by *"gratia gratum faciens"* ("grace that makes one graceful") or other appropriate internal motions and modifications. The effect of the sacrament becomes internalized in a way that can do real damage. The gospel character of the supper is lost.

2. Schwarz, "Last Supper," 396.
3. See the article by James S. Preus, "Neglected Problems in the Eucharistic Dialogue," *Currents in Theology and Mission* 3 (1976): 279–87, for an enlightening account of the hermeneutical problems involved.

SYSTEMATIC CONSIDERATIONS

We cannot here engage in an exhaustive treatment of the advantages of the conceptuality of testament for the more systematic problems always attending reflection on the supper. They are many. I shall only allude to some of them here. First and foremost, of course, the supper as testament firmly establishes the proper direction. The testament grants the inheritance from the testator Jesus to the heirs. This also should be insisted upon over against the covenantal language that has become so prevalent today.[4] If covenantal language is used it should be understood as a testament, not vice versa. As Luther observed, a testament differs from a covenant in that it goes into effect upon the death of the testator whereas a covenant depends upon the continued existence of the covenantor. Since, however, in this case Jesus is raised and lives forever, testament and covenant can be taken as equivalent.[5] That means that testament provides the interpretative key. The new testament is the new covenant, not vice versa. This guards against lapsing once again into sacrificial language.

Second, the language of testament does much better in what we might call the "reality check." Lutheranism has always insisted on the reality of what transpires in the doing of the supper. It is not a representation, not a repetition, not a mere symbolic proceeding, but real. If it is not real it is not gospel. How can this reality be perceived? Where the supper is interpreted in terms of the sacrifice one always runs afoul of the time question. How can the present celebration be a real reoccurrence of an event that happened so long ago? An event, indeed, that was said to be "once for all"? If it is truly once for all, why does it have to be made present again, and how is that possible? Various devices have to be constructed for the time gap between the ancient sacrifice and the present to be transcended. One must somehow be initiated, so to speak, into a special time warp so as to become contemporary with a sacrifice buried in the sands of time. How can this be done? The ritual is the answer. The sacrifice must be ritually "repeated," or "remembered," or in the preferred liturgical jargon of today, "re-presented" (made present again) by exact observation of prescribed ritual action, usually by priests who have the proper ontological qualification to do it. Such interpretations, of course, only pile more difficulties upon already existing ones.

No such difficulties arise if the supper is understood as Jesus' last will

---

4. The substitution of "covenant" for "testament" in recent liturgies of the supper (as in "This cup is the new covenant") was *not* a happy development.
5. Schwarz, "Last Supper," 394.

and testament. What happens when Jesus' followers meet to "do this in remembrance of me" is simply the same thing that happened in the night in which he was betrayed: the last will and testament is distributed to his heirs. What is "repeated" is not Golgotha but exactly the same thing that was done at the Last Supper. "Repeated" is even here a bad word. Rather, the will of Jesus is carried out, the supper *extended now through time* to include all Jesus' heirs in accordance with the will itself. It is not a symbol wrapped up in a ritual time warp, not a repetition, not a re-presentation, not merely a memory, but rather a real event in our time. It is what it says it is: the New Testament.

To conclude here, thirdly, just a word is in order about the question of "real presence" that has so plagued the understanding of the supper. This question too can be more adequately handled through the conceptuality of testament. Jan Lindhardt has attempted this in intriguing fashion.[6] Briefly, the bread and the wine hold a place equivalent to the piece of paper called a person's "last will and testament." The piece of paper "really" is the last will and testament, just as are the bread and wine. They are not mere symbols, just as the piece of paper establishing the testament is not merely symbolic. Yet the piece of paper as such is not the entire inheritance, the estate and all its goods. Still, without the piece of paper, the inheritance would not be an inheritance. It would not exist as such. So it is with the last will and testament of Jesus. The bread and the wine really are the testament and they mediate the body and blood because without them there would be no body and blood. Thus the body and blood are given "in, with, and under" the bread and the wine. In Luther's terms, the literary figure at work here is *synecdoche*: the part in reality "stands in" for the whole, not merely in a symbolic or representational sense—in which case the body and blood would "really" exist somewhere else. The presence of our Lord's body and blood "in, with, and under" the bread and the wine is real because it is given to us as the inheritance he has bequeathed to us. It is the New Testament.

Such is what a Lutheran understanding of the Lord's Supper ought to look like. In a time when the pressure is on in ecumenical circles to adopt views of the supper, the liturgy, the ministry, ordination, and the church which quite obviously rest on presuppositions of an entirely different sort, we would do well to pay some heed to these roots.

---

6. See the important discussion by Jan Lindhardt in *Martin Luther: Knowledge and Mediation in the Renaissance* (Lewiston, NY: Edwin Mellen, 1986), 193–203.

Bibliographies

BY GERHARD O. FORDE

Forde, Gerhard O. *The Captivation of the Will: Luther vs. Erasmus on Freedom and Bondage.* Edited by Steven D. Paulson. Grand Rapids: Eerdmans, 2005.
———. *Justification by Faith: A Matter of Death and Life.* Philadelphia: Fortress, 1982.
———. *The Law-Gospel Debate: An Interpretation of Its Historical Development.* Minneapolis: Augsburg, 1969.
———. *A More Radical Gospel: Essays on Eschatology, Authority, Atonement, and Ecumenism.* Edited by Mark C. Mattes and Steven D. Paulson. Minneapolis: Fortress Press, 2017.
———. *On Being a Theologian of the Cross: Reflections on Luther's Heidelberg Disputation, 1518.* Grand Rapids: Eerdmans, 1997.
———. *The Preached God: Proclamation in Word and Sacrament.* Edited by Mark C. Mattes and Steven D. Paulson. Minneapolis: Fortress Press, 2017.
———. *Theology Is for Proclamation.* Minneapolis: Fortress Press, 1990.
———. *We Preach Christ Crucified: Sermons by Gerhard O. Forde.* Edited by Marianna Forde. Minneapolis: Lutheran University Press, 2016.
———. *Where God Meets Man: Luther's Down-to-Earth Approach to the Gospel.* Minneapolis: Augsburg, 1972.
Forde, Gerhard O., and James Nestingen. *Free to Be: A Handbook to Luther's Small Catechism.* Minneapolis: Augsburg, 1975; revised 1993.

Articles, Chapters in Books, and Editorials

Forde, Gerhard O. "Bound to Be Free." In *Encounters with Luther*, edited by Eric Gritsch, 2 vols., 2:67–80. Gettysburg, PA: Lutheran Theological Seminary at Gettysburg, 1976.

———. "Bultmann: Where Did He Take Us?" *Dialog* 17 (1978): 27–30.

———. "Called to Freedom." *Lutherjahrbuch* 62 (1995): 13–27. Also in *The Preached God: Proclamation in Word and Sacrament*, edited by Mark C. Mattes and Steven D. Paulson, 254–69. Grand Rapids: Eerdmans, 2007.

———. "The Catholic Impasse: Reflections on Lutheran–Roman Catholic Dialogue Today." In *Promoting Unity: Themes in Lutheran-Catholic Dialogue*, edited by H. George Anderson et al., 67–78. Minneapolis: Augsburg, 1989.

———. "Caught in the Act: Reflections on the Work of Christ." *Word and World* 3 (1983): 22–31.

———. "The Christian Life." In *Christian Dogmatics*, edited by Carl E. Braaten and Robert W. Jenson, 2 vols., 2:391–470. Philadelphia: Fortress, 1984.

———. "Confessional Subscription: What Does It Mean for Lutherans Today?" *Word and World* 11 (1991): 316–20.

———. "The Critical Response of German Theological Professors to the Joint Declaration on Justification." *Dialog* 38 (1999): 71–72.

———. "Does the Gospel Have a Future? Barth's *Romans* Revisited." *Word and World* 14 (1994): 67–77.

———. "The Exodus from Virtue to Grace: Justification by Faith Today." *Interpretation* 34 (1980): 32–44.

———. "Fake Theology: Reflections on Antinomianism Past and Present." *Dialog* 22 (1983): 246–51.

———. "Forensic Justification and the Christian Life." in *A More Radical Gospel: Essays on Eschatology, Authority, Atonement, and Ecumenism*, edited by Mark C. Mattes and Steven D. Paulson, 114–36. Grand Rapids: Eerdmans, 2004.

———. "Forensic Justification and the Law in Lutheran Theology." In *Justification by Faith*, edited by H. George Anderson, T. Austin Murphy, and Joseph A. Burgess, 287–303. Lutherans and Catholics in Dialogue 7. Minneapolis: Augsburg, 1985.

———. "The Formula of Concord Article V: End or New Beginning?" *Dialog* 15 (1976): 184–91.

———. "Full Communion?" *Dialog* 28 (1989): 85–86.

———. "Infallibility Language and the Early Lutheran Tradition." In *Teaching Authority and Infallibility in the Church*, edited by Paul C. Empie, T. Austin Murphy, and Joseph A. Burgess, 120–37. Lutherans and Catholics in Dialogue 6. Minneapolis: Augsburg, 1980.

———. "Is Forgiveness Enough? Reflections on an Odd Question." *Word and World* 16 (1996): 302–8.

———. "Is Invocation of Saints an Adiaphoron?" In *The One Mediator, the Saints, and Mary*, edited by H. George Anderson, J. Francis Stafford, and Joseph

A. Burgess, 327–38. Lutherans and Catholics in Dialogue 8. Minneapolis: Augsburg, 1992.

———. "Justification." In *A New Handbook of Christian Theology*, edited by Donald W. Musser and Joseph L. Price, 271–73. Nashville: Abingdon, 1992.

———. "Justification by Faith Alone." In *In Search of Christian Unity: Basic Consensus/Basic Differences*, edited by Joseph A. Burgess, 64–76. Minneapolis: Fortress, 1991.

———. "Justification by Faith Alone: The Article by Which the Church Stands or Falls?" *Dialog* 27 (1988): 260–67.

———. "Law and Gospel as the Methodological Principle of Theology." In *Theological Perspectives: A Discussion of Contemporary Issues in Theology by Members of the Religion Department at Luther College*, 50–69. Decorah, IA: Luther College Press, 1964.

———. "Law and Gospel in Luther's Hermeneutic." *Interpretation* 37 (1983): 240–52.

———. "Law and Sexual Behavior." *Lutheran Quarterly* 9 (1995): 3–22.

———. "*Lex semper accusat*? Nineteenth-Century Roots of Our Current Dilemma." *Dialog* 9 (1970): 265–74.

———. "The Lord's Supper as the Testament of Jesus." *Word and World* 17 (1997): 5–9.

———. "Loser Takes All: The Victory of Christ." *Lutheran Standard*, September 2, 1975, 3–5.

———. "Luther and the Jews." *Lutheran Quarterly* 27, no. 2 (Summer 2013): 125–42.

———. "Luther and the *Usus Pauli*." *Dialog* 32 (1993): 275–82.

———. "Lutheran Ecumenism: With Whom and How Much?" *Lutheran Quarterly* 17 (2003): 436–55.

———. "Lutheran Faith and American Freedom." *Lutheran Quarterly* 31, no. 4 (Winter 2017): 424–35.

———. "The Lutheran View." In *Christian Spirituality: Five Views of Sanctification*, edited by Donald L. Alexander, 13–32. Downers Grove, IL: InterVarsity, 1988. Forde's responses to the other views can be found on pp. 77–82, 119–22, 155–57, and 190–93.

———. "Lutheranism." In *The Blackwell Encyclopedia of Modern Christian Thought*, edited by Alister McGrath, 354–58. Cambridge, MA: Blackwell, 1993.

———. "Martens on the Condemnations." *Lutheran Quarterly* 10 (1996): 67–69.

———. "The Meaning of *satis est*." *Lutheran Forum* 26 (1992): 14–18.

———. "A Movement without a Move?" *Dialog* 30 (1991): 83–84.

———. "Naming the One Who Is Above Us." In *Speaking the Christian God:*

The Holy Trinity and the Challenge of Feminism, edited by Alvin F. Kimmel, 110–19. Grand Rapids: Eerdmans, 1992.

———. "The Newness of the Gospel." *Dialog* 6 (1967): 87–94.

———. "The Newness of the New Testament." In *All Things New: Essays in Honor of Roy A. Harrisville*, edited by Arland J. Hultgren, Donald H. Juel, and Jack D. Kingsbury, 175–80. St. Paul: *Word and World* Supplement, 1992.

———. "The Normative Character of Scripture for Matters of Faith and Life: Human Sexuality in Light of Romans 1:16–32." *Word and World* 14 (1994): 305–14.

———. "The 'Old Synod': A Search for Objectivity." In *Striving for Ministry: Centennial Essays Interpreting the Heritage of Luther Seminary*, edited by Warren Quanbeck et al., 67–80. Minneapolis: Luther Theological Seminary / Augsburg, 1977.

———. "On Being a Theologian of the Cross." *Christian Century* 114 (1997): 947–49.

———. "Once More into the Breach? Some Questions about Key 73." *Dialog* 12 (1973): 7–14.

———. "The One Acted Upon." *Dialog* 36 (1997): 54–61.

———. "The Ordained Ministry." In *Called and Ordained: Lutheran Perspectives on the Office of the Ministry*, edited by Todd Nichol and Marc Kolden, 117–36. Minneapolis: Fortress, 1990.

———. "Outside the Gate: Atonement as Actual Event." *Dialog* 18, no. 4 (Autumn 1979): 247–54.

———. "The Place of Theology in the Church." *Dialog* 22 (1983): 121–30.

———. "The Power of Negative Thinking: On the Principle of Negation in Luther and Hegelianism." *Dialog* 23 (1984): 250–56.

———. "Preaching the Sacraments." *Lutheran Theological Seminary Bulletin* 64, no. 4 (1984): 3–27.

———. "Proclamation: The Present Tense of the Gospel." *Dialog* 29 (1990): 167–73.

———. "Public Ministry and Its Limits." *Dialog* 30 (1991): 102–10.

———. "Radical Lutheranism: Lutheran Identity in America." *Lutheran Quarterly* 1 (1987): 5–18.

———. "Response to James Nestingen's Article." *Dialog* 31 (1992): 34–35.

———. "The Revolt and the Wedding: An Essay on Social Ethics in the Perspective of Luther's Theology." In *The Reformation and the Revolution: A Series of Lectures Celebrating the Protestant Reformation and Commemorating the Bolshevik Revolution*, 79–88. Sioux Falls, SD: Augustana College Press, 1970.

———. "Robert Jenson's Soteriology." In *Trinity, Time, and Church: A Response* to the Theology of Robert W. Jenson, edited by Colin Gunton, 126–38. Grand Rapids: Eerdmans, 2000.

———. "Romans 8:18–27." *Interpretation* 38 (1984): 281–85.

———. "Sacraments as Eschatological Gift and Promise." *Lutheran Quarterly* 31, no. 3 (Autumn 2017): 310–19.

———. "Sense and Nonsense about Luther." *Dialog* 10 (1971): 65–67.

———. "A Short Word." *Dialog* 20 (1981): 88–92.

———. "Some Remarks on Peters' Review of *Christian Dogmatics*." *Dialog* 24 (1985): 297–99.

———. "Something to Believe: A Theological Perspective on Infant Baptism." *Interpretation* 47 (1993): 229–41.

———. "Theology as *modus operandi*." *Dialog* 21 (1982): 175–79.

———. "Unity without Concord." *Dialog* 20 (1981): 166–73.

———. "The Viability of Luther Today: A North American Perspective." *Word and World* 7 (1987): 22–31.

———. "What Finally to Do about the (Counter-)Reformation Condemnations." *Lutheran Quarterly* 11 (1997): 3–16.

———. "What Next?" *Dialog* 37 (1998): 163.

———. "What's in a Name? Eucharist or Lord's Supper." *Word and World* 9 (1989): 52–55.

———. "When Old Gods Fail: Martin Luther's Critique of Mysticism." In *Piety, Politics, and Ethics: Reformation Studies in Honor of George Wolfgang Forell*, edited by Carter Lindberg, 15–26. Kirksville, MO: Sixteenth Century Journal Publishers, 1984.

———. "The Word on Quotas." *Lutheran Quarterly* 6 (1992): 119–26.

———. "The Word That Kills and Makes Alive." In *Marks of the Body of Christ*, edited by Carl E. Braaten and Robert W. Jenson, 1–12. Grand Rapids: Eerdmans, 1999.

———. "The Work of Christ." in *Christian Dogmatics*. Edited by Carl E. Braaten and Robert W. Jenson. 2 vols. Philadelphia: Fortress, 1984. Vol. 2, pp. 5–100.

Forde, Gerhard O., et al. "A Call for Discussion of the 'Joint Declaration on the Doctrine of Justification.'" *Dialog* 36 (1997): 224–29.

Forde, Gerhard O., and Eric Gritsch. "Discussion." In *Encounters with Luther*, edited by Eric Gritsch, 2 vols., 2:81–83. Gettysburg, PA: Lutheran Theological Seminary at Gettysburg, 1976.

Forde, Gerhard O., and James Nestingen. "Beware of Greeks Bearing Gifts." *Dialog* 39 (2000): 291–92.

Translations

Schwarz, Reinhard. "The Last Supper: The Testament of Jesus." Trans. Gerhard O. Forde. *Lutheran Quarterly* 9 (1995): 391–403.

Book Reviews

Forde, Gerhard O. Review of *Christianity and Humanism: Studies in the History of Ideas*, by Quirinus Breen. *Lutheran World* 16 no. 2 (1969): 193–94.

———. Review of *Creation and Law*, by Gustaf Wingren. *Dialog* 1 (1962): 78–79.

———. Review of *Critical Issues in Modern Religion*, by Roger A. Johnson. *Dialog* 13 (1974): 232–33.

———. Review of *Dogmatics*, by Hermann Diem. *Dialog* 1 (1962): 69–70.

———. Review of *Eberhard Jüngel: An Introduction to His Theology*, by John Webster. *Lutheran Quarterly* 2 (1988): 531–33.

———. Review of *Faith and the Vitalities of History: A Theological Study Based on the Work of Albrecht Ritschl*, by Philip J. Hefner. *Interpretation* 21 (1967): 486–89.

———. Review of *Formation of Historical Theology: A Study of Ferdinand Christian Baur*, by Peter Crafts Hodgson. *Una sancta* 24 (1967): 69–72.

———. Review of *God as the Mystery of the World*, by Eberhard Jüngel. *Word and World* 4 (1984): 458–61.

———. Review of *Gospel and Church*, by Gustaf Wingren. *Dialog* 5 (1966): 150–53.

———. Review of *The Göttingen Dogmatics: Instruction in the Christian Religion*, vol. 1, by Karl Barth, trans. Geoffery Bromiley. *Pro Ecclesia* 2 (1993): 240–42.

———. Review of *Luther and Staupitz: An Essay in the Intellectual Origins of the Protestant Reformation*, by David C. Steinmetz. *Interpretation* 36 (1982): 196–99.

———. Review of *Luther in Mid-Career, 1521–1530*, by Heinrich Bornkamm. *Interpretation* 39 (1985): 436.

———. Review of *The Place of Bonhoeffer: Problems and Possibilities in His Thought*, by Martin E. Marty, ed. *Dialog* 2 (1963): 334–35.

———. Review of *The Reality of the Devil: Evil in Man*, by Ruth Nanda Anshen. *Dialog* 12 (1973): 156–58.

———. Review of *Revolt against Heaven: An Enquiry into Anti-Supernaturalism*, by Kenneth Hamilton. *Dialog* 5 (1966): 312–14.

———. Review of *The Structure of Lutheranism*, by Werner Elert. *Dialog* 3 (1964): 77–78.

———. Review of *Theology and Preaching*, by Heinrich Ott. *Dialog* 5 (1966): 150–53.

———. Review of *Theology and Proclamation: Dialogue with Bultmann*, by Gerhard Ebeling. *Dialog* 6 (1967): 299–302.

———. Review of *Word and the Spirit: Essays on the Inspiration of the Scriptures*, by Regin Prenter. *Dialog* 4 (1965): 304–6.

ABOUT GERHARD O. FORDE

Baker, Robert. "Natural Law, Human Sexuality, and Forde's 'Acid Test.'" In *Natural Law: A Lutheran Reappraisal*, edited by Robert Baker and Roland Ehlke, 135–56. St. Louis: Concordia, 2011.

Burgess, Joseph, and Marc Kolden, eds. *By Faith Alone: Essays on Justification in Honor of Gerhard O. Forde*. Grand Rapids: Eerdmans, 2004.

Forde, Marianna. *Gerhard O. Forde: A Life*. Minneapolis: Lutheran University Press, 2014.

Hopman, Nicholas. "Luther's *Antinomian Disputations* and *lex aeterna*." *Lutheran Quarterly* 30, no. 2 (Summer 2016): 152–80.

Kilcrease, Jack. *The Doctrine of Atonement: From Luther to Forde*. Eugene, OR: Wipf & Stock, 2018.

———. "Gerhard Forde's Doctrine of the Law: A Confessional Lutheran Critique." *Concordia Theological Quarterly* 75, nos. 1–2 (January/April 2011): 151–79.

———. "Gerhard Forde's Theology of Atonement and Justification: A Confessional Lutheran Response." *Concordia Theological Quarterly* 76, nos. 3–4 (July/October 2012): 269–93.

Koch, John D., Jr. *The Distinction between Law and Gospel as the Basis and Boundary of Theological Reflection*. Dogmatik in der Moderne. Edited by Christian Danz, Jörg Dierken, Hans-Peter Grosshans, and Fredericke Nüssel. Vol. 16. Tübingen: Mohr Siebeck, 2016.

Mattes, Mark C. "Gerhard Forde on Re-Envisioning Theology in Light of the Gospel." *Lutheran Quarterly* 13, no. 4 (Winter 1999): 373–93.

Mattes, Mark C., and Steven D. Paulson. Introduction to *A More Radical Gospel: Essays on Eschatology, Authority, Atonement, and Ecumenism*, by Gerhard O. Forde, x–xxviii. Minneapolis: Fortress Press, 2017.

Mattes, Mark C. and Steven D. Paulson. "Introduction: Taking the Risk to Proclaim." In *The Preached God: Proclamation in Word and Sacrament*, by Gerhard O. Forde, 1–29. Minneapolis: Fortress Press, 2017.

Murray, Scott. *Law, Life, and the Living God: The Third Use of the Law in Modern American Lutheranism*. St. Louis: Concordia, 2002.

Nygard, Mark Lewellyn. *The Missiological Implications of the Theology of Gerhard Forde*. Minneapolis: Lutheran University Press, 2011.

Peterson, Cheryl M. *Who Is the Church? An Ecclesiology for the Twenty-First Century*. Minneapolis: Fortress Press, 2013.

Wong, Jonathan. "Born Free? Recovering the Doctrine of the Bound Will for the Sake of Preaching in the Church." In *Comfortable Words: Essays in Honor of Paul F. M. Zahl*, edited by John D. Koch Jr. and Todd H. W. Brewer. Eugene: Pickwick, 2013.

Dissertations and Theses

Bowers, Dianne Virginia. "Martin Luther and the Joyful Exchange between Christ and His Christian: Implications for the Doctrine of Justification and the Christian Life." PhD diss., Graduate Theological Union Berkeley, 2008.

Hannan, Shauna Kay. "Lutheran Preachers and the Third Use of the Law: A Homiletical Approach to Overcome the Impasse." PhD diss., Princeton Theological Seminary, 2010.

Hiller, Timothy M. "Justification and Moral Value: Martin Luther on Good, Evil, and the Moral Self." PhD diss., University of Chicago, 2016.

Kilcrease, Jack. "The Self-Donation of God: Gerhard Forde and the Question of Atonement in the Lutheran Tradition." PhD diss., Marquette University, 2009.

Lazerte, Steele. "Dying and Behold We Live." MTh thesis, Waterloo Lutheran Seminary, 2007.

Peterson, Cheryl M. "The Question of the Church in North American Lutheranism: Toward an Ecclesiology of the Third Article." PhD diss., Marquette University, 2004.

Rawn, Gregory Thorwald. "The Wondrous Duel: The Interpretation and Reconstruction of Luther's Theology of the Atonement in Gustaf Aulén's *Christus Victor* and Gerhard Forde's 'The Work of Christ.'" MA thesis, Luther Seminary, 2005.

Thompson, Erick J. "'Christ Crucified Brings All These Things with Him': Proclamation as Response to the Theology of Gianni Vattimo." PhD diss., The Lutheran School of Theology at Chicago, 2013.

Index

Anselm, 39, 68–69, 71
antinomianism, 23–26, 31, 33, 61, 63–65, 152–54, 165, 245–48, 251, 253
Arendt, Hannah, 237
Augsburg Confession, 15, 43, 133, 149, 167–77
Augustine, 116, 120, 133–34, 136, 213
Aulén, Gustav, 39, 68–69, 72

Barth, Karl, 8, 10, 19, 23, 59, 61, 73, 75, 204, 210, 258–61
Bauer, Bruno, 188
Becker, Ernest, 12, 84, 107
Berdyaev, Nicolas, 210
Berge, Wolfgang, 73
Bloom, Allen, 260
Brown, Joanne Carlson, 238
Brunner, Emil, 210
Burtness, James, 150

Calvinism, 33, 171, 176
Carlson, Edgar, 68
Cobb, John, 210
Cone, James, 210
Cortes, Donoso, 188

de Chardin, Pierre Teilhard, 210
de Unamuno, Miguel, 210
devil, 23, 31–32, 55, 57, 64, 70, 123, 139–41, 143, 145, 172, 174, 241, 246, 260, 263–64
docetism, 47, 49

Ebeling, Gerhard, 8, 60–61, 63, 66, 73, 79
election, 16, 93, 221–27, 229, 251, 253, 266
Elert, Werner, 8, 42, 180
Enlightenment, 42–43, 180, 186, 202, 246, 251, 267
Erasmus (of Rotterdam), Desiderius, 3, 13–14, 26, 111–17, 119–22, 124, 140, 213, 215–16
eternal law. *See lex aeterna*
Evangelical Lutheran Church in America (ELCA), 3, 15, 158, 169–70, 176–77, 245

Forde, Marianna (née Carlson), xiv–xv, 2–3

Gaiser, Frederick, 164–65
Goetz, Ronald, 209–11
Grane, Leif, 133
Gritsch, Eric, 87, 277

Haikola, Lauri, 8, 38–39, 59–60, 63, 69–72, 150, 154
Hall, Douglas John, 107
Halperin, David, 150
Hanigan, James P., 160–63
Harnack, Theodosius, 8–9, 53–58, 63, 65–66, 72, 75–76, 189
Hegel, G. W. F., 183–91
Hengstenberg, E. W., 42–43
Hirsch, Emanuel, 42–43
historical criticism, 41–43
Holl, Karl, 69, 75, 77–78
Hollaz, David, 39
Hoover, J. Edgar, 178, 181
Hopman, Nicholas, 31
Hudson, Winthrop, 171

idealism, 49, 63–64, 140, 176, 183, 222–24
immutability, 13, 111–19, 122–23, 125, 207, 209–10, 223, 227, 229–30, 262
infallibility, 40–42, 169, 202–3

Jenson, Robert, xv, 87
Joest, Wilfried, 73
Juel, Donald H., 159
Jüngel, Eberhard, 260

Kant, Immanuel, 9, 180–82, 202, 223, 246
Kattenbusch, Ferdinand, 75, 77
Koester, Craig R., 155, 159
Küng, Hans, 210

Lazareth, William H., 156
Lessing, Gotthold Ephraim, 202
lex aeterna/eternal law, 8–9, 21–23, 27, 31, 38–39, 49, 60, 76
Lindhardt, Jan, 275
Löwith, Karl, 188–89

Marx, Karl, 187–88
McLellan, David, 188
Melanchthon, Philip, 23–25, 27–30, 38, 41, 45–46, 49, 53–54, 60, 63, 64–72, 76, 144, 167, 171, 179, 192
Mencken, H. L., 143
Mercadante, Linda A., 105
Moltmann, Jürgen, 210

necessity, 13, 111–19, 122–23, 215, 262
Nestingen, James Arne, xiv–xv, 2–4, 107
Niebuhr, Reinhold, 176, 210

Ozment, Steven, 168

Pannenberg, Wolfhart, 210
Parker, Rebecca, 238
Paul (apostle), 6, 10–12, 16, 19, 23, 30, 84, 86, 89–90, 94, 97, 100, 104, 117–18, 133–34, 143–44, 151–53, 167, 217, 226, 231, 233
Platonism, 12, 19, 103
Prager, Dennis, 155
predestination, 94, 114, 222–24, 226, 229, 253
Prenter, Regin, 222
Preus, James S., 273
promise, 1, 10–11, 13, 15, 20–21, 31–33, 40, 87–89, 91–92, 97, 117–20, 122, 125, 143, 175, 182, 187, 197, 202–3, 215, 218, 221, 234, 242, 247, 262, 264–65, 268, 271–73

Rahner, Karl, 204
Rasmussen, Larry, 133, 236
Reid, J. K. S., 86

repristination theology, 10, 42–43, 51
Ritschl, Albrecht, 8–9, 51, 58, 59, 61, 72, 75–78, 189
Root, Michael, 177
Ruether, Rosemary, 210
Rusch, William G., 169, 176

Satan, 32, 55, 144, 208, 212, 214, 217
Schleiermacher, Friedrich, 182–84
Schlink, Edmund, 264–66
Schultz, Robert, 50–51, 54, 189
Schwarz, Reinhard, 272–74
Schwarzwäller, Klaus, 217, 240
simul, 91–95, 96, 152
spontaneity, 8, 14, 84, 86, 98–99, 141–42, 190
Stirner, Max, 188
Strasbourg, 176

Tanzania, 268
Taylor, Charles, 11
Temple, William, 210
Thielicke, Helmut, 73
third use of the law, 27, 63, 74, 121, 134, 143–44, 150, 153, 176–77, 179, 180

Thomasius, Gottfried, 48
Tillich, Paul, 162
Turner, James, 212–13, 237

universalism, 19, 42–43, 184–88, 199, 215, 224–25, 229

Vercruysse, Jos E., 107, 138
Vischer, Lukas, 176
vocation, xv, 5, 14, 98–99, 139–40, 162–63
von Harnack, Adolf, 189
von Harnack, Theodosius. *See* Harnack, Theodosius
von Hofmann, J. C. K., 8–9, 23, 37, 44
von Loewenich, Walther, 173

Walther, C. F. W., 10
Wendebourg, Ernst-Wilhelm, 49
Weth, Gustav, 52
Wingren, Gustav, 150, 156, 164
Wolf, Ernst, 74, 174
Wolff, Otto, 72
wrath, 7, 9–11, 24, 27, 30, 32, 39, 45–58, 62, 68–78, 133, 151, 206–7, 212, 220, 224, 238, 241, 249, 254

Sources

The editors thank Professor Marianna Forde for sharing her photos of her husband, Gerhard. We also thank William B. Eerdmans Publishing Company and Fortress Press for granting us permission to reprint previously published works.

We gratefully acknowledge permission to reprint materials previously published as:

Part I. The Law-Gospel Distinction in Modern Lutheranism

All excerpts from *The Law-Gospel Debate: An Interpretation of Its Historical Development* (Minneapolis: Augsburg, 1969), 3–11, 69–78, 88–94, 175–99.

Part II. Death and Resurrection

"The Lutheran View (of Sanctification)," in *Christian Spirituality: Five Views of Sanctification*, ed. Donald L. Alexander (Downers Grove, Ill.: InterVarsity, 1988), 13–32; and in *The Preached God: Proclamation in Word and Sacrament*, ed. Mark C. Mattes and Steven D. Paulson (Grand Rapids: Eerdmans, 2007; Minneapolis: Fortress Press, 2017), 226–44.

"Two Ways of Being a Theologian," in *On Being a Theologian of the Cross: Reflections on Luther's Heidelberg Disputation, 1518* (Grand Rapids: Eerdmans, 1997), 10–19.

Part III. The Bondage of the Will

Excerpts from *The Captivation of the Will: Luther vs. Erasmus on Freedom and Bondage*, ed. Steven Paulson (Grand Rapids: Eerdmans, 2005; Minneapolis: Fortress Press, 2017), 31–45, 77–79.

"Heidelberg Disputation: Thesis 15," in *On Being a Theologian of the Cross: Reflections on Luther's Heidelberg Disputation, 1518* (Grand Rapids: Eerdmans, 1997), 56–58.

Part IV. Good Works

"Heidelberg Disputation: Theses 26–28," in *On Being a Theologian of the Cross: Reflections on Luther's Heidelberg Disputation*, 1518 (Grand Rapids: Eerdmans, 1997), 107–15.

"Luther's 'Ethics,'" in *A More Radical Gospel: Essays on Eschatology, Authority, Atonement, and Ecumenism*, ed. Mark C. Mattes and Steven D. Paulson (Grand Rapids: Eerdmans, 2004; Minneapolis: Fortress Press, 2017), 148–55.

Part V. Controversies Concerning the Law

"Law and Sexual Behavior," *Lutheran Quarterly* vol. 9, no. 1 (Spring 1995): 3–22.

"The Meaning of *Satis Est*," *Lutheran Forum* 26 (1992): 14–18; and in *A More Radical Gospel: Essays on Eschatology, Authority, Atonement, and Ecumenism*, ed. Mark C. Mattes and Steven D. Paulson (Grand Rapids: Eerdmans, 2004; Minneapolis: Fortress Press, 2017), 159–70.

"Lex Semper Accusat," *Dialog* 9, no. 4 (Autumn 1970): 265–74; and in *A More Radical Gospel: Essays on Eschatology, Authority, Atonement, and Ecumenism*, ed. Mark C. Mattes and Steven D. Paulson (Grand Rapids: Eerdmans, 2004; Minneapolis: Fortress Press, 2017), 33–49.

Part VI. Theological Method

"Introduction" and "The Preached God," in *Theology Is for Proclamation* (Minneapolis: Augsburg Fortress, 1990), 1–9, 13–37.

"Heidelberg Disputation: Theses 19–21," in *On Being a Theologian of the Cross: Reflections on Luther's Heidelberg Disputation*, 1518 (Grand Rapids: Eerdmans, 1997), 72–90.

Part VII. The Ministry

"Speaking the Gospel Today," in *The Preached God: Proclamation in Word and Sacrament*, ed. Mark C. Mattes and Steven D. Paulson (Grand Rapids: Eerdmans, 2007; Minneapolis: Fortress Press, 2017), 165–94.

"Something to Believe: A Theological Perspective on Infant Baptism," *Interpretation* 47 (1993): 229–41; and in *The Preached God: Proclamation in Word and Sacrament*, ed. Mark C. Mattes and Steven D. Paulson (Grand Rapids: Eerdmans, 2007; Minneapolis: Fortress Press, 2017), 131–45.

"The Lord's Supper as the Testament of Jesus," *Word & World* 17 (1997): 5–9; and in *The Preached God: Proclamation in Word and Sacrament*, ed. Mark C. Mattes and Steven D. Paulson (Grand Rapids: Eerdmans, 2007; Minneapolis: Fortress Press, 2017), 146–51.

www.ingramcontent.com/pod-product-compliance
Lightning Source LLC
Chambersburg PA
CBHW020356080526
44584CB00014B/1048